The Ultimate
Disney Trivia Book 2

Other Books by Kevin Neary and Dave Smith

The Ultimate Disney Trivia Book

The Ultimate

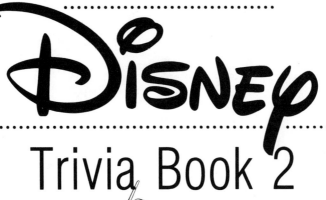

Trivia Book 2

Kevin Neary and Dave Smith

HYPERION

New York

Library of Congress Cataloging-in-Publication Data

Neary, Kevin F.
The ultimate Disney trivia book 2 / Kevin Neary and Dave Smith.—1st ed.
    p.   cm.
  ISBN 1-7868-8024-4
  1. Walt Disney Company—Miscellanea. I. Smith, Dave. II. Walt Disney Company. III. Title.
NC1766.U52D5542 1994
741.5'09794'93—dc20   94-2207
                                                                CIP

FIRST EDITION

10 9 8 7 6 5 4 3 2 1

ACKNOWLEDGMENTS

· ·

We would like to take this opportunity to especially thank the following colleagues and friends without whose advice, cooperation, and encouragement these trivia books would not have been nearly as successful: Russell and Karen Brower, Steven Clark, Becky Cline, Bill and Sharon Cox, Jennifer Hendrickson, Rose Motzko, Russell Schroeder, Paula Sigman, Tracy Terhune, Sue Thoma, Robert Tieman, Mike Troyan, our families, and fellow cast members.

CONTENTS

· · · · · · · · · · · · · · · · · ·

INTRODUCTION

....

by Dave Smith, Archives Director,
The Walt Disney Company

Owing to the great success of the first volume of *The Ultimate Disney Trivia Book,* Kevin Neary and I were asked to prepare a second volume. Since we began working on the first book, interest in Disney has not diminished; in fact, quite the contrary. Even The Walt Disney Company has jumped on the Disneyana bandwagon. The Company held its first Disneyana Convention at the Walt Disney World Resort in September 1992, and it was a huge success attended by 750 avid Disney fans. The second Disneyana Convention, held in September 1993, convened at the Disneyland Hotel on the other side of the continent and attracted almost double the number of registrants as the first.

In 1995 the Walt Disney Archives reaches its twenty-fifth anniversary. Back in 1970, when I joined the Disney staff to establish the Archives, I could not have imagined how much we would grow in a quarter of a century. Because of the interest in Disney's past, The Walt Disney Company constantly delves into that past to reissue classic films, and to create merchandise, educational materials, television specials, CDs, books, videos, and theme park attractions based on the company's early characters and films. These many projects often involve detailed research in the Archives.

Beginning its sixth year is the Disney Stores trivia competition for store cast members (the Disney term for employees), which is where the idea for this trivia book originated—and it shows no signs of waning interest. As I write this, there are upward of 225 Disney Stores throughout the world, and more are being added on a regular basis. Since these stores tend to attract cast members who have a sincere fondness for Disney lore, the annual trivia competitions have been gaining even greater success. Monthly competitions are held in the individual stores, and all stores that maintain an 85 percent score are entitled to select a cast member to compete in the district competitions. In the fall of 1993, twenty district competitions were held all around the United States and Canada. As a result of the competitions, the eight individuals with the highest scores were selected to go to Disneyland in October for the finals, where a national winner was chosen. At the district competitions, each participating cast member had a large, enthusiastic rooting section from his or her store to cheer at each correct answer and groan at each one that was incorrect. Kevin Neary, my co-author, was the national winner in 1991 and contines to work as a Disney Store cast member in Cherry Hill, New Jersey.

As before, Kevin prepared most of the questions for this book. They then came to me for extensive editing. We tried to make sure that there were no ambiguities and that there was not more than one correct answer. Some questions were replaced and new ones were created. Then we submitted our manuscript to a number of Disney experts, who each made generous contributions to the effort.

We would like to thank all of the Disney fans around the world who have encouraged us to compile this second volume of Disney trivia. We hope we have succeeded in properly challenging them and increasing their Disney knowledge.

April 1994

Animated
Cartoons and
Featurettes

Animated Cartoons and Featurettes

Questions

1. What song does Mickey play with the help of some musical animals in the cartoon classic *Steamboat Willie* (1928)?
2. What kind of animal proves to be a constant irritation to Mickey in the galley in *Steamboat Willie*?
3. What friend of Walt Disney's from Kansas City helped convince Walt to start the Silly Symphony series?
4. What is Mickey Mouse's profession in the 1929 cartoon *The Karnival Kid*?
5. Mickey's early pal, Clarabelle, is easily recognized by what item worn around her neck?
6. Who are Mickey's opponents in the 1932 cartoon *Touchdown Mickey*?
7. What is Mickey's profession in the 1932 cartoon *The Klondike Kid*?
8. According to the song "Who'll Buy a Box Lunch?," which Minnie sings in the 1933 Academy Award–nominated cartoon *Building a Building*, she sells bologna, macaroni, and what type of pie?
9. In the Academy Award–winning cartoon *Three Little Pigs*, what is so unusual about the portraits of the pigs' father?
10. From what three materials do the Three Little Pigs make their houses?
11. What U.S. President asked that a Mickey Mouse cartoon be shown before each movie he viewed?
12. In the 1934 cartoon *Shanghaied*, what characters are kidnapped by the evil Captain Pete and his crew?
13. Besides Donald Duck, who does the Wise Little Hen ask for help in the 1934 cartoon of that title?
14. According to animation historians, the character Max Hare from the Academy Award–winning cartoon *The Tortoise and the Hare* (1935) helped inspire what famous non-Disney animated character?
15. Who originally wrote the fable that helped inspire *The Tortoise and the Hare*?

16. In what year did Mickey Mouse first achieve his entry in the *Encyclopaedia Britannica*?

17. When Mickey is accidentally doused by some insecticide spray, what does he dream happens to his garden in the 1935 cartoon *Mickey's Garden*?

18. In *Mickey's Fire Brigade* (1935), whom do Mickey and the gang save from a burning building?

19. What does Goofy use as bait to help catch fish in the 1935 cartoon *On Ice*?

20. What two kingdoms are represented in the 1935 Silly Symphony *Music Land*?

21. After a battle has taken place between the two kingdoms in *Music Land*, a truce is declared. What is the name of the bridge that is built between these two kingdoms to represent that unity?

22. What object from a magician's bag of tricks does Pluto attempt to catch in the 1936 cartoon *Mickey's Grand Opera*?

23. Whom does Elmer Elephant rescue in the 1936 Silly Symphony *Elmer Elephant*?

24. Who challenges Mickey Mouse to a sword fight in the 1936 cartoon *Thru the Mirror*?

25. What type of object seems to develop its own identity and make life miserable for Goofy in the 1936 cartoon *Moving Day*?

26. In *Alpine Climbers* (1936), Donald throws one of his major tantrums when he tangles with what types of creatures?

27. As a result of the success of *The Tortoise and the Hare*, a sequel was made entitled *Toby Tortoise Returns* (1936). What type of event does this famous duo square off in?

28. In what MGM musical does Mickey Mouse make a cameo appearance with comedian Jimmy Durante?

29. What is the name of the little elephant featured in the 1936 cartoon *Mickey's Elephant*?

30. What character plays the vicious dogcatcher from the City Pound that attempts to catch Pluto in the 1937 cartoon *The Worm Turns*?

31. In *Don Donald* (1937), Donald trades his little burro to El Trading Post for what in order to win the heart of the lovely señorita, Donna?

32. In the 1937 short *Moose Hunters*, what two characters disguise themselves as a moose in order to lure their prey?

33. What is the name of the ostrich that gave the Wahoo Railroad stationmaster, Donald Duck, so much grief in *Donald's Ostrich* (1937)?

34. The Seven Dwarfs, who appeared first in *Snow White and the Seven Dwarfs* in 1937, went on to star in four short films. Can you name any of them?

35. In the 1938 cartoon *Boat Builders,* what do Mickey, Donald, and Goofy name their boat, and what happens to this boat as it is about to embark on its maiden voyage?

36. What two characters join Mickey on a thrill-packed, topsy-turvy ride while vacationing in the 1938 cartoon *Mickey's Trailer*?

37. According to the radio announcer in *Mickey's Parrot* (1938), what is the name of the gangster who just escaped from jail?

38. In *Mickey's Parrot,* what was the name of Mickey's goldfish?

39. Who wrote the story that inspired the cartoon classic *Brave Little Tailor* (1938)?

40. In the 1939 cartoon *The Autograph Hound,* what Hollywood stars does Donald Duck ask for their autographs?

41. What song does Donald Duck sing as he heads for work in *The Riveter* (1940)?

42. What type of dance do Donald and Daisy engage in while the three nephews do everything in their power to interrupt them in *Mr. Duck Steps Out* (1940)?

43. What does Mickey offer to do for Minnie in *The Little Whirl-wind* (1941), until a tornado ruins the day?

44. What is the name of the unfinished cartoon short on which Walt Disney collaborated with the surrealist painter Salvador Dali?

45. In the 1941 cartoon classic *The Nifty Nineties,* what was notable about the pair of tap-dancing comedians referred to as "Fred and Ward—Two Clever Boys from Illinois" at the vaudeville show?

46. Much to his embarrassment, what does Donald discover when he takes Huey, Dewey, and Louie to the schoolhouse in the 1941 Academy Award–nominated cartoon *Truant Officer Donald*?

47. In *Chef Donald* (1941), what ingredient does Donald accidentally pour into his waffle mix instead of baking powder?

48. What does the gang give to Mickey as a gift on his special day in the 1942 cartoon *Mickey's Birthday Party*?

49. Which character makes one incredible mess in the kitchen while attempting to bake Mickey's three-layer cake in *Mickey's Birthday Party*?

50. What happens to the orchestra's instruments prior to the big performance at the Wiz Theater in the classic cartoon *Symphony Hour* (1942)?

51. When *Donald Gets Drafted* (1942), who is his drill instructor?
52. What was the code word used by the Allied forces for D day, the June 6, 1944, invasion of Normandy during World War II?
53. What kind of animals are Monte and Vidi?
54. What was *Donald's Crime* in the 1945 Academy Award–nominated cartoon of the same name?
55. In the 1945 cartoon *Canine Casanova*, whom does Pluto save from the Municipal Dog Pound?
56. Along with a share of riches and glory, what does the winner of the Canterbury Tournament of Thunderstone Castle receive in the 1946 cartoon *A Knight for a Day*?
57. Whom does Donald recruit to help him win the hand of Daisy in the 1946 cartoon *Donald's Double Trouble,* and what goes wrong?
58. What gift does Daisy hint for Donald to bring back for her in *Dumb Bell of the Yukon* (1946)?
59. What character plays the Wild Man of the jungle in the 1946 cartoon *Frank Duck Brings 'em Back Alive*?
60. What type of creature becomes a rather unlikely opponent to the bulldog Butch and an ally to Pluto in the 1947 cartoon *Pluto's Housewarming*?
61. What exotic and neurotic bird foils Donald's attempts at photography in *Clown of the Jungle* (1947)?
62. What famous character was first introduced in the 1947 comic book *Christmas on Bear Mountain*?
63. In an attempt to get a good night's sleep, with what object does Donald battle in the 1947 cartoon *Wide Open Spaces*?
64. What is the name of Goofy's duck decoy in *Foul Hunting* (1947)?
65. What kind of animal is Flutter Foot in the 1947 cartoon *Mail Dog*?
66. What famous museum once maintained that Mickey Mouse was the "greatest historical figure in the development of American art?"
67. What kind of animals are Snapshot III and Old Moe?
68. What song does Donald sing while preparing lunch in the 1948 cartoon *Soup's On*?
69. Why does a seal decide to follow Mickey home in the Academy Award–nominated cartoon *Mickey and the Seal* (1948)?
70. What character tangles with a rather angry little bumblebee in the 1949 cartoon *Bubble Bee*?
71. Why does Goofy battle a lion in the 1951 cartoon *Lion Down*?

72. What was the stage name of Cliff Edwards, who provided the original voice of Jiminy Cricket?

73. What was the name of the beautiful nightclub singer at the Acorn Club who gets the attention of both Chip and Dale in the 1952 cartoon *Two Chips and a Miss*?

74. While on vacation in Mexico, what is Goofy recruited to do by a mob of his adoring fans in the 1953 cartoon *For Whom the Bulls Toil*?

75. What are the names of Donald's menacing neighbor and his dog in the 1953 cartoon *The New Neighbor*?

76. In which cartoon does Donald Duck contemplate marriage to Daisy during a dream?

77. What do Chip an' Dale mistake Donald's steam shovel for in *Dragon Around* (1954)?

78. What character is described as "the kind of character that thought very hard and long about everything he did and then did it wrong"?

79. What object do Chip an' Dale confiscate from Donald Duck in order to transport their nuts in the 1956 cartoon *Chips Ahoy*?

80. What character comes to mind when one hears the phrase, "Oh, bother"?

81. Name three Disney characters that have been honored on the Hollywood Walk of Fame.

82. For which country did Goofy become the Official Olympic Mascot in 1980?

83. Which character disguises himself as a jailer in an attempt to rescue Mickey and Donald in *The Prince and the Pauper* (1990)?

84. Scrooge McDuck and his nephews, Huey, Dewey, and Louie, are in search of whose lost treasure in *DuckTales: The Movie—Treasure of the Lost Lamp* (1990)?

85. What is the name of the evil wizard who is also in search of the treasure in *DuckTales: The Movie—Treasure of the Lost Lamp* (1990)?

Animated Cartoons
and Featurettes

....

Answers

1. Mickey plays "Turkey in the Straw."
2. An annoying parrot proves an irritant to Mickey.
3. Studio musician Carl Stalling first suggested to Walt Disney the Silly Symphony series.
4. Mickey plays a hot-dog vendor.
5. A cowbell.
6. A team of alley cats matches up against Mickey.
7. Mickey is a piano player in a tavern.
8. Along with bologna and macaroni, Minnie is also selling huckleberry pie in her box lunches.
9. The portraits of the Three Little Pigs' father show a ham and a string of hot dogs.
10. Fifer builds his house of straw, Fiddler builds a house of sticks, and Practical has the sense to build his house of brick.
11. Franklin Delano Roosevelt.
12. The evil Captain Pete and his crew kidnap Mickey and Minnie but, naturally, Mickey saves the day.
13. The Wise Little Hen asks Peter Pig for help. Peter Pig is the president of the Idle Hour Club and Donald Duck is the vice president.
14. Max Hare supposedly helped inspire Warner Brothers' Bugs Bunny.
15. Aesop first wrote down the fable "The Tortoise and the Hare."
16. Mickey Mouse first gained an entry in the *Encyclopaedia Britannica* in 1934.
17. Mickey believes the garden and its inhabitants have all grown to huge size and the insects are now after him and Pluto.
18. Mickey and the gang save Clarabelle Cow—against her will.
19. Goofy uses chewing tobacco as bait, so when the fish jump out of the water in order to spit, Goofy can then club them.
20. The Land of Symphony and the Isle of Jazz.
21. As a sign of their unity, the two kingdoms build the Bridge of Harmony.
22. A magic hat and all of its inhabitants.
23. Elmer Elephant saves Tillie Tiger.

24. Mickey battles the King of Hearts after the King spots Mickey dancing with the Queen.
25. Goofy tangles with a stubborn piano.
26. Donald throws a major tantrum over a goat and then an eagle family.
27. This time Max Hare and Toby Tortoise are involved in a boxing match.
28. Mickey makes a cameo appearance in the 1934 film *Hollywood Party*.
29. The little elephant is named Bobo.
30. Peg Leg Pete plays the role that befits him: dogcatcher from the City Pound.
31. Donald trades his little burro for a shiny motor car to impress Donna Duck. Donna was actually the original name of Daisy Duck.
32. Goofy plays the front of the moose and Donald the backside.
33. Hortense is the name of the ostrich, and she had a ferocious appetite.
34. The Seven Dwarfs appeared in four cartoon shorts: *The Standard Parade* (1939), *the Winged Scourge* (1943), *The Seven Wise Dwarfs* (1941), and *All Together* (1942), the last two being produced for the Canadian War Bond Campaign.
35. The *Queen Minnie* is the name of the boat. When Minnie breaks the ceremonial bottle on the bow, the boat completely falls apart.
36. Mickey is joined by Donald and driver Goofy, who decides to take a food break inside the trailer while the car is still in motion.
37. Machine Gun Butch is on the loose.
38. Mickey's goldfish is named Bianca.
39. *Brave Little Tailor* was inspired by a Brothers Grimm fairy tale.
40. Donald asks Mickey Rooney, the Ritz Brothers, Sonja Henie, and Shirley Temple for their autographs.
41. Donald sings "Heigh Ho" originally featured in *Snow White and the Seven Dwarfs* (1937).
42. Donald and Daisy dance the jitterbug.
43. Mickey offers to clean Minnie's yard, but then a little tornado, followed by a big tornado, frustrates his efforts.
44. *Destino.*
45. The characters Fred and Ward were caricatures of two of Walt Disney's leading animators at that time, Fred Moore and Ward Kimball.
46. School is out for summer vacation.

47. Donald uses rubber cement instead of baking powder.
48. Minnie and the gang give Mickey an electric organ.
49. Goofy makes a mess baking a cake for Mickey.
50. Goofy, who is responsible for the instruments, falls down the elevator shaft and the elevator crushes the instruments.
51. Pete plays Donald's drill instructor.
52. "Mickey Mouse."
53. They are the two title stars of the 1944 cartoon *The Pelican and the Snipe*.
54. Donald robs the nephews' piggy bank so that he can take Daisy out on a date, but guilt gets the better of him, causing him to hallucinate the life of a gangster—and finally he gives the money back.
55. Pluto saves one of his great loves, Dinah the dachshund.
56. The hand of the fair Princess Esmeralda.
57. Donald recruits his debonair look-alike to win the hand of Daisy, but Daisy falls for the impostor.
58. Daisy asks Donald to bring her back a fur coat, but when Donald attempts to take a baby bear cub to make this request possible, mother bear enters and is not at all happy.
59. Goofy is the Wild Man of the jungle.
60 A little turtle.
61. The Aracuan Bird, who earlier appeared in the animated feature *The Three Caballeros* (1945), and is also in *Melody Time* (1948).
62. Scrooge McDuck first appeared in *Christmas on Bear Mountain*.
63. Donald battles with an air mattress.
64. Goofy's duck decoy is named Clementine.
65. A snowshoe rabbit.
66. New York's Metropolitan Museum of Art.
67. Snapshot III and Old Moe were two horses that starred in *They're Off* (1948).
68. Donald sings "Zip-A-Dee-Doo-Dah," originally featured in *Song of the South* (1946).
69. While at the zoo, Mickey feeds fish to a group of seals, and a little seal is confident that there is more where that came from. The little seal also enjoys taking a bath in Mickey's tub.
70. The little bumblebee makes life miserable for Pluto after the dog takes the little bee's supply of bubble gum.
71. Goofy has taken the lion's tree in order to support one end of his hammock. The lion also needs the tree for his sleeping arrangements.
72. Cliff Edwards was also known as Ukulele Ike.

73. The nightclub singer was named Clarice.
74. Goofy is transformed into a matador by his adoring fans.
75. Donald's new neighbor is Pete and his dog is Muncey.
76. *Donald's Diary* (1954).
77. Chip an' Dale think Donald's steam shovel is actually a medieval dragon intent on destroying their castlelike tree house.
78. Who else but Goofy! This description actually came from Art Babbitt, an animator who has been given credit for helping make Goofy a star.
79. Chip an' Dale "borrow" Donald Duck's ship in a bottle.
80. Winnie the Pooh.
81. Mickey Mouse, Donald Duck, and Snow White.
82. Goofy was the official mascot for France in 1980.
83. Goofy.
84. The treasure of Collie Baba.
85. The evil wizard is named Merlock, voiced by Christopher Lloyd.

Animated Features

Snow White and the Seven Dwarfs

December 21, 1937

Questions

1. What was so unusual about the special 1939 Academy Award presented to Walt Disney for this film?
2. Who is the only Dwarf with blue eyes?
3. What song does Snow White sing as she cleans the Dwarfs' cottage?
4. What time do the Dwarfs end their workday at the diamond mine, and what song do they sing?
5. After cleaning the cottage, Snow White decides to take a nap. Whose beds does she fall asleep on?
6. Which two Dwarfs were voiced by the same individual?
7. After arriving at their cottage, the Dwarfs fear an intruder has broken in and is still upstairs. Which Dwarf is sent upstairs to chase the intruder out?

8. According to Grumpy, all females are full of "wicked wiles." When asked by Bashful what "wicked wiles" are, what is Grumpy's response?

9. On which Dwarf's shoulders does Dopey stand in order to become a suitable dance partner for Snow White?

10. What song does Snow White sing when she tells the Dwarfs a story?

11. Whose pie is Snow White preparing when the Queen, disguised as the old peddler woman, enters the scene?

12. What are the six ingredients that the Queen uses to make up her disguise as the old peddler woman?

13. What character was described in production notes as a mixture of Lady Macbeth and the Big Bad Wolf?

14. What famous authors wrote the fairy tale on which *Snow White and the Seven Dwarfs* was based?

15. In 1979 a stage version of *Snow White and the Seven Dwarfs* was performed. At what famous New York City theater did it play?

Snow White and the Seven Dwarfs

Answers

1. The award presented by actress Shirley Temple consisted of one large Oscar and seven dwarf Oscars.
2. Dopey is the only Dwarf with blue eyes.
3. "Whistle While You Work" by Frank Churchill and Larry Morey.
4. The Dwarfs end their day at 5:00 P.M., and the song they sing is "Heigh Ho."
5. Snow White falls asleep on the beds of Dopey, Sneezy, and Happy.
6. Pinto Colvig provided the voices for Grumpy and Sleepy. Colvig is better known as the original voice of Goofy.
7. Dopey is sent upstairs to chase out the intruder. At this point the Dwarfs do not realize that the intruder is Snow White, who is asleep.
8. Grumpy responds, "I don't know but I'm agin' 'em!"
9. Dopey stands on the shoulders of Sneezy.
10. "Some Day My Prince Will Come."
11. Snow White is busy preparing Grumpy's pie.
12. Ingredient one: Mummy Dust (to make me old); Ingredient two: Black of Night (to shroud my clothes); Ingredient three: Old Hag's Cackle (to age my voice); Ingredient four: Scream of Fright (to whiten my hair); Ingredient five: A Blast of Wind (to fan my hate); Ingredient six: a Thunderbolt (to mix it well).
13. The evil Queen.
14. The Brothers Grimm.
15. Radio City Music Hall.

Pinocchio

February 7, 1940

Questions

1. Which author wrote the book on which *Pinocchio* is based?
2. When Jiminy Cricket arrives at Geppetto's house, what two items does he carry?
3. What type of business does Geppetto run?
4. According to the song, what is the only thing Pinocchio has to do when he wants his conscience to be his guide?
5. What character uses the words, "Little puppet made of pine, wake, the gift of life is thine"?
6. What character is dubbed the "lord high keeper of the knowledge of right and wrong, counselor in moments of temptation, and guide along the straight and narrow path"?
7. From what object does Jiminy Cricket make his bed in Geppetto's workshop?
8. What does Pinocchio wear in his hat?
9. What song includes the phrase, "an actor's life for me"?
10. Who saves Pinocchio from the evil puppeteer and showman, Stromboli?
11. Who tricks Pinocchio into thinking that he needs a vacation on Pleasure Island?
12. What is the name of the obnoxious boy whom Pinocchio befriends on Pleasure Island?

13. What game is Pinocchio playing when Jiminy Cricket eventually finds him on Pleasure Island?

14. How do Pinocchio and Jiminy Cricket discover that Geppetto has been swallowed by a whale?

15. What type of fish is Geppetto attempting to catch while inside the whale when he discovers Pinocchio?

Pinocchio

Answers

1. Collodi (Carlo Lorenzini) published *Pinocchio* in serial form in 1880 and as a book in 1883.
2. Jiminy is seen carrying his umbrella and his carpetbag.
3. Geppetto runs a wood-carving shop specializing in clocks, music boxes, and toys.
4. According to the song, all Pinocchio has to do is "give a little whistle."
5. The Blue Fairy uses these words in order to bring Pinocchio to life.
6. Jiminy Cricket, who also acts as Pinocchio's conscience.
7. Jiminy Cricket uses a matchbox for a bed after first trying a violin handle.
8. Pinocchio's hat has a red feather in it.
9. "Hi Diddle Dee Dee" by Leigh Harline, Ned Washington, and Paul J. Smith.
10. The Blue Fairy saves Pinocchio from Stromboli's bird-cage prison.
11. Helped by Giddy, Honest John tricks Pinocchio into going to Pleasure Island, and gives him an Ace of Spades playing card, claiming that it is his ticket.
12. Lampwick.
13. Pinocchio is playing pool when Jiminy discovers him.
14. They read it in a note from the Blue Fairy, delivered by a dove.
15. Geppetto is attempting to catch tuna.

Dumbo

··

October 23, 1941

Questions

1. As the film opens, what song do we hear that describes a friendly delivery man?
2. What is the name of the circus train featured in the film?
3. Whose baby is the last to be delivered by Mr. Stork?
4. How does Dumbo first reveal the fact that he has rather large ears?
5. During Dumbo's first attempt at becoming a circus star, what happens when he tries to springboard to the top of a pyramid of elephants?
6. What color hat does Dumbo wear in the movie?
7. After the disaster that Dumbo causes involving the pyramid of elephants, what group is he then teamed up with?
8. Who convinces the Ringmaster that Dumbo could become the circus's newest star?
9. What event displaced Dumbo's planned appearance on the cover of *Time* magazine?
10. What eventually happens to Dumbo and his mother at the conclusion of the film?

Dumbo

1. "Look Out for Mr. Stork."
2. Casey Junior.
3. Mr. Stork makes his last delivery to Mrs. Jumbo.
4. Dumbo's large ears are revealed only after he sneezes, causing them to spring out.
5. Dumbo trips over his ears, causing the pyramid of elephants to fall and the Big Top to collapse.
6. Dumbo wears a yellow hat.
7. Dumbo has been reduced to a member of the clown act, and is forced to jump into a vat of plaster.
8. Timothy acts as a subconscious voice and inspiration while the Ringmaster is asleep one evening.
9. The entry of the United States into World War II.
10. Dumbo is the circus's newest and brightest star, and he and his mother are given their own private car on the circus train.

Bambi

August 13, 1942

Questions

1. What is the name of the Academy Award–nominated song from the film *Bambi*?
2. What place does Bambi's mother call wonderful, but also a place where they are unprotected and must be careful?
3. Why is Bambi's father known as the Great Prince of the Forest?
4. Who does Thumper constantly quote throughout the film, with some encouragement from his mother?
5. Who informs Bambi of the fate of his mother?
6. Whom does Bambi fight for the affection of Faline?
7. From what danger does Bambi save Faline?
8. How do Bambi and his father escape the great fire in the forest?
9. How is Bambi injured during the great fire?
10. How many children does Thumper eventually have?

Bambi

Answers

1. "Love Is a Song," written by Frank Churchill and Larry Morey.
2. Bambi's mother is referring to the meadow.
3. "Everyone respects him, for of all the deer in the forest, not one has lived half so long. He's very brave and very wise. That's why he is known as the Great Prince of the Forest."
4. His father.
5. Bambi's father breaks the unfortunate news.
6. Bambi fights the bully Ronno.
7. Bambi saves Faline from a pack of hunting dogs.
8. Bambi and his father jump down a waterfall.
9. A bullet hits Bambi as he attempts to jump over a ridge.
10. Thumper has four children, all of which look like their father and possess his ability to thump.

Cinderella

....
February 15, 1950

Questions

1. Who helps Cinderella wake up each morning?
2. What is the name of the vicious and spiteful cat who makes life downright miserable for Cinderella?
3. According to the King, who is to be invited to the ball held in honor of his returning son?
4. What Disney voice actor spoke for both mice, Gus and Jaq?
5. What song does Cinderella sing as she washes the floor?
6. What items were discarded by the two ugly stepsisters, then eventually retrieved by Gus and Jaq to prepare Cinderella's dress?
7. Which actress provided the voice for Cinderella?
8. What song do Cinderella and Prince sing and dance to at the ball?
9. What is actually the last word uttered by Cinderella to the Prince at the ball?
10. How does Cinderella lose one of the glass slippers?

Cinderella

·················

Answers

1. Cinderella is awakened with the help of some bluebirds, as we hear the clock strike six A.M.
2. The haughty and spiteful cat is named Lucifer.
3. According to the King, "every eligible maiden" is to be invited to the ball.
4. The characters Gus and Jaq were both voiced by James Macdonald. In addition to providing the voice of these two mice, Macdonald was also responsible then for voicing another mouse, named Mickey.
5. Cinderella sings a beautiful rendition of "Oh Sing, Sweet Nightingale" while her two ugly stepsisters sing the same song a little off key.
6. The two ugly stepsisters' sash and beads were confiscated by Gus and Jaq and used for Cinderella's dress.
7. Ilene Woods.
8. Cinderella and the Prince dance to and sing "So This Is Love."
9. "Good-bye."
10. Cinderella hears the bell in the tower as it begins to strike twelve. She then runs to her coach in order to flee. However, in her haste to leave, she loses a glass slipper.

Alice in Wonderland

July 28, 1951

Questions

1. What is the White Rabbit's song, and what two items is he carrying when Alice first encounters him?
2. One of the first characters Alice stumbles upon is Dodo. What type of race does he organize?
3. What is another name for thc story of "The Walrus and the Carpenter" sung to Alice by Tweedledum and Tweedledee?
4. When Alice first arrives at White Rabbit's house, he refers to her by another girl's name. What is that name?
5. While in White Rabbit's house, Alice indulges in some wafers. Alice then grows to a huge size. Who is recruited to chase the now monstrous Alice out through the chimney?
6. According to the sign, what is the name of the woods into which Alice wanders?
7. What character asks Alice the curious riddle, "Why is a raven like a writing desk?"
8. What is the only way to calm down the Dormouse after one mentions the word "cat"?
9. As sung by the Queen of Hearts' gardeners, what color are they painting the roses?
10. What two earlier films made by Walt Disney were inspired by Lewis Carroll's classic *Alice's Adventures in Wonderland*?

Alice in Wonderland

Answers

1. White Rabbit sings "I'm Late," and he carries an umbrella and a large pocket watch.
2. Dodo organizes a "Caucus Race."
3. "The Story of the Curious Oysters."
4. White Rabbit calls Alice "Maryanne."
5. Bill, a lizard with a ladder who happens to be a chimney sweep.
6. Tulgey Wood.
7. The Mad Hatter asks Alice this curious riddle and then, to make matters worse, doesn't provide her the answer.
8. The only way to calm down the Dormouse is by placing jam on his nose.
9. The Queen's gardeners are "painting the roses red."
10. In 1923 the series of Alice Comedies began with a short film called *Alice's Wonderland*, and in 1936 Mickey went *Thru the Mirror*.

Peter Pan

February 5, 1953

Questions

1. Why did Walt Disney thank the Hospital for Sick Children on Great Ormond Street in London at the beginning of the film?
2. Which one of the Darling children carries an umbrella and wears a top hat on his journey to Never Land?
3. What is Wendy's full name?
4. What song do Peter Pan and the Darling children sing over the city of London as they make their way to Never Land?
5. Why is Tinker Bell banished from Never Land?
6. What nickname does Peter Pan use to refer to Captain Hook?
7. Who are Foxy, Rabbit, Skunk, Cubby, and the Raccoon Twins?
8. Who does Captain Hook trick into telling him the secret hide-out of Peter Pan?
9. How does Captain Hook attempt to eliminate Peter Pan after he discovers Peter's hiding place?
10. What song for the film *Peter Pan* was only sung on recordings?

Peter Pan

Answers

1. Walt Disney thanked the hospital because it owned the copyright to the play *Peter Pan*. The rights were bequeathed to the hospital by the author, Sir James M. Barrie.
2. John.
3. Wendy Moira Angela Darling.
4. Peter Pan and the children sing "You Can Fly, You Can Fly, You Can Fly," which was written by Sammy Cahn and Sammy Fain.
5. Tinker Bell is charged with "high treason," according to Peter Pan, for having attempted to have Wendy killed.
6. Peter calls Captain Hook a "codfish."
7. The six were known as Peter Pan's Lost Boys.
8. Captain Hook tricks Tinker Bell into revealing Peter Pan's hideout.
9. Captain Hook places a time bomb in a gift-wrapped package in an attempt to dispose of Peter Pan.
10. The song "Never Smile at a Crocodile," by Frank Churchill and Jack Lawrence, is heard as an instrumental, but is never sung in the film. However, it did appear on recordings.

Lady and the Tramp

June 22, 1955

Questions

1. What special gift does Lady receive from her owners?
2. How does Tramp describe the neighborhood in which Lady lives?
3. In what month do Lady's owners have their baby, and what is the name of the doctor who delivers it?
4. What is the name of the song Aunt Sarah's cats sing as they proceed to wreak havoc around the house?
5. Why does Aunt Sarah take Lady to the pet shop to buy her a muzzle?
6. From what danger does Tramp save Lady after she runs out of the pet store?
7. Who does Tramp recruit to help remove the muzzle that has been placed on Lady, and where does this take place?
8. What do the dogs first call Lady when she is brought to the City Pound?
9. What do the dogs in the pound call Lady's license and dog collar?
10. As a sign of their appreciation, what gift do Lady's owners present to Tramp as a symbol that he is now part of the family?

Lady and the Tramp

Answers

1. Lady receives a brand-new dog collar and license.
2. Tramp refers to Lady's neighborhood as "snob hill."
3. Darling has her baby in the month of April, and he is delivered by Old Doc Jones, who apparently "hasn't lost a father yet."
4. "The Siamese Cat Song" by Peggy Lee and Sonny Burke.
5. Aunt Sarah thinks Lady has attacked her two darling cats.
6. Tramp saves Lady from a pack of vicious dogs.
7. Tramp convinces a beaver at the zoo that the muzzle would prove to be of great assistance in his log-moving chores.
8. "Miss Park Avenue."
9. The dogs refer to Lady's dog collar and license as "a dog's passport to freedom."
10. Tramp is given his own dog collar and license and becomes an official member of the family.

Sleeping Beauty

January 29, 1959

Questions

1. According to the three good fairies, what are the three qualities Maleficent will never understand?
2. What song does the Princess sing to the forest animals and then with Prince Phillip?
3. What century provides the setting for *Sleeping Beauty*?
4. Which one of the good fairies bakes a cake for the Princess' birthday celebration?
5. Who eventually discovers the secret location of the Princess for the evil Maleficent?
6. What becomes of the Prince after he arrives at the cottage to meet Briar Rose?
7. What gift do the three good fairies present to the Princess after she is returned to the castle?
8. What spell do the three good fairies place on the inhabitants of the castle?
9. What becomes of Maleficent's raven?
10. What are the Prince and Princess doing in the final scene of the film?

Sleeping Beauty

1. According to the good fairies, Maleficent will never understand, "love, kindness, and the joy of helping others."
2. "Once Upon a Dream" by Sammy Fain and Jack Lawrence.
3. According to the Prince, it's the fourteenth century.
4. Fauna attempts to bake a cake for the Princess while Flora and Merryweather work on the dress for her birthday celebration.
5. Maleficent's pet raven discovers the Princess' secret hiding place when it spies flashes of magic during a dispute between Flora and Merryweather over the color of the dress they are to give to the Princess.
6. The Prince is attacked by Maleficent's goons, then kidnapped and thrown into her dungeon.
7. The three good fairies present the Princess with a crown for her to wear with grace and beauty.
8. They put the inhabitants of the castle into a deep sleep.
9. Merryweather turns the raven into a stone gargoyle.
10. The two start out dancing on the ballroom floor and then eventually in the clouds, which becomes an illustration in a book.

One Hundred and One Dalmatians

••

January 25, 1961

Questions

1. What is the title of Roger Radcliff's first hit song?
2. According to the story, in which month were Perdita's puppies born?
3. Who is the first person to discover the puppies missing?
4. The humans enlist the help of whom in an effort to recover their missing puppies?
5. Which character is the first to discover the actual whereabouts of the kidnapped puppies?
6. What is the title of the two bumbling kidnappers' favorite television show?
7. According to Cruella De Vil, what is her "only true love"?
8. In an attempt to not leave telltale paw prints, where do Pongo, Perdita, and the puppies walk?
9. Why does the evil Cruella De Vil have to give up the chase?
10. What photocopying process was used to simplify the work in this film?

One Hundred and One Dalmatians

Answers

1. "Cruella De Vil" is Roger Radcliff's first hit.
2. The puppies were born on a stormy night in October.
3. Nanny.
4. Roger and Anita Radcliff enlist the help of Scotland Yard.
5. Sergeant Tibs first discovers the missing puppies.
6. The two bumbling kidnappers, the Baduns, enjoy watching "What's My Crime?"
7. Cruella De Vil's only true love is fur coats, and she hopes to utilize the coats of the puppies to make them.
8. Pongo, Perdita, and the puppies walk on the frozen creek.
9. Cruella De Vil crashes her car into the Baduns' truck and careens off an embankment.
10. The Xerox process was utilized in *One Hundred and One Dalmatians* to copy the animator's drawings onto cels, which helped establish the uniformity that existed throughout the film. It was especially useful in this film because of the dalmatians' spots. For instance, thirty-two spots appear on each puppy, seventy-two on Pongo, and sixty-eight on Perdita.

The Sword in the Stone

December 25, 1963

Questions

1. How does Wart first encounter the wizard, Merlin?
2. What two words does Merlin use in order to start his spells?
3. How does Merlin convince Sir Ector, Wart's foster father, that he truly is a great wizard and wishes to instruct Wart?
4. What are the names of Sir Ector's two dogs?
5. What form of discipline is Wart constantly receiving from his foster father, Sir Ector?
6. What song does Wart and Merlin sing while in the water after the two are transformed into fish?
7. What important news does Sir Pelinore bring to Sir Ector and his son, Sir Kay, about the tournament to be held on New Year's Day?
8. What does Merlin's owl attempt to teach Wart?
9. What does mad Madam Mim hate more than anything?
10. What does Merlin call "the greatest force on earth"?

The Sword in the Stone

Answers

1. Wart, whose real name is Arthur, falls through Merlin's roof as he attempts to retrieve Sir Kay's misguided arrow.
2. "Higitus Figitus."
3. Merlin places a snowstorm over Sir Ector's head, which he describes as a "wizard blizzard."
4. Tiger and Talbot.
5. Wart is constantly receiving demerits from Sir Ector.
6. "That's What Makes the World Go Round" by the Sherman Brothers.
7. The winner of the tournament would be crowned "King of all England."
8. Merlin's highly educated owl, Archimedes, first instructs Wart in the elements of the ABCs. Then Archimedes teaches Wart to fly, because Merlin had turned him into a bird in an effort to teach him a valuable lesson.
9. Mad Madam Mim hates sunshine.
10. Love.

The Jungle Book

October 18, 1967

Questions

1. What famous author wrote the book on which *The Jungle Book* is based?
2. How old is Mowgli, the man cub, when he is taken back to the man village?
3. Who offers to take Mowgli to the "man village" after the wolf pack has decided that he can no longer stay with the pack because they fear the return of the evil Shere Khan?
4. How does Bagheera refer to Baloo?
5. What cunning crew kidnaps Mowgli while he and Baloo take their peaceful float down the river?
6. Whom does Bagheera ask for help during his search to find Mowgli?
7. Who provided the voice for the evil Shere Khan?
8. The four vultures have often been rumored to be patterned after what other "fab four," and what is the song they sing with their new friend, Mowgli?
9. How does Mowgli manage to scare off Shere Khan?
10. What is Baloo referring to when he says to Mowgli, "Forget about those, they ain't nothing but trouble"?

The Jungle Book

Answers

1. Rudyard Kipling.
2. Ten years old.
3. Bagheera offers to take the reluctant Mowgli back to the "man village."
4. Bagheera calls Baloo a "jungle bum."
5. A group of chimpanzees kidnap Mowgli from Baloo so that they can take him back to their leader, King Louie.
6. Bagheera asks Colonel Hathi for his assistance, but it takes the colonel's wife, Winifred, to eventually convince her husband to help in the search to retrieve Mowgli before he is discovered by Shere Khan.
7. Shere Khan was voiced by George Sanders.
8. The four vultures have often been compared to the Beatles. The song they sing with Mowgli is "That's What Friends Are For" by Richard and Robert Sherman.
9. Mowgli ties Shere Khan's tail around a burning bush.
10. Females.

Robin Hood

November 8, 1973

Questions

1. What kinds of animals are Robin Hood, Little John, and Friar Tuck?
2. Who provided the voice of Prince John?
3. How did Prince John gain control of King Richard's throne?
4. What song does Little John sing about the present leader of England, Prince John?
5. What is the name of Maid Marian's lady-in-waiting?
6. What type of game are Maid Marian and her lady-in-waiting playing in the courtyard?
7. What is the name of the hound dog, and what does he hide in the cast of his broken leg?
8. What is the name of the crossbow belonging to Trigger, the prison guard?
9. As the film concludes, what happens to Prince John?
10. What is the name of the Academy Award–nominated song from the film?

Robin Hood

Answers

1. Robin Hood is a fox, Little John is a bear, and Friar Tuck is a badger.
2. Peter Ustinov provided the voice of both Prince John and King Richard.
3. Sir Hiss hypnotized King Richard and sent him off on his Crusade.
4. "The Phony King of England" by John H. Mercer, sung by Phil Harris.
5. Lady Kluck.
6. They are playing a game of badminton.
7. The hound dog, Otto, hides his money so that the Sheriff of Nottingham will not find it.
8. Old Betsy, the same name used by Davy Crockett for his rifle.
9. Prince John, Sir Hiss, and the Sheriff of Nottingham are sentenced to the Royal Rock Pile for punishment. As for our hero, Robin Hood, he and Maid Marian are married and the real King of England, King Richard, resumes his reign.
10. "Love" by George Bruns and Floyd Huddleston.

The Rescuers

June 22, 1977

Questions

1. What is the motto of the Rescue Aid Society founded by Euripides Mouse in 405 B.C.?
2. What do Bernard and Bianca have to use as a pssenger seat while aboard the albatross, Orville?
3. Who is sent out to retrieve Penny when she attempts to escape the first time?
4. Why is Penny kidnapped by Madame Medusa in the first place?
5. What group helps Bernard and Bianca rescue Penny from the evil Madame Medusa?
6. What type of vehicle does Madame Medusa use to get around the swamp?

7. In what type of object is the diamond that everyone is searching for located?
8. What do Bernard and Bianca use to lure Madame Medusa's two crocodiles into a cage?
9. What type of vessel does Madame Medusa use as her hideout, the very place where Penny is being held?
10. What joyous event happens to Penny as the film concludes?

The Rescuers

....

1. "We Never Fail to Do What's Right."
2. Bernard and Bianca travel in a sardine can aboard Orville.
3. Madame Medusa's two crocodile henchmen, Nero and Brutus.
4. Penny was apparently the only one small enough to fit down the black hole, the alleged hiding place of the diamond.
5. The swamp folks, which included Luke and Ellie Mae, along with Digger, Deacon, Deadeye, and Gramps.
6. Medusa travels in her swamp mobile.
7. The diamond is located inside a skull.
8. Madame Medusa's two crocodiles are lured into the cage with a little help from Bianca's perfume.
9. Madame Medusa uses an abandoned riverboat as her hideout.
10. Penny is adopted.

Oliver & Company

November 18, 1988

Questions

1. Who sings the opening song, "Once Upon a Time in New York City"?
2. What actor provides the voice of Fagin, the dogs' master?
3. What are the names of the evil Sykes's two vicious Doberman pinschers?
4. What form of transportation do Fagin and his dogs use to get around New York City?
5. What character sings the song "Perfect Isn't Easy"?
6. What is the name of Jenny's butler and chauffeur?
7. What does Tito attempt to steal from the limousine after Einstein and Francis cause a distraction for the driver?
8. What is so familiar, for Disney fans, about one of the watches worn by Fagin?
9. What very special event is being celebrated by Jenny and her new friends as the film ends?
10. What author's work provided the inspiration for the film *Oliver & Company*?

Oliver & Company

Answers

1. Huey Lewis.
2. The voice of Fagin is provided by Dom DeLuise.
3. The two Dobermans are named Roscoe and DeSoto.
4. Fagin drives a scooter with a shopping cart attached to its back.
5. "Perfect Isn't Easy" is sung by the lavender poodle Georgette, voiced by Bette Midler.
6. Winston.
7. In an effort to raise money for Fagin, Tito attempts to steal the car's radio.
8. Fagin is seen wearing a Mickey Mouse watch.
9. Jenny and her new friends are celebrating her birthday.
10. Charles Dickens's classic, *Oliver Twist*.

The Little Mermaid

November 17, 1989

Questions

1. How old is the Little Mermaid, Ariel?
2. Whom does King Triton instruct to keep constant supervision over Ariel?
3. What song does Ariel sing while she is in her secret cavern?
4. What actress provided the voice of the evil sea witch, Ursula?
5. The actor who supplied the voice of Eric's valet, Grimsby, also voiced what character in the 1961 film *One Hundred and One Dalmatians*?
6. What are the names of Ursula's two conniving eels?
7. What is the only nominated song from the film that did not capture an Academy Award?
8. What character dresses Ariel on the beach after Ursula gives her the opportunity to become human?
9. How does Eric eventually dispose of Ursula after she has gained control of King Triton's kingdom?
10. What gift does King Triton bestow upon his daughter, knowing the love she carries for Prince Eric?

The Little Mermaid

Answers

1. Ariel is sixteen years old.
2. King Triton instructs Sebastian to keep constant supervision over his daughter, Ariel.
3. "Part of Your World" by Howard Ashman and Alan Menken.
4. Actress Pat Carroll voiced the evil sea witch, Ursula.
5. The voice of Grimsby was provided by Ben Wright, who also voiced Roger Radcliff in *One Hundred and One Dalmatians* (1961) as well as the wolf, Rama, from *The Jungle Book* (1967).
6. Ursula's two eels are Flotsam and Jetsam.
7. The song was "Kiss the Girl."
8. Scuttle, the scatterbrained seagull, dresses Ariel.
9. Prince Eric boards a shipwrecked boat that is brought to the surface with the swirling eddy that Ursula conjures, and uses the boat's splintered bowsprit to kill her.
10. King Triton permanently turns his daughter, Ariel, into a human.

Beauty and the Beast

November 22, 1991

Questions

1. What actors provide the voices of Cogsworth and Lumiere?
2. Where is Maurice headed when he is forced to escape from a pack of wolves to the Beast's castle?
3. What is the name of Maurice's horse?
4. While riding in the woods with his new invention, Maurice stumbles upon a directional sign. What two cities, significant to Disney fans, can be seen written on the sign?
5. According to the Beast, where is the only place in the castle Belle is not permitted?
6. According to Lumiere, how long has the transformation been in effect?
7. What two characters escort Belle on a guided tour of the castle?
8. From what danger does the Beast save Belle when she decides to leave the castle?
9. After the transformed servants witness Belle and the Beast's new friendship, whom does Mrs. Potts promise, "I'll tell you when you're older"?
10. What three suggestions does Cogsworth make to the Beast in an effort to help him win the heart of Belle?
11. What does the Beast give to Belle when she leaves the castle?
12. What is so unusual about Le Fou's appearance when Belle and her father return to the cottage?

13. What do the people who provide the voices of the Little Mermaid (Ariel) and the Beast have in common?
14. What do Pinocchio, the Little Mermaid, and the Beast all have in common?
15. Beginning in 1993, a stage version of Disney's *Beauty and the Beast* was produced. In what Texas city did it make its debut?

Beauty and the Beast

Answers

1. David Ogden Stiers provides the voice of the clock, Cogsworth, and is also the film's narrator. Jerry Orbach voices the candelabrum, Lumiere.
2. Maurice is headed to a fair.
3. Philippe.
4. The two California cities are Anaheim, home of Disneyland, and Valencia, home of CalArts, a famous art school attended by many of Disney's current animators.
5. Belle is not permitted in the West Wing.
6. Ten years.
7. Cogsworth and Lumiere give Belle a guided tour of the castle.
8. The Beast saves Belle from a pack of wolves.
9. Mrs. Potts promises to tell her son, Chip.
10. According to Cogsworth, they are "flowers, chocolates, promises you don't intend to keep."
11. The Beast gives Belle a magic mirror so that she will "always have a way to look back and remember" him.
12. Le Fou appears to be a snowman.
13. Even though unrelated, their last names are both Benson. Jodi Benson provides the voice of the Little Mermaid, Ariel, and Robby Benson voices the Beast.
14. All three characters want to be human.
15. Houston.

Aladdin

November 25, 1992

Questions

1. What is the name of the fictional city that provides the setting for the film?
2. Who provided the musical score for the feature *Aladdin*?
3. According to the ancient law, what does one need to be in order to marry a princess?
4. What is the name of Jasmine's pet tiger?
5. According to the Genie, besides not allowing wishes for more wishes, what are the only three types of wishes he cannot perform?
6. How long has the Genie been in the lamp before Aladdin finds it?
7. What song includes the words, "they're just lousy with loyalty"?
8. How do Jafar and his henchmen attempt to dispose of Aladdin after he and Jasmine have the Magic Carpet ride?
9. What character fools Aladdin into leaving the room so that he can remove the lamp and deliver it to the evil Jafar?
10. After taking possession of the lamp, what is Jafar's first wish of the Genie?
11. Where does Jafar place Princess Jasmine after she attempts to foil his plans?

12. What type of animal does Jafar change himself into during the battle with Aladdin?
13. What does Aladdin trick Jafar into wishing as his third wish of the Genie?
14. After regaining control of the lamp, what does Aladdin use as his third wish?
15. How many Academy Awards did the film *Aladdin* receive?

Aladdin

· · · · · · · · · · · · ·

Answers

1. Agrabah.
2. The Academy Award–winning team of Howard Ashman and Alan Menken, whose other film credits include *The Little Mermaid* (1989) and *Beauty and the Beast* (1991). However, during production of *Aladdin,* Ashman passed away and Tim Rice was called in to provide additional lyrics.
3. One needs to be a prince.
4. Rajah.
5. The three wishes the Genie cannot perform are: He can't kill anyone; he can't make anybody fall in love with anybody else; and he can't bring people back from the dead.
6. According to the Genie, "Ten thousand years will give you such a crick in the neck."
7. "Prince Ali."
8. Jafar's henchmen tie Aladdin up, attach a ball and chain to him, and then throw him into the sea.
9. Jafar's annoying little sidekick, Iago, who disguises himself as a flamingo.
10. Jafar's first wish is to be Sultan and to rule on high.
11. Jafar places Princess Jasmine in an hourglass.
12. Jafar transforms himself into a giant cobra snake.
13. Aladdin tricks Jafar into wishing that he were an all-powerful Genie.
14. Aladdin uses his third wish to free the Genie.
15. The film received two Academy Awards, one for Best Song, "A Whole New World," and one for Best Musical Score.

The Lion King

June 24, 1994

Questions

1. What joyous ceremony takes place as the film opens?
2. What is the name of the wise old mystic baboon who is friend to Mufasa?
3. Where do Mufasa and his family live?
4. Jonathan Taylor Thomas, who provides the voice for the young lion cub, Simba, is known for his continuing role in what popular television series?
5. What relation is Scar to the lion cub, Simba?
6. Where is Simba forbidden to go by his father, Mufasa?
7. What is the name of the lioness with whom Simba forms a romantic attachment?

8. What group of animals does Scar enlist in his campaign to destroy Mufasa and Simba?
9. Who composed the songs for *The Lion King*?
10. *The Lion King* has an all-animal cast. What are the only two other full-length animated features that have this distinction?

The Lion King

1. The newborn lion cub, Simba, is presented to the animals of the kingdom as the future king.
2. Rafiki.
3. Mufasa and his family live at Pride Rock.
4. Jonathan Taylor Thomas portrays Randy on "Home Improvement," starring Tim Allen.
5. Scar is his uncle, the brother of Simba's father, Mufasa.
6. The Elephant Graveyard.
7. Nala.
8. Scar forms an alliance with a group of hyenas.
9. The team of legendary singer-songwriter Elton John and the Tony Award–winning lyricist Tim Rice. Rice also won an Academy Award for "A Whole New World."
10. To date, the only two films besides *The Lion King* to have an all-animal cast are *Bambi* (1942) and *Robin Hood* (1973).

Live-Action Films

The Reluctant Dragon

June 20, 1941

Questions

1. *The Reluctant Dragon* features a tour of the Disney Studios, along with several animated cartoons that are incorporated into the story. In the first of these cartoons, we encounter a train battling the elements of nature. What is this train's name?

2. What popular humorist was used in live action sequences to provide a framework for this film?

3. What is so special about the baby in the *Baby Weems* sequence?

4. What three famous men—a scientist, a president, and an author—appear in the *Baby Weems* sequence?

5. In one sequence, Goofy teaches us *How to Ride a Horse*. What is the name of the horse that tangles with Goofy?

6. The final cartoon is the story of the Reluctant Dragon. What is the dragon doing the first time we see him?

7. What musical instrument does the dragon like to play?

8. What is the name of the dragon fighter who comes to town in order to fight the dragon?

9. What author wrote the story on which the *Reluctant Dragon* section is based?

10. Clarence Nash and Florence Gill play what roles in the film?

The Reluctant Dragon

1. Casey Junior. Later that same year, this train also appeared in *Dumbo,* playing an even more significant role.
2. Robert Benchley is shown on a tour of the Walt Disney Studios. The cartoons helped demonstrate steps in the animation process as Benchley visited various departments.
3. Baby Weems is a child prodigy who, as an infant, is able to talk intelligently and apparently is ready to solve all of mankind's problems.
4. Albert Einstein, Franklin Delano Roosevelt, and George Bernard Shaw appear in the sequence.
5. Percy is determined to give Goofy all kinds of problems.
6. He is taking a bath.
7. A flute.
8. Sir Giles.
9. Kenneth Grahame wrote the story "The Reluctant Dragon." This author also wrote *The Wind in the Willows,* which provided the inspiration for the *Mr. Toad* section in the 1949 animated feature *The Adventures of Ichabod and Mr. Toad.*
10. They are shown as themselves in a recording doing the voices of Donald Duck and Clara Cluck.

Song of the South

November 12, 1946

Questions

1. What author wrote the stories on which *Song of the South* is based?
2. What actor plays the role of the beloved Uncle Remus?
3. Why does Johnny's father have to leave the family and go back to Atlanta?
4. How does Uncle Remus convince Johnny to stay at the plantation and not run away to follow his father?
5. What is the name of the little boy who is instructed by the grandmother to look after Johnny?
6. In one of the first cartoon sequences, Brer Rabbit is shown trapped in a noose. How does he convince Brer Bear to get him down?
7. According to Uncle Remus, where does Brer Fox live?
8. What is the name of Academy Award–winning song from the film?
9. What popular young actor plays the part of Johnny?
10. What Academy Award–winning actress portrays the part of Aunt Tempy?
11. Why did the Favers boys make fun of Johnny during their first encounter?
12. What is the name of the little girl who befriends Johnny, and what gift does she give to him?
13. In a cartoon sequence, Brer Rabbit tells Brer Fox and Brer Bear that "Everybody's Got a Laughing Place." Where does Brer Rabbit lead them?
14. In another cartoon sequence, Brer Rabbit tangles with a figure made of tar. What trouble does this lead to for Brer Rabbit?
15. How does Brer Rabbit use reverse psychology to get him out of trouble with Brer Fox and Brer Bear?
16. According to Johnny, where is *his* laughing place?
17. What happens to Johnny as he attempts to stop Uncle Remus from leaving?
18. The actor who played the role of Uncle Remus also voiced what animated character?

19. According to the song, what does Uncle Remus discover on his shoulder?
20. What type of Academy Award was presented to the actor who portrayed Uncle Remus?

Song of the South

Answers

1. Joel Chandler Harris wrote *Uncle Remus* in 1880 and *Nights with Uncle Remus* in 1883, which are the basis for *Song of the South.*

2. James Baskett plays the part of Uncle Remus.

3. Because he is a journalist and his work requires him to travel back to Atlanta.

4. Uncle Remus tells Johnny the story of Brer Rabbit and the problems that resulted when he decided to leave his Briar Patch.

5. Toby.

6. Brer Rabbit convinces Brer Bear that even though he was making a dollar a minute hanging in the trap, he was certainly willing to pass on the opportunity to Brer Bear so that he could keep crows out of the cornfield.

7. Brer Fox lives atop Chickapin Hill.

8. "Zip-A-Dee-Doo-Dah," written by Allie Wrubel and Ray Gilbert.

9. Bobby Driscoll, who later did several other films for Disney.

10. Hattie McDaniel, who had won an Academy Award for *Gone with the Wind* (1939).

11. The Favers boys ridiculed Johnny because of the clothes he was wearing—a velvet suit with a lace collar.

12. Ginny, played by actress Luana Patten, gives Johnny a dog because her brothers, the Favers boys, threatened to drown it.

13. Brer Rabbit tricks Brer Bear into disturbing a beehive in a bush, stating that his laughing place was just beyond it.

14. The Tar Baby was placed there by Brer Fox and Brer Bear as a trick to capture Brer Rabbit. Brer Rabbit tangles with the Tar Baby and gets stuck.

15. Brer Rabbit pleads with Brer Fox and Brer Bear not to throw him in the Briar Patch. Naturally, they do, and Brer Rabbit hops away, tricking them once again.

16. Uncle Remus's cabin.

17. Johnny runs across a field, where a bull chases him and knocks him down.

18. In addition to playing the role of Uncle Remus, James Baskett voiced Brer Fox.
19. Mr. Bluebird.
20. James Baskett won a Special Award presented to him by the Academy of Motion Picture Arts and Sciences for his heart-warming characterization of Uncle Remus. The award was presented to him by Ingrid Bergman.

So Dear to My Heart

January 19, 1949

Questions

1. The film begins and ends looking at the same scene. What is this scene?
2. What is the name of the great race horse, often referred to as the Champion of Champions, that arrived in town one day?
3. What is the name of the Kincaid family's mule?
4. What is the name of the small town in which the film is set?
5. What is the name of the town's blacksmith, and what gift does he make for Jeremiah from a horseshoe nail he gets from the great race horse?
6. What actor plays the role of Jeremiah Kincaid?
7. What does Jeremiah name the lamb that becomes his pet?
8. What type of animal serves up proverbs from his Wishing Book to Jeremiah?
9. What two songs does this animal sing in order to make his point?
10. What does Jeremiah sell at Grundy's Mercantile Store so that he can afford to go to the County Fair?
11. What is the name of the Academy Award–nominated song from the film?
12. Who permits Jeremiah to keep a lamb as a pet?
13. What is the name of the little girl who accompanies Jeremiah and his lamb in their adventure?
14. What award do Jeremiah and his lamb win at the County Fair?
15. What special Academy Award did the actor who portrayed the character of Jeremiah Kincaid win?

So Dear to My Heart

Answers

1. The film begins and ends with a look at the attic at the Kincaid farm.
2. The great race horse is known as Dan Patch.
3. The family's mule is named General Jackson.
4. Fulton Corners.
5. Uncle Hiram, played by Burl Ives, is the town's blacksmith, and he gives Jeremiah a ring that he makes from the horseshoe nail.
6. Bobby Driscoll plays the part of Jeremiah Kincaid. Driscoll became somewhat of a regular for Disney, playing in a variety of films such as *Treasure Island, Song of the South,* and the animated feature *Melody Time,* and providing the voice of Peter Pan.
7. Danny.
8. The Wise Old Owl comes to life out of Jeremiah's scrapbook and attempts to teach him the lessons of life.
9. The two lesson songs the Wise Old Owl sings are "Stick-to-it-ivity" and "It's Whatcha Do with Whatcha Got."
10. Jeremiah sells honey for which Grundy was willing to pay him ten cents a pound.
11. "Lavender Blue (Dilly, Dilly)" by Eliot Daniel and Larry Morey.
12. Granny Kincaid.
13. The little girl is named Tildy.
14. A Special Award for Merit.
15. Bobby Driscoll won the Academy Award for Outstanding Juvenile Actor of 1949.

Treasure Island

July 19, 1950

Questions

1. Which star from *Treasure Island* was sent home to the United States from the filming in England because he did not have extended working papers to complete the project?
2. What is given to Captain Billy Bones at the Admiral Benbow Inn?
3. From what port does the ship sail to begin the adventure?
4. How does Long John Silver get on board the ship?
5. What is found in the possesion of George Merry that causes him to receive twelve lashes as a punishment?
6. What item does Long John Silver give to Jim Hawkins, instructing him to keep it a secret between the two of them?
7. What happens to the first mate of the ship?
8. How does the Captain first discover that a mutiny is about to take place?
9. Why don't the pirates attempt their mutiny sooner?
10. During the pirates' mutiny, who is taken as a hostage?
11. As soon as the pirates gain control of the ship, what action signifies their success?
12. What do the pirate crew give to Long John Silver as they grow impatient to find the treasure?
13. As the pirate crew are being prepared to return to England to stand trial, what gift does Long John Silver try to give to Jim Hawkins?

14. Instead of returning to England to stand trial, what happens to Long John Silver?
15. What author wrote the book on which *Treasure Island* was based?

Treasure Island

1. Bobby Driscoll, who portrayed Jim Hawkins, was a juvenile actor to whom working papers were not extended.
2. A blind man enters the Admiral Benbow Inn and gives Captain Billy Bones a piece of paper with a "black spot" on it, signifying that he will be the next to die that night.
3. The ship *Hispaniola* sailed from Bristol, England.
4. Long John Silver convinces Squire Trelawney to hire him as the ship's cook.
5. Before the mutiny the pirate crew were acting as part of the ship's crew. George Merry is given twelve lashes because he was concealing a knife.
6. Long John Silver gives Jim Hawkins his gun, fearing a punishment may come to him.
7. Long John Silver poisons the first mate and then throws the body overboard.
8. Jim Hawkins tells the Captain after he accidentally falls into an apple barrel and overhears the pirates planning their mutiny.
9. The pirates do not have the map and are allowing Captain Smollett to take them to the treasure site.
10. Jim Hawkins.
11. The pirates replace the British Union Jack with their own Jolly Roger (the skull and crossbones).
12. The dreaded "black spot."
13. His parrot, Captain Flint.
14. Long John Silver escapes and manages to sail off in a small boat.
15. Robert Louis Stevenson wrote the classic tale *Treasure Island*.

20,000 Leagues Under the Sea

December 23, 1954

Questions

1. What is the name of the ship that is destroyed as the film opens?
2. Professor Aronnax, the famous scientist from the National Museum of Paris, is asked by whom to investigate reports of the mysterious sea monster?
3. What actor plays the role of Professor Aronnax's assistant, Conseil?
4. According to the song Ned Land sings, "A Whale of a Tale," what does he swear by?
5. Why does Captain Nemo decide to spare the life of Professor Aronnax, Conseil, and Ned Land?
6. What musical piece, which was also used in one of the segments of *Fantasia* (1940), does Captain Nemo play on his organ?

7. What is the name of the prison camp from which Captain Nemo escaped?
8. Why does Professor Aronnax instruct Conseil to spy on Ned Land?
9. How does Ned Land get a message to the mainland concerning Captain Nemo and the ship's intended destination?
10. According to Captain Nemo, what is the giant squid's only vital spot?
11. Who saves Captain Nemo from the clutches of the giant squid?
12. What was Captain Nemo forced to do to his South Sea hideaway?
13. How does Captain Nemo receive his fatal injuries?
14. What becomes of Captain Nemo and the crew of the *Nautilus*?
15. What famous author wrote the book on which *20,000 Leagues Under the Sea* was based?

20,000 Leagues
Under the Sea

Answers

1. The *Golden Arrow.*
2. The United States Government asks Professor Aronnax to investigate because they fear the reports of the sea monster might be true.
3. Peter Lorre.
4. By his tattoo.
5. Captain Nemo spares the life of the three because of Professor Aronnax's loyalty to his companions.
6. Bach's Toccata and Fugue in D Minor.
7. Rorapandi.
8. Professor Aronnax instructs Conseil to spy on Ned Land because he doesn't trust him and fears that he would get all three of them into danger.
9. With a message in a bottle.
10. The giant squid's only vital spot is directly between the eyes.
11. Ned Land saves Captain Nemo from the giant squid.
12. The South Sea hideaway of Vulcania had to be destroyed because Captain Nemo feared that the world would learn his secrets.
13. Captain Nemo is shot by a crewman of a warship as he returns from Vulcania.
14. With the apparent death of Captin Nemo, the crew of the *Nautilus* carries out their suicide pact and the submarine is flooded as it sinks to the bottom of the sea.
15. Jules Verne wrote the book *20,000 Leagues Under the Sea.*

Davy Crockett, King of the Wild Frontier

May 25, 1955

Questions

1. According to the story, who wrote *Davy Crockett's Journal*?
2. In one of the opening scenes, Davy Crockett encounters a bear. How does Davy first attempt to capture the bear?
3. What was Davy Crockett's motto?
4. What is the first name of Davy Crockett's wife?
5. Whom does Davy rescue from Chief Red Stick and the Creek Indians?
6. What is the name of the character Davy beats in the town's shooting match?
7. Who is Davy Crockett's opponent when he runs for state legislator?
8. What sad and troubling news does Davy Crockett receive while exploring a new frontier for his family?
9. When Davy is asked to go to Washington as a congressman, what state does he represent?
10. Who asked Davy to tour the country on speaking engagements to tell some of his tales and exploits?
11. What is the name of the riverboat gambler who accompanies Davy Crockett and George Russel to the Alamo?
12. Whom does Davy fight against while defending the Alamo?
13. Who ventures out one night in order to get more troops to fight at the Alamo?
14. What military rank does Davy Crockett hold?
15. As the film concludes, what happens to Davy Crockett?

Davy Crockett, King of
the Wild Frontier

∙∙∙

Answers

1. *Davy Crockett's Journal* was written by Crockett himself.
2. Davy attempts to grin the bear to death.
3. Davy Crockett's motto was, "Be sure you're right, then go ahead."
4. Davy Crockett's wife is named Polly.
5. George Russel.
6. Davy beats the town's troublemaker, Bigfoot Mason.
7. Amos Thorpe.
8 Davy receives news that his wife, Polly, has died.
9. The state is Tennessee.
10. Tobias Norton. However, this was a trick to get Davy out of town so that Congress could pass a bill that would take away land from the Indians.
11. The riverboat gambler was named Thimblerig, portrayed by actor Hans Conried, who also provided the voice of Captain Hook in the 1953 feature *Peter Pan*.
12. Davy fights General Santa Anna and his army.
13. George Russel.
14. Davy Crockett is a colonel.
15. In the final scene, we see Davy Crockett swinging his rifle just prior to his death, although his legend was to live on.

Johnny Tremain

June 19, 1957

Questions

1. What actor plays the part of Johnny Tremain? What is Johnny's profession?
2. What is the setting for the film?
3. Why can't Johnny continue to work in his profession any longer?
4. Why is Johnny Tremain put on trial by the evil aristocrat Jonathan Lyte?
5. What actor plays the part of Jonathan Lyte?
6. What does Jonathan Lyte fear most about Johnny Tremain?
7. After the trial, what patriotic organization does Johnny Tremain join?
8. What is the name of the tree that becomes the symbol of this group's struggle for independence?
9. Who directed the film *Johnny Tremain*?
10. What author wrote the book on which *Johnny Tremain* was based?

Johnny Tremain

Answers

1. Hal Stalmaster plays the role of Johnny Tremain, who is an apprentice silversmith by trade.
2. The film is set in Boston at the time of the start of the Revolutionary War.
3. Johnny Tremain's hand is injured when molten silver is accidentally poured on it.
4. Jonathan Lyte accuses Johnny of stealing one of his silver cups.
5. Jonathan Lyte is played by Sebastian Cabot, who later went on to provide the voice of Bagheera in the 1967 animated feature *The Jungle Book*. Cabot was also the narrator for the 1963 animated film *The Sword in the Stone*.
6. He fears that Johnny by his birthright is actually a Lyte.
7. The Sons of Liberty.
8. The Liberty Tree.
9. The film was directed by Robert Stevenson, who is best known for his direction of *Mary Poppins* (1964).
10. Esther Forbes wrote the book *Johnny Tremain*.

Old Yeller

December 25, 1957

Questions

1. How does Old Yeller come to be the Coateses' new family dog?
2. What was the name of the dog they had prior to Old Yeller?
3. What actress plays the role of the mother, Katie Coates?
4. What is the title of the catchy song from the film that tells the story of "the best doggone dog in the West"?
5. What does Jim Coates, the father, promise to bring his boys, Travis and Arliss, when he returns?
6. What is the name of the family's mule?
7. Which of the two Coates children does Old Yeller save from a charging bear?
8. Who promises not to tell anyone that Old Yeller is stealing meat, bread, and eggs from some of the town's residents?
9. What does Travis trade with this person in order to ensure her silence about Old Yeller's stealing?
10. Why do Travis Coates and Old Yeller sleep in the corn patch one evening?
11. What is the name of the individual who shows up at the Coateses' house to reclaim his dog, Old Yeller?
12. What does the Coates family trade with this stranger for possession of Old Yeller?
13. What happens to Travis Coates when he attempts to capture hogs?
14. What gift does Lisbeth Searcy present to Travis?
15. From what danger does Old Yeller save the mother, Katie Coates, one night while in the field?

Old Yeller

Answers

1. Old Yeller shows up on the doorstep of the Coateses' house one day after chasing a rabbit through the corn patch.
2. Old Bell.
3. Katie Coates is played by actress Dorothy McGuire.
4. The name of the song is simply "Old Yeller," written by Oliver Wallace and Gil George.
5. Jim Coates promises to bring Travis a horse, and Arliss a tomahawk and an Indian headdress.
6. Jumper is the name of the family's mule.
7. Old Yeller saves Arliss from a charging bear.
8. Lisbeth Searcy informs Travis that she will keep the secret that Old Yeller was stealing.
9. Travis gives Lisbeth a Comanche arrowhead to keep her silent.
10. Travis sleeps in the corn patch with Old Yeller to help keep out the raccoons that were damaging the crop.
11. Old Yeller's real owner is Burn Sanderson, played by actor Chuck Connors.
12. Burn Sanderson agrees to leave Old Yeller behind in exchange for Arliss's "horny toad" and one good cooked family meal. He also warns Travis about an outbreak of rabies that has scourged the town.
13. Travis falls from a tree limb, is bitten by a hog, and is then saved by Old Yeller.
14. Lisbeth presents Travis with a puppy resembling Old Yeller.
15. Old Yeller saves Katie Coates from a charging wolf, but the dog is infected with rabies and eventually has to be destroyed.

The Shaggy Dog

March 19, 1959

Questions

1. What famous author wrote the book that provided the inspiration for *The Shaggy Dog*?
2. What young Disney actor plays the role of Wilby Daniels's kid brother Moochie?
3. What is the name of the professor at the museum who informs Wilby about the mysterious ring?
4. What is the name of the pretty girl who moves in next door?
5. What popular actor from the "Mickey Mouse Club" serials plays the part of Buzz Miller?
6. What does Wilson Daniels, the father, hate more than anything?
7. What is the name of the dog that continues to switch places with Wilby?
8. According to the professor at the museum, what is Wilby's hope of breaking the spell?
9. What happens to Wilson Daniels after Wilby tells him that he has turned into a dog?
10. What two girls does Buzz Miller take to the Country Club Dance?
11. What happens to Wilson Daniels when he tells the authorities about his son, the dog?
12. While Wilby is transformed into the Shaggy Dog, whose car does he borrow in order to chase the spy ring?

13. Who is the leader of the spy ring?
14. Whom does the town of Springfield honor as a hero for uncovering the spy ring?
15. Seventeen years after the release of *The Shaggy Dog*, a sequel was made. What was its title?

The Shaggy Dog

Answers

1. Felix Salten's book *The Hound of Florence* provided the inspiration for *The Shaggy Dog*.
2. Kevin Corcoran plays the part of Moochie in *The Shaggy Dog* as well as on TV's "Mickey Mouse Club" serials.
3. Professor Plumcutt tells Wilby about the mysterious Borgia ring.
4. Franceska Andrassy, played by actress Roberta Shore, is the girl who moves in next door.
5. Tim Considine, who played in a variety of serials including *The Hardy Boys* and *The Adventures of Spin and Marty*, portrays Buzz.
6. Wilson hates dogs more than anything.
7. Franceska's dog, Chiffon.
8. According to Professor Plumcutt, "an act of heroism could break the spell."
9. Naturally, he faints.
10. Buzz attempts to trick both Allison D'Allessio, played by Annette Funicello, and Franceska into going with him to the Country Club Dance.
11. After telling the authorities that his son is a dog, Wilson Daniels is sent for psychiatric testing.
12. Wilby first borrows Buzz Miller's car and then a police car.
13. Franceska's father, Doctor Mikhail Andrassy, is the head of the spy ring.
14. The town honors Wilson Daniels and Chiffon, even though it was Wilby all along.
15. *The Shaggy D.A.*, starring Dean Jones, was the 1976 sequel.

Darby O'Gill and the Little People

··

June 26, 1959

Questions

1. As the film opens, we see a quote from Walt Disney. What does it say?
2. What causes Darby O'Gill to fall down a well?
3. According to the legend, how old was the King of the Leprechauns?
4. What is Darby O'Gill's profession?
5. What popular actor played the role of Michael McBride?
6. What happens when one wishes a fourth wish of the leprechauns?
7. Why has Michael McBride come to the town of Rathcullen?
8. What was the name of the inn where Darby O'Gill would tell his tales of the leprechauns?
9. What is the name of the song that is sung by Michael McBride?
10. What musical instrument does the King of the Leprechauns ask Darby to play for his subjects?
11. According to the legend, when does the King lose his power?
12. Why has the King brought Darby O'Gill to his fairy mountain kingdom?
13. What is the name of the dreaded "death coach" that comes to collect Katie O'Gill after she has taken a serious fall and lies close to death?
14. How does Darby O'Gill convince the driver of the death coach not to take his daughter Katie?
15. What is the name of the town's troublemaker whom Michael McBride fights?

Darby O'Gill and the Little People

Answers

1. "My thanks to King Brian of Knocknasheega and his lepre-chauns, whose gracious co-operation made this picture possible. . . . Walt Disney."
2. Darby is frightened by a bucking horse who seems to be enchanted.
3. King Brian was 5,000 years old.
4. Darby O'Gill is the caretaker for Lord Fitzpatrick's estate.
5. Sean Connery.
6. One loses the previous three.
7. Michael McBride is the new caretaker for Lord Fitzpatrick.
8. Darby tells his stories at the Rathcullen Arms.
9. Sean Connery, who plays Michael, sings "Pretty Irish Girl."
10. Darby plays the violin for King Brian and his people.
11. King Brian loses his power with the coming of daylight.
12. Darby is taken to the fairy mountain kingdom so that he would not have to break the news to his daughter, Katie, that he has lost his job and the house.
13. The Costa Bower.
14. Darby uses his third wish and insists that the death coach take him instead.
15. Michael McBride fights the troublemaker Pony Sugrue.

Pollyanna

May 19, 1960

Questions

1. What is the name of the town that provides the setting for the film?
2. Why does Pollyanna have to come and live with her Aunt Polly?
3. What is Pollyanna's favorite game?
4. What is the name of the little orphan boy who befriends Pollyanna?
5. What is the name of the doctor and former sweetheart of Aunt Polly who comes back to town after a long absence?
6. What is the name of the town's reverend, who was always known for his fire-and-brimstone sermons?
7. According to Aunt Polly, what time is dinner served each evening?
8. What actress played the role of Aunt Polly?
9. What happens to the Harrington House Orphanage?
10. What intrigues Pollyanna and Jimmy at the home of the hermitlike Mr. Pendergast?
11. What does the charm that Pollyanna wears around her neck say?
12. What is the name of the old crotchety hypochondriac who is constantly feeling sorry for herself?
13. What does Pollyanna win at the town's Charity Bazaar fishpond?
14. Why has the town organized a Charity Bazaar?
15. What part does Pollyanna play while at the Charity Bazaar?
16. Who eventually adopts the orphan boy who befriended Pollyanna?
17. How does Pollyanna injure herself, resulting in paralysis?
18. Where is Pollyanna sent to receive treatment?
19. As a symbol of their support, the townspeople hang a sign from the railroad station platform. What does it say?
20. What special Academy Award did Hayley Mills receive for her portrayal of Pollyanna?

Pollyanna

Answers

1. The town of Harrington.
2. Pollyanna's father has passed away and Aunt Polly takes her in.
3. The "Glad Game," a game that always finds something glad in everything that happens.
4. The orphan boy is Jimmy Bean, played by Kevin Corcoran.
5. Doctor Edmund Chilton returns to Harrington after a long absence.
6. Reverend Paul Ford, played by Karl Malden.
7. According to Aunt Polly, dinner is served at "six o'clock sharp!"
8. Aunt Polly was played by actress Jane Wyman.
9. The pipes break, causing extensive damage to the town's orphanage.
10. Glass prisms.
11. "When you look for the bad in mankind expecting to find it, you surely will. . . . Abraham Lincoln."
12. Mrs. Snow, played by actress Agnes Moorehead.
13. Pollyanna wins a doll at the Charity Bazaar.
14. The Charity Bazaar was organized to help build a new orphanage.
15. Pollyanna is one of the children who make up the American flag.
16. Mr. Pendergast adopts the orphan, Jimmy Bean.
17. Pollyanna is injured when she falls from her third-floor window in an attempt to reach for the doll she won at the Charity Bazaar.
18. Pollyanna travels with Aunt Polly and Doctor Chilton to a children's hospital in Baltimore so the doctors can try to correct her paralysis.
19. "Harrington—The Glad Town."
20. Hayley Mills received the Academy Award for the Most Outstanding Juvenile Performance of 1960.

Swiss Family Robinson

December 21, 1960

Questions

1. Why did the family decide to leave Switzerland for a new land of opportunity?
2. What does Mr. Robinson rename the island?
3. What are the names of the two Great Danes that go with the family to the tropical island?
4. What does Mr. Robinson do to successfully chase away the pirates during their first confrontation?
5. What does the youngest Robinson boy name the baby elephant that he captures?
6. What kind of home does the family build on their island?
7. According to Mrs. Robinson, what is the only thing that the island lacks?
8. Which two Robinson boys set sail to explore the other side of the island?
9. How do the pirates know that the family is on the island, and who first spots their approach?
10. What is the name of the captain who eventually comes to the family's rescue and offers to take them to England?

Swiss Family Robinson

Answers

1. The family feared the current reign of Napoleon and his plans for expansion.
2. New Switzerland.
3. Turk and Duke.
4. He raises a quarantine flag on one of the ship's masts to indicate that black death is aboard.
5. Francis names his new pet Rocky.
6. A tree house.
7. Girls, knowing that she has two grown boys.
8. Fritz and Ernst.
9. The pirates learn the family is on the island when the boys rescue their prisoner. After the pirates leave, it is Roberta, the rescued prisoner, who first sights their return.
10. Captain Moreland.

The Absent-Minded Professor

March 16, 1961

Questions

1. What is the name of the school where the absent-minded professor teaches, and what is his field of study?
2. Who wrote the school's "Fight Song"?
3. What nickname do the students give to the absent-minded professor?
4. What was the name of the crooked company run by Alonzo Hawk?
5. Why does Alonzo Hawk want to tear down the school?
6. What is the name of the professor's sweetheart whom he has planned to marry?
7. To what object does the professor first apply his new invention?
8. What is the name of the opposing team's school in the big basketball game?
9. How does the professor help his school's basketball team against its highly favored opponent?

10. What is the name of the troublemaking and rather obnoxious English teacher from the opposing college, who also seeks the affection of the professor's sweetheart?

11. What does Alonzo Hawk do in an attempt to steal the professor's new invention?

12. What popular actor plays the part of the town's fire chief?

13. The professor decides to fly to Washington using his new invention. What do the authorities think of his arrival?

14. What Disney landmark can be seen as the professor makes his way to Washington?

15. Instead of the traditional "Just Married" sign that appears on a newly married couple's car, what does the sign read when the professor and his sweetheart are married?

The Absent-Minded Professor

Answers

1. Professor Ned Brainard teaches physical chemistry at Medfield College of Technology.
2. The "Medfield Fight Song" was written by Robert and Richard Sherman. This marked the Disney motion picture debut by the Academy Award–winning songwriting team.
3. The students refer to the professor as "Neddy the Nut."
4. Alonzo Hawk's crooked company is known as the Auld Lang Syne Loan Company.
5. The school owes Hawk money for a loan he made. The school does not have the money to repay him, so he plans to tear down the school and build a housing development.
6. The professor's sweetheart is Betsy Carlisle. However, he has missed several attempts at marriage already.
7. The professor applies his new invention, known as Flubber, to his Model T Ford.
8. Rutland College.
9. The professor gives his team a lift by applying Flubber to the team's sneakers. Medfield wins the basketball game with a score of 47 to 46 over Rutland College.
10. Shelby Ashton.
11. Alonzo Hawk switches Model T cars on the professor.
12. Ed Wynn plays the town's fire chief. His real-life son, Keenan, plays Alonzo Hawk.
13. Not knowing what to think of a flying Model T, the authorities treat the professor as an Unidentified Flying Object and are ready to shoot him down.
14. One can see the Walt Disney Studios in Burbank as the professor flies over.
15. After a successful fourth attempt at marriage, the sign reads "Finally Married."

The Parent Trap

June 21, 1961

Questions

1. As the film opens, we see a sign indicating the family's present situation. Instead of the traditional "Bless Our Happy Home," what does the sign read?
2. What two singers perform the title song from the film *The Parent Trap*?
3. Who play the roles of the parents, Maggie McKendrick and Mitch Evers?
4. What is the name of the boys' camp and what event do they plan together with the girls' camp?
5. What nasty trick do Sharon and her roommates play on Susan one night that causes the girls to fight?
6. What penalty does the camp's leader, Miss Inch, impose on Susan and Sharon for fighting?
7. How old are Susan and Sharon, and what date is their birthday?
8. How do Susan and Sharon finally come to the realization that they are twin sisters?
9. As camp concludes, what do Susan and Sharon do in order to try to reunite their parents?
10. What embarrassing nickname does Mitch call his daughter, Susan?
11. According to Maggie, where did she and Mitch go on their first date?
12. Why does Vicky Robinson want to marry Mitch?
13. What is in the telegram that Sharon sends to Susan?
14. While in Boston, who is the first individual to realize what the two girls had done?
15. Why does Maggie have to travel to California?
16. What is the name of the reverend who finds the entire situation involving the family very amusing?
17. What are the names of the ranch foreman and housekeeper who work for Mitch?
18. What do the girls attempt to re-create during the first evening their parents are together again?
19. In an effort to keep their parents together, the two girls re-

fuse to tell them which one is Sharon and which one is Susan unless they agree to do what?

20. What trick do the girls play on Vicky Robinson one night while she is sleeping?

The Parent Trap

Answers

1. The sign reads, "Bless Our Broken Home."
2. The title song is sung by Annette Funicello and Tommy Sands.
3. The mother, Maggie McKendrick, is played by actress Maureen O'Hara, and the father, Mitch Evers, is played by Brian Keith.
4. The Thunderhead Boys' Camp and Camp Inch for Girls plan a Saturday night dance.
5. Sharon cuts off a large piece from the back of Susan's dress, which naturally causes her humiliation at the Saturday night dance.
6. According to Miss Inch, "Let the punishment fit the crime." Therefore, for the remaining four weeks of camp, the two are placed in isolation and forced to do everything together.
7. Susan and Sharon are thirteen years old and their birthday is November 12.
8. The two finally realize they are sisters when Sharon reveals a picture of their mother.
9. They switch places. Susan goes to Boston and Sharon to California.
10. Mitch calls Susan "Peanut Face."
11. To Martinelli's, an Italian restaurant in New York City.
12. Vicky Robinson wants to marry Mitch just for his money.
13. The telegram reads, "ALEXANDER GRAHAM 3 A.M. IMPORTANT."
14. The girls' grandfather, Charles McKendrick, played by actor Charles Ruggles, overhears a telephone conversation the girls are having.
15. After realizing what the two girls have done, Maggie takes Susan back to Mitch.
16. Reverend Mosby.
17. Hecky and Verbena.
18. The girls attempt to re-create the first date their parents had together at Martinelli's Restaurant.
19. The girls refuse to tell their parents which girl is which un-

less the parents agree to go on a camping trip. However, Vicky goes in place of Maggie.

20. The two girls tie string around Vicky's tent and pour honey on her feet, which results in two young bear cubs trying to lick off the honey.

Babes in Toyland

December 14, 1961

Questions

1. As the film opens, we are introduced to Mother Goose and her rather chatty goose. What is the name of the goose?
2. In one of the opening scenes, we see members of the town gathering to celebrate what important event in Mother Goose village?
3. The film *Babes in Toyland* is based on an operetta by whom?
4. Who play the roles of Tom Piper and Miss Mary Quite Contrary?
5. What actor plays the role of the evil Barnaby?
6. What are the names of Barnaby's two bumbling accomplices?
7. The story is about the evil Barnaby and his attempts to wed Mary. Why was this marriage so important to Barnaby?
8. What does Barnaby tell his two accomplices to do with Tom Piper?
9. What happens to Little Bo Peep's sheep?
10. What song does Barnaby sing to Mary about how their life would be if she would only marry him?
11. What is so unusual about the trees in the Forest of No Return?
12. Who play the roles of the Toymaker and his assistant, Grumio?
13. Why do Tom, Mary, and the children help the Toymaker with the making of his toys?
14. While at the Toymaker's house, what object does Tom ride as he attempts to conquer the evil Barnaby?
15. What event takes place as the film concludes?

Babes in Toyland

Answers

1. The chatty goose is named Sylvester J. Goose.
2. The town is celebrating the upcoming wedding of Tom and Mary.
3. Victor Herbert and Glenn McDonough.
4. Mary Quite Contrary is played by Disney regular Annette Funicello, and Tom Piper is played by Tommy Sands.
5. The evil Barnaby is played by actor Ray Bolger.
6. Barnaby's two bumbling accomplices were Roderigo and Gonzorgo, played by Gene Sheldon and Henry Calvin, teamed up again after their roles on "Zorro."
7. Barnaby wants to wed Mary because she will receive a large sum of money when she marries, and he wants to be the beneficiary of her good fortune.
8. Roderigo and Gonzorgo are instructed to kidnap Tom and throw his body into the sea so that he will be unable to marry Mary. However, the two decide to sell Tom to a band of gypsies.
9. They were stolen by Roderigo and Gonzorgo and placed in the Forest of No Return. The part of Little Bo Peep was played by actress Ann Jillian (then spelled Jilliann).
10. "Castle in Spain" by George Bruns and Mel Leven.
11. They sing, talk, walk, and dance, and force Tom, Mary, and the children to follow them to the Toymaker.
12. The Toymaker is played by Ed Wynn and his assistant Grumio is Tommy Kirk. In addition to being the Toymaker, Wynn was also the mayor of Toyland and the police chief.
13. Toyland was CLOSED FOR ALTERATIONS, and a deadline had to be met.
14. Tom rides a toy horse.
15. The actual wedding of Tom Piper and Mary Quite Contrary.

In Search of the Castaways

December 19, 1962

Questions

1. What famous author wrote the book that inspired the film?
2. How does Captain Grant manage to get a message to the mainland that he is still alive?
3. What is the name of the Frenchman who helps Captain Grant's children search for their father?
4. Who is the owner of the boat that Captain Grant was commanding before he was lost at sea?
5. What popular Disney actress played the part of Captain Grant's daughter, Mary?
6. What is the name of the ship commanded by Captain Grant that was lost at sea?
7. To what continent does the search for Captain Grant first take the search party?
8. After a huge earthquake disrupts the search party, what type of creature captures the younger of the Grant children?
9. What is the name of the former crew member who convinces the search party that Captain Grant is being held prisoner in New Zealand?
10. Why is this former crew member so anxious to inform the search party of the whereabouts of Captain Grant?

In Search of the Castaways

Answers

1. Jules Verne wrote *Captain Grant's Children,* on which the film was based.
2. With a message in a bottle that is actually thrown by Bill Gaye, a crew member on Captain Grant's ship.
3. Professor Paganel of the University of Paris, who is played by actor Maurice Chevalier, helps the two children.
4. Lord Glenarvan is the owner of the ship that was commanded by Captain Grant.
5. Hayley Mills.
6. The *Britannia.*
7. The search party travels first to South America, where they have adventures in the Andes Mountains.
8. A giant condor.
9. Thomas Ayerton, played by actor George Sanders.
10. Because Ayerton is a gunrunner and he organized the mutiny of Captain Grant's ship in the first place. He wants to dispose of the search party so they will not discover his secret.

Son of Flubber

· ·

January 18, 1963

Questions

1. In the opening scene we see the professor and Biff flying over Washington. Why are the two there?
2. Who is the president of the college where the professor taught?
3. This time around our absent-minded professor invents a weather gun that, when pointed in a certain direction, produces artificial rain. What does the professor call this new phenomenon?
4. What is the disappointing side effect to the professor's new invention?
5. What does Biff Hawk discover after he is tinkering around with the Professor's equipment?
6. Who takes the professor to court as a result of his new invention?
7. What type of sporting event does the professor's school compete in this time around with its archrival?
8. How does the professor get his revenge on the obnoxious Shelby Ashton?
9. What is the name of the agricultural agent who testifies in court about the benefits of the professor's new invention?
10. How does the professor's team eventually win its big game against their archrival?

Son of Flubber

Answers

1. The professor and Biff are seeking money for Medfield College.
2. Medfield College's president is Professor Daggett.
3. "Dry rain."
4. The new invention shatters every piece of glass within its range.
5. Biff discovers a by-product of the professor's first invention, Flubber, which is named Flubbergas.
6. Alonzo Hawk takes the professor to court because his machine broke all of the windows.
7. Medfield College plays its archrival, Rutland College, in a game of football.
8. The professor causes a rain cloud to burst in his car.
9. The agricultural agent A. J. Allen testifies in court and brings evidence that the professor's new invention causes vegetables to grow to extraordinary size.
10. With the assistance of Flubbergas, Medfield College beats highly favored Rutland College on a ninety-eight-yard field goal.

Mary Poppins

August 29, 1964

Questions

1. Who wrote the stories on which the film is based?
2. What is the address of the Bankses' house?
3. According to Mary Poppins's tape measure, what was said about the two children?
4. What did Mary Poppins's tape measure say about herself?
5. In the movie, what time of day does Admiral Boom fire his cannon?
6. Besides the tape measure, name the other eight items that Mary Poppins pulls from her carpetbag.
7. What reverse psychology song does Mary Poppins sing to the Banks children to make them fall asleep?
8. According to Mary Poppins, what is the special word that one would say when there is nothing else to say?
9. What laughable character does Ed Wynn play?
10. What does Mary Poppins order during the "Jolly Holiday" sequence at the tea shop?
11. According to Bert, what brings one luck?
12. When does Mary Poppins say it is time for her to leave the Bankses' house?
13. What do we see the Banks family doing as the film concludes?
14. Who provided the musical score for the film?
15. How many Academy Awards did *Mary Poppins* win?

Mary Poppins

Answers

1. P. L. Travers wrote the stories that inspired the film *Mary Poppins*.
2. The Banks family lives at number 17 Cherry Tree Lane.
3. Michael is "extremely stubborn and suspicious," and Jane is "inclined to giggle and doesn't put anything away."
4. "Mary Poppins—Practically Perfect in Every Way."
5. Admiral Boom fires his cannon at eight A.M. and at six P.M.
6. The eight items are a hat stand, a hand mirror, a plant, a lamp, a wall mirror, shoes, a coat, and an apron.
7. The song is "Stay Awake."
8. "Supercalifragilisticexpialidocious."
9. The laughable character is Uncle Albert.
10. Mary Poppins orders raspberry ice, cakes, and tea.
11. Shaking hands with a chimney sweep, or blowing him a kiss.
12. Mary Poppins says it is time to leave when the wind changes.
13. We see the Banks family flying a kite and singing the song "Let's Go Fly a Kite."
14. The Academy Award–winning song writing team of Robert and Richard Sherman, who won for Best Score and Best Song, "Chim-Chim-Cher-ee."
15. *Mary Poppins* won five Academy Awards, including Best Actress for Julie Andrews, plus a technical award for the traveling matte process that allowed the combination of live action and animation in the film.

That Darn Cat!

December 2, 1965

Questions

1. Who sings the title song for the film?
2. What actor makes his Disney screen debut playing the role of FBI agent Zeke Kelso?
3. What is the cat's name?
4. What does the cat bring home one night that causes Patti Randall to suspect that someone is in danger and that the FBI should be called in?
5. Where are Patti and Ingrid's parents when all this is going on?

That Darn Cat!

Answers

1. Bobby Darin sings the title song, "That Darn Cat."
2. Dean Jones plays Agent Zeke Kelso, who happens to be allergic to cats.
3. The Siamese cat's name is simply D.C.
4. The cat comes home wearing a wristwatch around its neck, with part of a word scratched on the surface of the watch. Patti could only think that this means someone has been kidnapped and needs help.
5. In Venice, Italy.

Follow Me, Boys!

December 1, 1966

Questions

1. The story concerns a saxophone player named Lem Siddons who decides to settle down. What is the name of the group that he leaves?
2. What is the name of the small town in which the film is set?
3. What actor made his Disney screen debut in the role of Whitey?
4. While at the Civic Club meeting, what does Lem propose?
5. What honor does Lem receive from the town near the conclusion of the film?

Follow Me, Boys!

Answers

1. Lem Siddons played for Melody Murphy's Collegians.
2. The small town is known as Hickory (population 4951).
3. Kurt Russell played the role of Whitey.
4. Lem proposes the creation of a Boy Scout troop.
5. The town honors Lem with his own day, renaming the camp "Camp Siddons" and presenting to him an honorary law degree.

The Happiest Millionaire

··

June 23, 1967

Questions

1. The story surrounds a rather eccentric millionaire named Anthony J. Drexel Biddle and his daughter, Cordelia, who is coming into her own as a lady. What is the name of the actress who makes her screen debut in the role of Cordelia?

2. As the film opens, we are introduced to the Biddles' new butler singing a song about his byword which combines a little bit of luck and good fortune. What is the title?

3. What is the name of the employment agency that sends the butler to the Biddle household?

4. According to the housekeeper, Mrs. Worth, what type of diet is Anthony J. Drexel Biddle currently on?

5. What is the name of Cordelia's gentleman caller, who is knocked unconscious by her two brothers?

6. What is Anthony J. Drexel Biddle's favorite sport?

7. What is the name of the school Cordelia is sent off to study at?

8. What actress plays the role of the mother, Mrs. Biddle?

9. What is the name of the individual whom Cordelia meets while at school and plans to marry?

10. Where does Cordelia's future husband dream of going to start their life together?

11. Throughout the film, Anthony J. Drexel Biddle is heard singing a song. What is its title?

12. What happens to Anthony J. Drexel Biddle's alligators one night, after someone leaves some windows open?

13. Who plays the role of Cordelia's future mother-in-law, an individual who is not at all pleased with her son's future plans?

14. What happens to Cordelia's husband-to-be after he pays a visit to Clancy's Irish Pub?

15. As a sign of the Marine Corps's appreciation for all of his help in the World War I effort, what honor is bestowed upon Anthony J. Drexel Biddle as the film concludes?

The Happiest Millionaire

Answers

1. Cordelia Drexel Biddle is played by Lesley Ann Warren, in her screen debut.
2. "Fortuosity."
3. The Mayflower Employment Agency sends John Lawless to the Biddle household that day.
4. Anthony J. Drexel Biddle is apparently on a chocolate cake diet!
5. Charlie Taylor comes to see Cordelia. However, Tony and Livingston accidentally knock him unconscious.
6. Boxing.
7. Cordelia attends the Loretta Wingfield School for Girls in Lakewood, New Jersey.
8. The role of Mrs. Biddle is played by Greer Garson.
9. Cordelia meets Angier Buchanan Duke, played by John Davidson in his screen debut.
10. Angier is fascinated with automobiles and dreams of going to Detroit.
11. "What's Wrong with That?"
12. The alligators freeze, but after a night in front of the fire, they eventually thaw.
13. Mrs. Duke is played by Geraldine Page. She also provides the voice of Madame Medusa in the animated feature *The Rescuers* in 1977.
14. Angier gets involved in a pub brawl and is thrown in jail.
15. The Marine Corps awards Anthony J. Drexel Biddle a Provisional Captaincy.

The Gnome-Mobile

July 12, 1967

Questions

1. What famous author wrote the book on which *The Gnome-Mobile* is based?
2. Besides playing the role of the lumber tycoon, D. J. Mulrooney, what other part is played by Walter Brennan?
3. What provides the setting for the film *The Gnome-Mobile*?
4. By what name do the gnomes refer to humans?
5. The story deals with the plight of two gnomes who are in search of more of their kind. The gnome named Jasper also has another problem, which he reveals to D. J. Mulrooney's niece, Elizabeth. What is that problem?
6. D. J. Mulrooney offers to take the two gnomes to a part of the forest untouched by humans, in the hope of finding other gnomes. What type of vehicle do they ride in and promptly redub "The Gnome-Mobile"?
7. What popular Disney pair play the roles of D. J. Mulrooney's niece and nephew, Elizabeth and Rodney?
8. What is the name of the 1,100-year-old gnome king, who is also the Gnomish Head of the Council of Elders?
9. As the film concludes, what eventually happens that enables the younger gnome's problem to be solved?
10. What gift does D. J. Mulrooney bequeath to the gnomes so that they may live in peace?

The Gnome-Mobile

Answers

1. Upton Sinclair.
2. A 943-year-old gnome named Knobby.
3. The American redwood forests.
4. Doo-deens.
5. He is having difficulty finding a bride.
6. A 1930 Rolls Royce.
7. Elizabeth is played by Karen Dotrice and Rodney by Matthew Garber. The pair teamed up earlier as brother and sister in *Mary Poppins* (1964).
8. The 1,100-year-old gnome is named Rufus.
9. Jasper marries Violet.
10. D. J. Mulrooney donates 50,000 acres of redwood forest to the gnomes.

The Love Bug

March 13, 1969

Questions

1. What town provides the main setting for the film?
2. According to Tennessee Steinmetz, where did he go in order to discover his inner self?
3. What actress plays the role of Carole Bennett?
4. What is the license plate number of Herbie?
5. What is the name of the evil Thorndyke's assistant and some-time driving partner?
6. How does Herbie the Volkswagen get to be Jim Douglas's car in the first place?
7. To show his dislike of the evil Thorndyke, what does Herbie do?
8. How does the Volkswagen get his name, Herbie?
9. What was Herbie's first motor race?
10. According to Tennessee Steinmetz, where in Ireland was his mother from?
11. What does Thorndyke place in Herbie's engine in an attempt to sabotage the car?
12. What does Herbie attempt to do when Jim Douglas brings home a new car?
13. Who becomes Herbie's new owner after some storefronts have been destroyed?
14. How does Jim Douglas eventually get Herbie back?
15. What do we see Herbie doing for Jim and Carole at the end of the film?

The Love Bug

1. San Francisco.
2. Tennessee Steinmetz traveled to Tibet to find himself.
3. Carole Bennett is played by actress Michele Lee.
4. "OFP 857—California."
5. Havershaw, played by actor Joe Flynn, was Thorndyke's assistant.
6. Herbie decides to follow Jim Douglas home after Douglas sticks up for the VW at Thorndyke's car showroom.
7. Herbie is constantly squirting oil on Thorndyke's leg.
8. Tennessee Steinmetz names Herbie after his uncle, who was a middleweight boxer.
9. Herbie came in first at the Jack Rabbit Springs Raceway.
10. According to Tennessee Steinmetz, his mother was from Coney, Ireland.
11. Thorndyke places Irish coffee in Herbie's engine.
12. Herbie first runs away and then attempts to jump off the Golden Gate Bridge.
13. Mr. Wu becomes the new owner of Herbie.
14. Jim Douglas makes a wager with Mr. Wu that if he would permit him to drive Herbie again in the El Dorado Race, he would give the prize money to Mr. Wu and Herbie would then become his once again.
15. Herbie is seen driverless, escorting Jim and Carole on their honeymoon.

Bedknobs and Broomsticks

December 13, 1971

Questions

1. What actress plays the part of Eglantine Price, and what is Eglantine aspiring to be?
2. What are the names of the three children taken in by Eglantine Price in order to escape the bombing over London?
3. When and Where is the setting for the film?
4. What is the name of Eglantine Price's cat?
5. What is the name of the spell Eglantine Price is searching for that can bring inanimate objects to life?
6. Who runs the Correspondence College of Witchcraft in London?
7. What is included in the package that Eglantine receives from London?
8. What vehicle does Eglantine Price use as her mode of transportation?
9. What does Eglantine give to the youngest of the three children so that her secret would be kept?
10. What is the name of the Academy Award–nominated song from the film *Bedknobs and Broomsticks*?
11. What is the name of the lost island to which Eglantine, the children, and the Professor travel in order to retrieve the Star of Astaroth?
12. What type of sporting event does the Professor volunteer to officiate?
13. What are the names of the two teams that compete?
14. What do Eglantine and the Professor win at "the Beautiful Briny Ballroom"?
15. Whom must they retrieve the Star of Astaroth from?

Bedknobs and Broomsticks

Answers

1. Eglantine Price, played by actress Angela Lansbury, is aspiring to be a full-fledged witch.
2. The three children are named Paul, Carrie, and Charlie Rawlings.
3. The film is set in 1940, in the little town of Pepperinge Eye.
4. Eglantine's black cat is named Cosmic Creepers.
5. The spell is known as "Substitutiary Locomotion."
6. Professor Emelius Browne runs the Correspondence College of Witchcraft.
7. Eglantine receives a Certificate of Apprenticeship and a broom from Professor Browne.
8. Eglantine rides a motorcycle with a sidecar.
9. Eglantine gives Paul a bedknob, which is used in her "traveling spell."
10. "The Age of Not Believing" by Richard and Robert Sherman.
11. The Isle of Naboombu.
12. Professor Browne officiates the Royal Cup Match (soccer).
13. The two teams are the Dirty Yellows and the True Blues.
14. At the Beautiful Briny Ballroom, Professor Browne and Eglantine win a loving cup in a dance competition.
15. They must retrieve the Star of Astaroth from King Leonidas, who wears it around his neck.

The World's Greatest Athlete

February 1, 1973

Questions

1. What actor plays the role of the jungle boy, Nanu, who is brought over from Africa by Coach Sam Archer so that he can compete for his school?
2. What is the name of the school for which Sam Archer coaches?
3. What is the name of Nanu's pet tiger?
4. What happens to Assistant Coach Milo Jackson as a result of the Witch Doctor's spell?
5. After Nanu has successfully competed and won many trophies for the college, what does he decide to do?

The World's Greatest Athlete

Answers

1. Nanu is played by actor Jan-Michael Vincent.
2. Coach Sam Archer's school is Merrivale College.
3. Nanu's pet tiger is Harri.
4. The Witch Doctor Gazenga, played by Roscoe Lee Brown, reduces Assistant Coach Jackson to a height of three inches.
5. Nanu decides to return to Africa, accompanied by his girl-friend, Jane.

Island at the Top
of the World

····································

December 20, 1974

Questions

1. The story is about the search by Sir Anthony Ross for his missing son, Donald. What is the name of the airship that the search party uses?
2. Why has Professor Ivarsson of the University of Minnesota been asked to go on the search by Sir Anthony Ross?
3. What is the name of the lost island on which Donald is found?
4. What is so fascinating about the inhabitants of this lost island?
5. The search party is taken prisoner, but is then permitted to leave the island under what condition?

Island at the Top of the World

1. The *Hyperion*.
2. Professor Ivarsson, played by David Hartman, is chosen for the search because he is an expert on the North. According to all reports, Donald was lost at sea somewhere near the Arctic.
3. Astrogard is the name of the lost island.
4. The lost island is inhabited by a Viking civilization.
5. The search party has to leave one member behind to ensure that they all keep their silence. Professor Ivarsson welcomes the opportunity.

Escape to Witch Mountain

March 21, 1975

Questions

1. What is the name of the children's home where Tia and Tony are sent to live after the death of their foster parents?
2. How do Tia and Tony communicate with each other?
3. What Disney film do we see the children attending during an outing?
4. Why does Aristotle Bolt want Tia and Tony?
5. How is Aristotle Bolt informed that the children possess special qualities?
6. What is the name of Tia and Tony's black cat?
7. What is the name of the camper who helps Tia and Tony escape from Aristotle Bolt?
8. As a sign of their appreciation, what do the children give to the camper who has helped them escape from Aristotle Bolt?
9. Why do the children possess these special powers in the first place?
10. As a result of the success of *Escape to Witch Mountain*, a sequel was released three years later. Can you name it?

Escape to Witch Mountain

Answers

1. Pine Woods Children's Home.
2. Tia and Tony communicate telepathically with one another.
3. The children are going to see *Snow White and the Seven Dwarfs.*
4. Because of their ability to predict upcoming events, Tony and Tia's information would be extremely valuable to the evil Aristotle Bolt.
5. Aristotle Bolt's right-hand man, Lucas Deranian, had been warned by the children about an upcoming accident that he was able to avoid.
6. Winky is the name of their cat.
7. The children meet camper Jason O'Day, played by actor Eddie Albert.
8. As a sign of their appreciation, the children give Jason O'Day their cat, Winky.
9. The children come from another planet. Their planet was dying and they chose Earth as their new home.
10. The sequel was *Return from Witch Mountain* (1978).

The Apple Dumpling Gang

July 4, 1975

Questions

1. Who played the roles of the two bumbling crooks, Theodore Ogelvie and Amos Tucker?
2. Besides acting as the town's sheriff, what other three professions does Homer McCoy hold?
3. Who tricks Russel Donavan into accepting the three children who were arriving the next day?
4. Who is the founder and president of The Butterfly Stage & Freight Company?
5. What is the name of the town that provides the setting for the film?
6. What is the name of the mine that the three children inherit from their father?
7. What is the full name of the stage coach driver who rides for The Butterfly Stage & Freight Company?
8. What do the children discover one day while digging in their mine?
9. What is the name of the gang organized by Theodore and Amos?
10. What gang did Theodore and Amos once belong to?
11. Why are Theodore and Amos arrested by Sheriff McCoy?
12. Where was Russel Donavan headed prior to stopping in the small town?
13. Why do the three children ask Theodore and Amos to form the Apple Dumpling Gang?
14. What does Russel Donavan receive for the capture of Frank Stillwell?
15. What are the names of the three Bradley children?

The Apple Dumpling Gang

Answers

1. Don Knotts played Theodore Ogelvie, and Tim Conway played Amos Tucker.
2. In addition to being the town's sheriff, Homer McCoy is also the town's judge, barber, and justice of the peace.
3. The scandalous John Wintle tricks Donavan into taking the children, pretending that the package Donavan was expecting was something other than children.
4. Colonel T. R. Clydesdale.
5. The town of Quake City.
6. The Commodore Mine is given to the children by their father.
7. Magnolia Dusty Clydesdale, played by actress Susan Clark, is the driver for The Butterfly Stage & Freight Company.
8. The children discover a 356-pound gold nugget.
9. Amos and Theodore form the Hash Knife Outfit.
10. Amos and Theodore were once gang members who rode with the notorious Stillwell Gang, until Amos shot the leader, Frank Stillwell, in the leg.
11. The two bumbling crooks are arrested for trying to steal the gold nugget from the Quake City Bank. They are sentenced to be hanged from an oak tree at high noon—and also receive a $10 fine for perjury. Sheriff McCoy also instructs the two to bring their own rope.
12. Russel Donavan was headed for New Orleans before stopping in the small town of Quake City.
13. The children ask Amos and Theodore to help form the Apple Dumpling Gang so they can steal the nugget themselves, as the gold has brought them nothing but trouble since they discovered it.
14. Russel Donavan receives $5,000 for the capture of Frank Stillwell.
15. The three children are Bobby, Clovis, and Celia Bradley.

Pete's Dragon

December 16, 1977

Questions

1. What actor provided the voice for the dragon, Elliott?
2. In the opening scene, we see Pete running away from whom?
3. What is Elliott doing when he makes his first appearance?
4. What actor plays the role of the lighthouse keeper, Lampie?
5. To what town do Pete and Elliott travel, where they meet Lampie and his daughter, Nora?
6. What happens to Lampie after he tells the town's residents that he has seen a dragon?
7. What does Doc Terminus want to do with Elliott?
8. What is the name of the Academy Award–nominated song from the film?
9. What is the name of Doc Terminus's bumbling assistant?
10. Whom was Nora scheduled to marry before he was lost at sea?

11. According to the song "It's Not Easy," how does Pete describe Elliott?
12. What does Doc Terminus attempt to trade Pete for his dragon?
13. Who eventually takes in the orphan, Pete?
14. Why does Elliott leave Pete after he has a home of his own?
15. What song do they sing as the film concludes?

Pete's Dragon

Answers

1. Charlie Callas provided the voice of Elliott the dragon.
2. Pete runs away from the Gogan family, who purchased him for $50 plus 50 cents in legal fees, and who were planning to enslave him.
3. Elliott is seen eating apples.
4. Mickey Rooney plays Lampie.
5. Pete and Elliott travel to the town of Passamaquoddy, Maine.
6. Naturally, anyone who reports a dragon would be laughed at!
7. Doc Terminus wants to cut Elliott up so that he can use him in his potions, tablets, and lotions.
8. "Candle on the Water" by Al Kasha and Joel Hirschhorn.
9. Doc Terminus's bumbling assistant is Hoagy, played by Red Buttons.
10. Nora was supposed to marry Paul.
11. Pete sings about Elliott having a "Head of a camel, neck of a crocodile, and the ears of a cow."
12. Doc Terminus is willing to trade Pete $5 plus a bottle of his potion.
13. Nora and Lampie.
14. Elliott has to leave Pete because another child is in trouble and needs his assistance.
15. "Brazzle Dazzle Day."

The Black Hole

December 21, 1979

Questions

1. What has become of the evil captain's crew?
2. What member of the ship, the *Palomino,* is able to communicate telepathically with the hovering robot, V.I.N.Cent?
3. What does Dr. Alex Durant call "the most destructive force in the universe"?
4. What is the name of the good-guy hovering robot that is found on board the evil captain's ship?
5. What does V.I.N.Cent compete with in a laser shoot-out?
6. Who boards the *Palomino* in an attempt to run away?
7. Where has the evil captain sent Kate McCrae in order to make her part of his crew?
8. What do the surviving members of the *Palomino* and V.I.N.-Cent use in order to escape?
9. How does the evil captain eventually meet his demise while on board his ship?
10. Whom does V.I.N.Cent save from entering the Black Hole?

The Black Hole

....

Answers

1. The evil captain has turned his entire crew into a zombielike race of subservient creatures.
2. Kate McCrae.
3. Dr. Durant refers to the Black Hole as "the most destructive force in the universe."
4. A robot named Old Bob.
5. V.I.N.Cent competes with the beats S.T.A.R. (Special Troops Arms Regulator).
6. Harry Booth, played by Ernest Borgnine.
7. The evil captain sends her to "the hospital," the place where he creates his zombielike force.
8. The remaining crew members of the *Palomino* escape on the probe ship.
9. Captain Reinhardt meets his demise when covered by falling debris after a meteor shower.
10. V.I.N.Cent saves Charlie Pizer.

Tron

July 9, 1982

Questions

1. What actor plays the title character in the film *Tron*?
2. Why is Kevin Flynn, a software engineer, fired by the corrupt business executive, Dillinger?
3. What is the name of the company run by Dillinger?
4. Why is Flynn transported into the game grid by the Master Control Program?
5. What is the name of Flynn's alter ego after he has been transported into the game grid, and in the climactic scene, whom is he challenged by?

Tron

········

Answers

1. Tron is played by actor Bruce Boxleitner.
2. Flynn discovers that Dillinger was responsible for some stolen programs. When Dillinger realizes Flynn has discovered his secret, he fires him.
3. Dillinger runs ENCOM.
4. Flynn is trying to gain evidence that Dillinger was responsible for stealing the game, Paranoids.
5. Flynn's alter ego is Clu, and he is challenged by Sark, the alter ego of Dillinger.

Flight of the Navigator

July 30, 1986

Questions

1. On what date was David Freeman declared missing?
2. Whom is David chasing when he is knocked unconscious and taken aboard the spacecraft?
3. What city provides the setting for the film?
4. Why does the spacecraft travel to Earth in the first place?
5. What does the robot inside the spacecraft call David?
6. What nickname does David call the robot on the spacecraft?
7. What is the name of the NASA official called in to investigate the flying saucer that has been discovered?
8. According to the NASA official who is assigned to investigate David, what planet has he apparently traveled to?
9. How does David escape from the NASA building where he is being held for observation?
10. What has the robot of the spacecraft placed in David's memory and now needs to retrieve in order to return home?

Flight of the Navigator

Answers

1. David was declared missing on July 4, 1978.
2. David is seen chasing his brother Jeff when he is knocked unconscious and falls in a ravine.
3. Fort Lauderdale, Florida.
4. The spacecraft has been instructed to analyze species from the various planets, and Earth happened to be one of its stops.
5. The robot refers to David as "the navigator."
6. Max.
7. Dr. Faraday, played by Howard Hesseman, is the NASA official.
8. According to NASA, David has apparently traveled to the planet Phaelon, some 550 light-years away.
9. David escapes in a device known as R.A.L.F. (Robotic Assistant Labor Facilitator).
10. The robot from the spacecraft has placed flight patterns inside David's memory. He now needs them back because his own were erased when his ship accidentally crashed into some electrical wires.

Honey, I Shrunk the Kids

June 23, 1989

Questions

1. What actor plays the role of the rather clumsy Professor Wayne Szalinski?
2. Thinking that his new invention is a complete failure, what does Professor Szalinski do to his reducing machine?
3. What does the neighbors' youngest boy hit through the window of the Szalinski house?
4. What objects are reduced first by Professor Szalinski's invention?
5. The story is about the adventures of four children who are reduced by Professor Szalinski's new invention. Besides the two Szalinski children, what other two children are reduced?
6. How do the children end up in the yard after being reduced?
7. Which of the two children takes a ride on a bee?
8. In an effort to get back to the house, the children run into many obstacles. What type of creature actually helps the children battle a scorpion?
9. What type of object do the children use for their sleeping quarters?
10. Where does Professor Szalinski finally discover the children after they have been reduced?

Honey, I Shrunk the Kids

Answers

1. Professor Wayne Szalinski is played by actor Rick Moranis.
2. Professor Szalinski attempts to destroy his invention with a baseball bat.
3. The next-door neighbors' youngest boy, Ron Thompson, accidentally hits a baseball through the window of the Szalinski house.
4. The professor's chair and sofa.
5. Along with Amy and Nick Szalinski, the Thompson children, Ron and Russ, are reduced.
6. Professor Szalinski sweeps them up in a dustpan, deposits them into a trash bag, and places them outside.
7. Nick gets picked up by the bee, and Russ attempts to save him.
8. An ant that befriends the children.
9. The children sleep in a LEGO block.
10. Professor Szalinski discovers one of the children in his cereal and the other children on the table.

Who Framed
Roger Rabbit

June 22, 1988

Questions

1. What is the title of the cartoon that Roger Rabbit and Baby Herman are making as the film opens?
2. What is the password required by patrons in order to gain access to the Ink & Paint Club?
3. On what street are the R. K. Maroon Studios located?
4. How was Eddie Valiant's brother killed?
5. Who purchases and takes charge of the Pacific Red Car?
6. What three components make up the dreaded "Dip"?
7. What color is Roger Rabbit's bowtie?
8. Who is Roger Rabbit's uncle?
9. What type of character plays the bouncer at the Ink & Paint Club?
10. Why does Judge Doom want to destroy Toontown?
11. What actress plays the role of Eddie Valiant's girlfriend, Dolores?
12. Who provides the voice of the Singing Sword?
13. In addition to providing the voice for Roger Rabbit, what other three voices are done by Charles Fleischer?
14. What actress provides the speaking voice of Jessica Rabbit but requested no screen credit?
15. How do the judge and the weasels meet their demise?
16. Who had Marvin Acme's will all along?
17. What is Roger Rabbit's favorite cake?
18. Who wrote the book on which the film *Who Framed Roger Rabbit* was based?
19. How many Academy Awards did the film receive?
20. In what year and where is the film set?

Who Framed Roger Rabbit

Answers

1. *Somethin's Cookin'.*
2. The password for the Ink & Paint Club is "Walt sent me!"
3. R. K. Maroon Studios are located on Sunset Boulevard.
4. A Toon killed Eddie's brother by dropping a piano on his head from fifteen stories while he was investigating a break-in at the First National Bank of Toontown.
5. The Pacific Red Car was purchased by Cloverleaf and its sole stockholder, Judge Doom.
6. The three ingredients of "Dip" are turpentine, acetone, and benzene.
7. Blue with yellow polka dots.
8. Thumper.
9. A gorilla named Bongo.
10. Judge Doom wants to tear down Toontown to build a freeway.
11. Joanna Cassidy.
12. The Singing Sword is voiced by Frank Sinatra.
13. In addition to Roger Rabbit, Charles Fleischer provides the voice for Benny the Cab and for two weasels named Greasy and Psycho.
14. Kathleen Turner provides the speaking voice for Jessica Rabbit.
15. The judge meets his demise as a result of his own invention, Dip. The weasels laugh themselves to death.
16. Roger Rabbit had Marvin Acme's will all along; he wrote a love letter to Jessica on it.
17. Naturally, carrot cake!
18. Gary K. Wolf wrote the book *Who Censored Roger Rabbit?*
19. *Who Framed Roger Rabbit* received four Academy Awards, including a Special Achievement Oscar.
20. Hollywood in 1947.

Dick Tracy

June 15, 1990

Questions

1. Who produced and directed the film *Dick Tracy*?
2. What is the name of Dick Tracy's ever-faithful girlfriend?
3. What two thugs are Big Boy Caprice's right-hand men?
4. Who plays the role of Mumbles?
5. What is the name of the club that Big Boy Caprice takes over from Lips Manlis?
6. According to Breathless Mahoney, what side is she always on?
7. What is the name of the piano player at the club?
8. What actor plays the part of D.A. Fletcher?
9. Who saves Dick Tracy from the building before it is blown up?
10. What is Dick Tracy's repeated expression whenever he speaks into his wristwatch?
11. Who is Dick Tracy accused of killing?
12. Who eventually confesses to Dick Tracy regarding the killing that "Big Boy did it"?
13. Which character is given an Honorary Detective Certificate and Badge?
14. What is the true identity of the character No Face?
15. Where did *Dick Tracy* have its world premiere?

Dick Tracy

Answers

1. Warren Beatty directed and produced *Dick Tracy*.
2. Dick Tracy's ever-faithful girlfriend is Tess Trueheart.
3. Itchy and Flattop are Big Boy Caprice's right-hand men.
4. Dustin Hoffman plays the role of Mumbles.
5. Big Boy Caprice takes control of the Club Ritz.
6. "The side I'm always on . . . mine."
7. The piano player at the Club Ritz is named 88 Keys.
8. After a twenty-two-year absence from a Disney film, Dick Van Dyke returns to play the role of D.A. Fletcher.
9. The Kid saves Dick Tracy.
10. "I'm on my way."
11. Dick Tracy has been framed for the killing of D.A. Fletcher.
12. Mumbles confesses to Dick Tracy that "Big Boy did it."
13. The Kid, because he saved Dick Tracy from the building that was about to blow up.
14. The true identity of No Face is Breathless Mahoney in disguise.
15. *Dick Tracy* had its premiere at the Walt Disney World Resort in Florida.

The Rocketeer

June 21, 1991

Questions

1. As the film opens, Cliff Secord is shown testing his plane for the upcoming Air Nationals. What happens to Cliff and his plane?
2. What is the name of the rocket pack developed by Howard Hughes that everyone is searching for?
3. What is the name of the Neville Sinclair movie Cliff and his girlfriend, Jenny, go to see?
4. What part does Neville Sinclair want Jenny to read for?
5. What is the name of the cafe that serves as a popular hangout for some of the local pilots?
6. What statue do Cliff and Peevy take in order to test the rocket pack they found?
7. What is on the sign that Bigelow reads when he coins the expression "Rocketeer"?
8. What is the headline of the "Extra" edition of the *Los Angeles Times* that Howard Hughes holds in his hands?
9. What is the name of Neville Sinclair's hired henchman?
10. At one point the rocket pack is hit by a stray bullet. What does Peevy use as a makeshift patch to fix a leak in the rocket pack?
11. What location does Cliff have to go to in order to trade the rocket pack for the safe release of Jenny?
12. Neville Sinclair is apparently one of "Hollywood's finest actors," but whom does he really work for?
13. What type of aircraft does Neville Sinclair take Jenny aboard to escape from the authorities?
14. How does Neville Sinclair eventually meet his demise?
15. As a symbol of his appreciation, what does Howard Hughes give to Cliff?

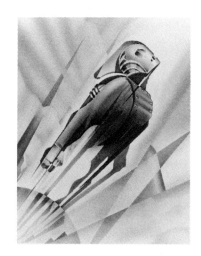

The Rocketeer

Answers

1. The crooks think Cliff is following them and attempt to shoot him down. Cliff's plane is hit, and crashes beyond repair.
2. Cirus X-3.
3. Cliff and Jenny go to see *Wings of Honor.*
4. The Saxon Princess.
5. The Bulldog Cafe.
6. Cliff and Peevy take a statue of Charles Lindbergh.
7. Bigelow spots a sign that reads "Pioneer."
8. The paper reads: "Flying Man Saves Pilot."
9. Lothar.
10. Peevy takes Cliff's gum from his mouth and places it over the leak.
11. Griffith Park Observatory.
12. Neville Sinclair is actually a Nazi spy for the Third Reich.
13. A Zeppelin.
14. Cliff removes the gum that was covering the leak in the rocket pack. When the fuel reaches the flame as Neville Sinclair attempts to fly away, he ignites.
15. A replica of the plane he lost, the *Gee Bee 5,* becomes his new plane.

The Mighty Ducks

···

October 2, 1992

Questions

1. Who plays the role of the selfish lawyer, Gordon Bombay, who is convicted of drunk driving and then required to coach a peewee hockey team as his debt to society?
2. What does Gordon Bombay's license plate read?
3. Who is the sponsor of the team that Bombay coaches?
4. What is the name of the opposing team that quickly becomes the archrival to Bombay's team?
5. What city provides the setting for the film?
6. What is the name of the individual the team recruits because of his unbelievable slap-shooting ability?
7. What does the team have to write on the blackboard one day during school detention?
8. What is the name of the obnoxious coach whose motto is, "It's not worth winning if you can't win big"?
9. As the film ends, where do we see Gordon Bombay going?
10. What National Hockey League team was inspired by the film?

The Mighty Ducks

Answers

1. Emilio Estevez plays the role of Gordon Bombay.
2. The plate reads: JUST WIN.
3. The team's sponsor is the owner of the law firm that employs Gordon Bombay. Its owner is Gerald Ducksworth.
4. The Hawks.
5. Minneapolis, Minnesota.
6. The team recruits Fulton Reed because of his awesome slap shot.
7. "I will not quack at the Principal."
8. The Hawks' coach, Reilly.
9. We see Gordon Bombay set to attend a minor league tryout with the Minnesota North Stars National Hockey League team.
10. The Disney Company's National Hockey League team, the Mighty Ducks, whose hometown is Anaheim, California.

Homeward Bound: The Incredible Journey

February 3, 1993

Questions

1. What is the name of the risk-taking bulldog that was orphaned at birth before being taken in by Bob, Laura, and the family?
2. Thinking that they are left behind, the family pets take off on a 250-mile journey to find their home. What mountain range do the three pets cross in order to return to the family?
3. What is the name of the wise golden retriever, and what actor provides the voice?
4. What is the final destination for the three pets?
5. What is the name of the prudish and pampered Himalayan cat that completes the threesome?

Homeward Bound:
The Incredible Journey

Answers

1. The bulldog, who always seemed to be in some sort of predicament, is named Chance, voiced by Michael J. Fox.
2. The Sierra Nevadas.
3. Don Ameche supplies the voice of the golden retriever, Shadow.
4. The animals are trying to return to their country home.
5. Sassy, voiced by Sally Field.

Hocus Pocus

July 16, 1993

Questions

1. What actresses play the roles of the three witches, Winifred, Sarah, and Mary Sanderson?
2. What is the name of the enchanted candle that brings the Sanderson sisters back to life?
3. What bewitching town provides the setting for the film?
4. What spell does Winifred place on the young boy, Thackery, as he attempts to save his sister, Emily?
5. What is so unusual about Winifred's Book of Spells?
6. What is Mary forced to ride after her broom is stolen?
7. According to the legend, what must one encircle onself with in order to be protected from witches and evil spirits?
8. What is the name of Max's sister whom the Sanderson sisters kidnap, and what do they want from her?
9. What is the name of the helpful zombie, and how did Winifred kill him back in 1693?
10. When does the spell that has brought the Sanderson sisters back to life come to an end?

Hocus Pocus

Answers

1. Winifred is played by Bette Midler, Sarah by Sarah Jessica Parker, and Mary by Kathy Najimy.
2. The Black Flame Candle lit by Max on Halloween night, 300 years after the Sanderson sisters were hanged.
3. The town of Salem, Massachusetts.
4. She turns him into a black cat named Binx, cursed with immortality.
5. Winifred's Book of Spells is covered in human skin and contains an evil eye.
6. Mary rides a vacuum cleaner.
7. Salt.
8. The three witches kidnap Dani, whom they want to suck the life out of to ensure their own immortality.
9. The helpful zombie is named Billy. Winifred poisoned him and also sewed his mouth shut so he could never tell his secrets or hers.
10. The light of day ends the spell.

Live-Action Potpourri

Live-Action Potpourri

Questions

1. What is the name of the 1943 Disney film based on a book by Major Alexander P. de Seversky that examined the military aspects of aviation?

2. In 1952 Walt Disney released his version of *Robin Hood*. What was its full title?

3. What actor plays the role of the legendary hero in Disney's version of *Robin Hood*?

4. What is the name of the 1953 film starring Glynis Johns, who portrays the role of Mary Tudor during the reign of King Henry VIII?

5. What is the title of Walt Disney's first full-length True-Life Adventure film?

6. Why did the State Censorship Board of New York want to ban the release of one True-Life Adventure, *The Vanishing Prairie* (1954)?

7. What is the name of the first Disney film to be filmed entirely in Mexico?

8. What 1956 film stars Fess Parker in the role of Union spy, James J. Andrews, who leads a raid in Confederate territory?

9. Which True-Life Adventure film features photography of an active volcano?

10. What 1956 film includes the catchy tune "Wringle, Wrangle"?

11. What kind of animal was Perri in the 1957 True-Life Fantasy of the same name?

12. What actor plays the role of Johnny Butler in *The Light in the Forest* (1958), and what is his Indian name?

13. What 1990 Academy Award–winning actress plays the role of Myra Butler in *The Light in the Forest*?

14. What True-Life Adventure pictures the legendary plight of the lemmings?

15. What kind of animal is *Tonka* in the 1958 film that bears that title?

16. In what 1959 Disney film do a real-life mother and son appear?

17. What feature is considered Walt Disney's first comedy film?

18. What 1960 film is based on a book by Robert Louis Stevenson?

19. What is the name of the film that retold the experiences of a

group of men who attempted to explore the Colorado River in 1869?

20. What is the title of the last full-length True-Life Adventure film?

21. What film is considered to be Walt Disney's first live-action musical?

22. What Disney feature is about a Skye terrier who is honored by the city of Edinburgh, Scotland?

23. Tom Tryon, star of the Disney miniseries *Texas John Slaughter,* plays the role of Captain Richmond Talbot in what 1962 film?

24. The 1962 film *Bon Voyage* tells the story of the Willard family from Terre Haute, Indiana, who go on vacation and discover that whatever can go wrong will. What is the family's vacation destination?

25. What feature was filmed in Austria, and tells a story about the Vienna Boys' Choir?

26. What kind of animal is Lobo in the 1962 film *The Legend of Lobo?*

27. What film used the slogan, "A Thousand Thrills and Hayley Mills"?

28. What 1963 film included the famous Lipizzaner stallions?

29. What film is considered to be the sequel to the 1957 classic, *Old Yeller?*

30. The song "The Ugly Bug Ball" appears in what film?

31. What popular Disney actor plays the curious Merlin Jones in *The Misadventures of Merlin Jones* (1964)?

32. What country provides the setting for the 1964 film *The Moon-Spinners,* starring Hayley Mills?

33. What is the name of the 1964 mystery set in Berlin about a band of juvenile detectives who thwart a gang of bank robbers?

34. What musical group sings the title song for the Disney film *The Monkey's Uncle* (1965)?

35. What is the name of the film that is set in sixteenth-century Ireland, as the country sought freedom from English rule?

36. What film features an American who inherits a French olive farm?

37. What 1967 feature is about a young boy from Boston who runs away to California during the days of the great Gold Rush?

38. Dean Jones plays the role of Steve Walker, a harried track coach from Godolphin College who conjures up the ghost of what famous pirate?

39. What is the name of the 1968 film in which actress Goldie Hawn and actor Kurt Russell first appear together?

40. Dick Van Dyke plays the role of actor Jack Albany in the 1968 film *Never a Dull Moment.* Unfortunately for our character, he is involved in a case of mistaken identity. What is Jack Albany accused of being?

41. What legendary actor plays the role of Joseph Smooth in the film *Never a Dull Moment* (1968), and what is Smooth attempting to steal?

42. What is the name of the horse from the film *The Horse in the Gray Flannel Suit* (1968)?

43. What kind of animal is Rascal in the 1969 film of the same name?

44. What actor plays the role of Dexter Riley in *The Computer Wore Tennis Shoes* (1969)?

45. Name the two sequels that followed the release of *The Computer Wore Tennis Shoes* (1969)?

46. What is the name of the college that was attended by Dexter and is featured in each of these three films?

47. What actor plays the role of Virgil in the 1971 feature *The Wild Country*?

48. What kind of animal is considered the Barefoot Executive in the 1971 film of that title?

49. What is the name of the duck who is able to lay golden eggs in the 1971 film *The $1,000,000 Duck*?

50. This 1972 film features the debut of Jodie Foster. What is the name of the film?

51. What is the name of the circus lion that the children run away with in *Napoleon and Samantha* (1972)?

52. Which film is about the straitlaced accountant Johnny Baxter and his family, who give up the demands of big city life and manage a ski resort in the Rockies?

53. What two actors play the title roles in the 1973 film *Charley and The Angel*?

54. What is the name of the 1973 film that starred Bob Crane in the role of Charlie McCready, a father who is jealous that his daughter is getting married?

55. What was the first sequel to the 1969 film *The Love Bug,* and who is Herbie's new driver?

56. Who wrote the song "Sweet Surrender" for the 1974 film *The Bears and I,* starring Patrick Wayne?

57. What actor plays the starring role in *The Castaway Cowboy,* a 1974 film about a Texas cowboy who finds himself in Hawaii?

58. What 1975 film stars Peter Ustinov as Hnup Wan from the Chinese London Intelligence Office, who is in search of a top secret formula called Lotus X?

59. What feature is about two youngsters who skip out on their Easter vacation with their grandfather and take up with two gangsters?

60. What is the name of the film that features a mule that kicks field goals for the California Atoms football team?

61. What film stars Jodie Foster as a teenager named Annabel Andrews, who miraculously exchanges bodies for a day with her mother, Ellen Andrews, played by actress Barbara Harris?

62. What was the only year in which two Disney songs from two different films were nominated for an Academy Award?

63. What is the name of the 1977 film that features Herbie, the Love Bug, falling in love with a Lancia Scorpion race car?

64. Name the two Disney films starring Bette Davis.

65. What 1978 film involves a cat named Jake who crash-lands his spacecraft on Earth and has only thirty-six hours to repair the ship or be stranded on Earth forever?

66. What film is about twin brothers who don't know each other but who must challenge one another in a winner-takes-all competition for their father's inheritance?

67. What is the profession of the leader in the film *The North Avenue Irregulars* (1979)?

68. What 1979 feature was inspired by Mark Twain's classic, *A Connecticut Yankee in King Arthur's Court*?

69. What film was originally dubbed *Space Probe One*?

70. What actor plays the role of Barney Satin, the devil's top man, in the 1981 film *The Devil and Max Devlin*?

71. Michael Crawford, the original Phantom from the Broadway production *The Phantom of the Opera,* stars in what 1981 comedy about a comic book writer named Woody Wilkins who assumes his character's identity to help a beautiful Russian agent escape to freedom?

72. What is the only Disney feature to be pulled after its initial brief theatrical release so that a new ending could be filmed?

73. What is the name of the 1982 feature that tells the true story of two families who risk their lives as they attempt to escape from communist East Germany in their homemade hot-air balloon?

74. What coming-of-age drama stars Matt Dillon as a teenager from Oklahoma?

75. What 1984 Touchstone film tells the tale of a mermaid, played

by Daryl Hannah, who surfaces in New York and befriends Allen Bauer, played by Tom Hanks?

76. What is the name of the short 1984 film by Tim Burton that tells the story of a young boy who brings his dead dog, Sparky, back to life?

77. What 1985 film begins in Chicago during the Depression and concerns a young girl who sets out on a 2,000-mile journey across America in search of her father?

78. Bette Midler stars in what 1986 Touchstone film in which she plays a shrewd wife who is abducted by a pair of bumbling amateur kidnappers?

79. What 1986 Touchstone film captured the prestigious Best Actor Academy Award for Paul Newman?

80. Who plays Paul Newman's protégé in this film?

81. What 1987 Touchstone film stars Tom Selleck, Steve Guttenberg, and Ted Danson, who discover a "little bundle of joy" outside their door one day?

82. What is the name of the hit song from the film *Beaches* (1988)?

83. What 1989 Touchstone film won the Academy Award for Best Original Screenplay?

84. Tom Hanks stars in what 1989 Touchstone film about a police officer who is teamed up with a rather unlikely new partner, a sloppy dog?

85. What feature involves two young Americans who visit a research station in Kenya, where they are befriended by a young Masai, Morogo, and his pet?

86. In 1990 The Walt Disney Company formed a new movie label, Hollywood Pictures. What was the label's first release?

87. What 1991 Disney film is based on a book by Jack London?

88. Besides the adventure thriller *Treasure Island,* what other Disney film features a boy in search of a treasure on a deserted island?

89. What is the only Disney feature to end in a question mark?

90. What 1991 film tells the true story of a young Georgia country girl who runs away from home to become a rider of diving horses with a traveling tent show, then wins fame as a legendary diving girl in Atlantic City?

91. *Father of the Bride* (1991) tells the story of the events that lead up to the wedding of George Banks's daughter. What actor plays the role of the father?

92. Who wrote the original songs for the 1992 Disney film *Newsies*?

93. What is the nickname of Jack Kelly, the leader of the news-

boys who helps organize the 1899 newsboys' strike in the film *Newsies*?

94. What actor plays the role of the powerful newspaper tycoon, Joseph Pulitzer, in the film *Newsies*?

95. What Touchstone film stars Whoopi Goldberg in the role of nightclub singer Dolores Van Cartier, who witnesses a mob murder and is therefore on the run?

96. What 1992 feature is a sequel to *Honey, I Shrunk the Kids*?

97. What 1993 film is based on a book by Mark Twain?

98. What is the name of the 1993 film that tells the story of the first Jamaican Olympic bobsled team?

99. In *Tim Burton's The Nightmare Before Christmas* (1993), what character is called "the Pumpkin King"?

100. What is the name of the 1993 feature in which you would find the phrase, "All for one and one for all!"?

Live-Action Potpourri

1. *Victory Through Air Power.*
2. *The Story of Robin Hood and His Merrie Men.*
3. Richard Todd plays the role of Robin Hood. Richard Todd became somewhat of a regular in early Disney live-action films. His credits include *The Sword and the Rose* (1953) and *Rob Roy, The Highland Rogue* (1954).
4. Glynis Johns plays the role of Mary Tudor in the 1953 Disney film *The Sword and the Rose.* Glynis Johns also starred as Winifred, the mother, in the 1964 classic, *Mary Poppins.*
5. *The Living Desert* (1953), which captured the Academy Award for Best Documentary.
6. Because the film showed the birth of a buffalo calf.
7. *The Littlest Outlaw* (1955).
8. *The Great Locomotive Chase.*
9. *Secrets of Life* (1956).
10. "Wringle, Wrangle" by Stan Jones appeared in *Westward Ho The Wagons!*
11. Author Felix Salten provided the inspiration for the film with his book, *Perri,* about a female squirrel who eventually falls in love with Porro. This film also marked the first feature credit for Roy E. Disney, the current vice-chairman of the board of The Walt Disney Company.
12. The role of Johnny Butler is played by James MacArthur, and his Indian name is True Son.
13. Academy Award—winning actress Jessica Tandy, who was honored for *Driving Miss Daisy,* plays the role of Myra Butler.
14. The plight of the lemmings and their mass suicide is featured in the 1958 Academy Award—winning film *White Wilderness.*
15. A horse.
16. *Third Man on the Mountain* features Helen Hayes in a cameo along with her son, James MacArthur.
17. Disney's first comedy is the 1959 classic *The Shaggy Dog.*
18. *Kidnapped,* directed by, appropriately, Robert Stevenson, who shared his name with the author.
19. *Ten Who Dared* (1960).

20. Disney's last full length True-Life Adventure was *Jungle Cat* (1960).
21. Disney's first musical was the 1961 film *Babes in Toyland.*
22. *Greyfriars Bobby* (1961).
23. Tom Tyron stars in *Moon Pilot.*
24. The Willard family heads for France. Mother Katie Willard is played by actress Jane Wyman, and Fred MacMurray plays the father, Harry.
25. *Almost Angels* (1962).
26. Lobo is a wolf.
27. "A Thousand Thrills and Hayley Mills" was used to describe the 1962 film *In Search of the Castaways.*
28. *Miracle of the White Stallions.*
29. *Savage Sam* (1963).
30. Burl Ives sings "The Ugly Bug Ball" in the 1963 film *Summer Magic.*
31. Tommy Kirk plays the role of the misfit inventor, Merlin Jones.
32. Greece provides the setting for the film *The Moon-Spinners.* This film also marked Hayley Mills's first real screen kiss, which she shared with Peter McEnery.
33. *Emil and the Detectives.*
34. "The Monkey's Uncle" is sung by Annette Funicello and The Beach Boys, and was written by Richard and Robert Sherman. The film was a sequel to *The Misadventures of Merlin Jones.*
35. *The Fighting Prince of Donegal* (1966).
36. *Monkeys, Go Home* (1967), starring Dean Jones.
37. The 1967 film *The Adventures of Bullwhip Griffin.*
38. Blackbeard, in the 1968 film *Blackbeard's Ghost.*
39. Goldie Hawn and Kurt Russell first appeared together in *The One and Only, Genuine, Original Family Band.*
40. A gangster.
41. Edward G. Robinson plays the role of the gangster, Joseph Smooth, and he attempts to steal a forty-two-foot picture known as *A Field of Sunflowers.*
42. Aspercel.
43. Rascal is a raccoon.
44. The likable college student is played by Kurt Russell.
45. The two sequels were *Now You See Him, Now You Don't* (1972) and *The Strongest Man in the World* (1975).
46. The college that provides the setting is Medfield College. This was the same name used for the college in *The Absent-Minded Professor* (1961) and its sequel, *Son of Flubber* (1963).

47. Ron Howard.
48. A chimpanzee named Raffles, who has the uncanny ability to pick successful television shows.
49. Charley was the star of *The $1,000,000 Duck.*
50. *Napoleon and Samantha.*
51. The circus lion is Major McTavish.
52. *Snowball Express* (1972), starring Dean Jones.
53. Fred MacMurray plays the role of Charley and Harry Morgan plays the angel. This also marked Fred MacMurray's last Disney film.
54. Bob Crane stars in *Superdad.*
55. The sequel was *Herbie Rides Again* (1974), with Ken Berry playing Willoughby. Helen Hayes plays the role of Tennessee Steinmetz's mother. The familiar villain from *The Absent-Minded Professor* and *Son of Flubber,* Alonzo Hawk, is played by Keenan Wynn.
56. John Denver.
57. James Garner plays the role.
58. *One of Our Dinosaurs Is Missing.*
59. *No Deposit, No Return* (1976).
60. *Gus* (1976).
61. *Freaky Friday* (1977).
62. It was in 1977 that two Disney songs from two different films ("Someone's Waiting for You" from *The Rescuers* and "Candle on the Water" from *Pete's Dragon*) were nominated for an Academy Award.
63. *Herbie Goes to Monte Carlo.*
64. Bette Davis's two films were *Return from Witch Mountain* (1978) and *The Watcher in the Woods* (1981).
65. *The Cat from Outer Space.*
66. *Hot Lead and Cold Feet* (1978).
67. A minister.
68. *Unidentified Flying Oddball.*
69. *Space Probe One* eventually became *The Black Hole* (1979).
70. Bill Cosby stars as Barney Satin.
71. Michael Crawford stars as *Condorman.*
72. *The Watcher in the Woods* (1981) is the only Disney film to be pulled for a rewrite of the conclusion.
73. *Night Crossing.*
74. *Tex* (1982).
75. *Splash.*
76. *Frankenweenie.*
77. This 1985 adventure film was *The Journey of Natty Gann.*
78. Bette Midler stars in *Ruthless People.* The problem for Mid-

ler's character is that her husband, played by Danny DeVito, has no desire to pay the ransom.

79. Paul Newman won the Academy Award for his role in *The Color of Money.*
80. Tom Cruise.
81. *Three Men and a Baby,* and the "little bundle of joy" was a baby named Mary.
82. The song was "Wind Beneath My Wings."
83. *Dead Poets Society.*
84. Tom Hanks stars in *Turner and Hooch.*
85. *Cheetah* (1989).
86. The film was *Arachnophobia,* and it tells the story of a highly poisonous spider from South America that relocates to a small town, where she and her offspring wreak havoc on the populace.
87. *White Fang,* based on the Jack London classic.
88. *Shipwrecked* (1991).
89. *What About Bob?* (1991). *Who Framed Roger Rabbit* did not use a question mark.
90. *Wild Hearts Can't Be Broken.*
91. Steve Martin plays the role of George Banks in *Father of the Bride.* The name George Banks was also used as the name of the father in the film *Mary Poppins* (1964).
92. The original songs were provided by Alan Menken and Jack Felden.
93. Jack Kelly is also known as "Cowboy."
94. Actor Robert Duvall plays the role of Joseph Pulitzer.
95. *Sister Act* (1992).
96. *Honey, I Blew Up the Kid.*
97. *The Adventures of Huck Finn.*
98. *Cool Runnings.*
99. "The Pumpkin King" is Jack Skellington.
100. *The Three Musketeers.*

Disney on Television

Disney on Television

Questions

1. When the *Mickey Mouse Club* first aired back in 1955, how many Mouseketeers made up the original cast?

2. Of the *Mickey Mouse Club* serials *Spin and Marty, The Hardy Boys,* and *Annette,* which young actor starred in all three?

3. A popular serial on the *Mickey Mouse Club* was *Corky and White Shadow.* What kind of animal was White Shadow?

4. What actor played Corky's sheriff father on the *Mickey Mouse Club* serial, *Corky and White Shadow?*

5. What city provided the setting for the popular television series "Zorro"?

6. What does the name Zorro mean in Spanish?

7. What character from an early *Walt Disney Presents* miniseries was known for a "tail on his hat"?

8. How many episodes of *The Scarecrow of Romney Marsh* were made?

9. Actor Robert Loggia, star of the film miniseries *The Nine Lives of Elfego Baca,* provided the voice of what villain in a full-length animated feature?

10. What actor starred in the Disney miniseries *The Saga of Andy Burnett?*

11. What is the name of The Disney Channel program from the mid-eighties that creatively combined Disney animation with popular songs?

12. What is the title of the 1984 film originally made for The Disney Channel that told the true story of Billy Young and the events surrounding the 1968 baseball season?

13. What Touchstone Television show used as its theme song "Why Should I Worry," from the 1988 full-length animated feature *Oliver & Company?*

14. What town provides the setting for Scrooge McDuck and Donald Duck's three nephews in *DuckTales?*

15. Which one of the Rescue Rangers is considered the "free spirit," and which is the "bold adventurer"?

16. Who are both Chip and Dale smitten with on *Chip 'n Dale Rescue Rangers?*

17. What character is a friend to Monterey Jack and commu-

nicates by buzzing and pantomime on *Chip 'n Dale Rescue Rangers*?

18. What character from *Chip 'n Dale Rescue Rangers* was flushed down the toilet when he was very young and grows up in the city sewers?

19. What author wrote the stories on which The Disney Channel's series "Avonlea" is based?

20. What is the name of Dr. Harry Weston's chatty nurse on the show "Empty Nest"?

21. How many daughters does Dr. Weston have on the show "Empty Nest"?

22. Actor Joey Lawrence from the television show "Blossom" provides the voice of what animated character in the full-length animated feature *Oliver & Company* (1988)?

23. What city provides the setting for the Touchstone Television series "Nurses"?

24. What is the name of the robot host featured on The Disney Channel's "Jump, Rattle, and Roll"?

25. What waterfront city provides the setting for "Darkwing Duck"?

26. What is the name of the ultrasecret intelligence agency that calls on Darkwing Duck's crimefighting expertise?

27. Only Goslyn, Darkwing's adopted daughter, along with Launchpad McQuack and Honker Muddlefoot, know the true identity of our crime-fighting hero. What is the true identity of Darkwing Duck?

28. Where is Darkwing Duck's crime-fighting headquarters?

29. What actress plays the title role of Blossom, a teenage girl coming of age in a male-dominated household?

30. The main character is named Herman Brooks, and he is surrounded by a collection of cerebral characters named Animal, Genius, Wimp, and Angel. What is the title of this show?

31. What is the name of The Disney Channel's entertaining and educational half-hour weekday series of Lewis Carroll's stories?

32. What is the name of Tim Allen's character on the show "Home Improvement"?

33. What is the name of Tim Allen's show within a show on "Home Improvement," and what is his co-host's name?

34. What is the name of the next-door neighbor that Tim Allen talks to through the fence on "Home Improvement"?

35. What is the name of the Walt Disney television program featuring a family named Sinclair?

36. What is the name of Goofy's son on the show "Goof Troop" who seems to follow in his father's footsteps?

37. Who currently provides the voice for Goofy?

38. What is the name of Goofy's troublemaking used-car salesman neighbor?

39. What is the name of Goofy's cat from the "Goof Troop" series?

40. What is the name of the high-flying adventure series that appears on "The Disney Afternoon," starring Baloo the Bear, King Louie, and Shere Khan?

41. What do the voices of Winnie the Pooh, Darkwing Duck, and Bonkers have in common?

42. What is the full name of Bonkers, the wildly enthusiastic and yet naive new recruit of the Hollywood Police Department?

43. What is the name of Bonkers's mismatched partner from the Hollywood Police Department?

44. What star from a 1989 full-length animated feature appears in her own weekly cartoon series?

45. What is the name of Marsupilami's best friend, the hulking and blissful ape whose entire vocabulary consists of grunts and belches?

Disney on Television

Answers

1. Twenty-four.
2. Tim Considine.
3. White Shadow was a dog.
4. Buddy Ebsen.
5. The Spanish-settled El Pueblo de Los Angeles in 1820.
6. Fox.
7. The Swamp Fox, General Francis Marion, who was played by Leslie Neilsen.
8. Three.
9. The evil Sykes in *Oliver & Company* (1988).
10. Jerome Courtland.
11. "DTV."
12. *Tiger Town.*
13. "The Fanelli Boys."
14. Duckburg.
15. Dale is the free spirit and Chip is the bold adventurer.
16. The highly resourceful Gadget.
17. Zipper.
18. The evil Sewernose, an alligator that lives under the opera house.
19. Lucy Maud Montgomery.
20. Laverne Todd, played by Park Overall.
21. Dr. Weston has three very different daughters: Barbara, Carol, and Emily.
22. The title character, Oliver.
23. Miami, Florida.
24. DECKS.
25. St. Canard.
26. SHUSH.
27. Drake Mallard.
28. Atop St. Canard's Audubon Bay Bridge.
29. Mayim Bialik.
30. "Herman's Head."
31. "Adventures in Wonderland," starring Elisabeth Harnois.
32. Tim Taylor.
33. "Tool Time," and Tim's co-host is Al Borland.
34. Wilson helps Tim answer those important questions of life.

35. "Dinosaurs."
36. His name is actually Goofy Jr., but he prefers Max.
37. Bill Farmer.
38. Pete.
39. Goofy's cat is named Waffles.
40. "Tale Spin."
41. They are all provided by the talented Jim Cummings.
42. Bonkers D. Bobcat.
43. Bonkers's partner is the streetwise detective Lucky Piquel.
44. Ariel stars in "Disney's The Little Mermaid."
45. Maurice.

Disneyland

Disneyland

....

Questions

1. What individual bought Disneyland's first general admission ticket for its public opening on July 18, 1955?
2. What message can be heard constantly being transmitted from the Disneyland Railroad Station's telegraph office in Frontierland?
3. What organ manufacturer sponsored a shop on Main Street U.S.A. during the 1950s and 1960s?
4. When Disneyland first opened in 1955, what year in the future was Tomorrowland supposed to represent?
5. The feature *Third Man on the Mountain* (1959) helped inspire what Fantasyland attraction?
6. What attraction opened in 1960 and was based on Walt Disney's True-Life Adventure series?
7. What popular singing group made its professional debut in 1961 at Carnation Gardens?
8. The location for the Disney Gallery in New Orleans Square was originally intended to serve what purpose?
9. Who helped inspire the development of the One-of-a-Kind Shop located in New Orleans Square?
10. What major attraction was Walt Disney unable to experience because it opened shortly after his passing?
11. What place devoted to our four-legged friends can guests find outside of the Haunted Mansion?
12. The Carousel of Progress was replaced by what *Audio-Animatronics* attraction saluting the Bicentennial and featuring the vocal talents of Burl Ives?
13. What attraction was added to Fantasyland during its complete renovation in 1983?
14. Monsanto's Adventure Thru Inner Space was replaced by what current attraction?
15. What two films can be seen at the World Premiere Circle-Vision Theatre?
16. Who is the magical Master of Ceremonies for the nighttime spectacular, Fantasmic?
17. What is the name of the trolley that transports guests through Disneyland's first completely new land in twenty years, Mickey's Toontown?

18. What is the name of Donald Duck's home, located in Toon Lake in Mickey's Toontown?

19. What is the name of the attraction featuring Roger Rabbit in Mickey's Toontown?

20. The Tahitian Terrace was replaced by what dinner-show restaurant?

Disneyland

Answers

1. Walt Disney's brother and business partner for over forty years, Roy O. Disney, bought the first general admission ticket for $1.
2. The land-line telegraphy code transmits Walt Disney's opening day speech for Disneyland.
3. Wurlitzer.
4. 1986.
5. Matterhorn Bobsleds.
6. Nature's Wonderland.
7. The Osmond Brothers.
8. The Disney Gallery location was planned as Walt Disney's private apartment to replace the one located above the Firehouse on Main Street, U.S.A. The initials W.D. (Walt Disney) and R.D. (Roy Disney) can be found in the wrought iron of the railing of the Disney Gallery balcony.
9. Walt Disney's wife, Lillian, because of her love of antiques.
10. Pirates of the Caribbean.
11. A pet cemetery.
12. America Sings. The Carousel of Progress was then transported to the Walt Disney World Magic Kingdom.
13. Pinocchio's Daring Journey.
14. Star Tours.
15. *Wonders of China* and *American Journeys.*
16. Mickey Mouse.
17. The Jolly Trolley.
18. Donald's home, in the shape of a boat, is called the *Miss Daisy.*
19. Roger Rabbit's Car Toon Spin.
20. Aladdin's Oasis.

Walt Disney World Magic Kingdom

Walt Disney World Magic Kingdom

....

Questions

1. What are the names of the counties in which Disneyland in California and the Walt Disney World Magic Kingdom in Florida are located?
2. Name the six vintage Mickey Mouse cartoons that can be seen at the Main Street Cinema.
3. What two airlines have sponsored attractions at the Magic Kingdom?
4. What attraction preceded Mission to Mars, using the same theater concept?
5. When did the Magic Kingdom's first thrill attraction, Space Mountain, open?
6. How many white horses can be found on Cinderella's Golden Carousel?
7. What Fantasyland attraction was inspired by Disney's 1951 full-length animated feature?
8. What is the largest living thing in the Magic Kingdom?
9. What is the theme song for the Haunted Mansion?
10. In what attraction can guests hear the songs "Belly Up to the Bar," "Lilly's Back in Town," "Orange Blossom Special," and "A Good Man Is Hard to Find"?
11. In what attraction can you find two vultures wearing top hats?
12. Where can guests find Boothill while visiting the Magic Kingdom?
13. Where can *Orinoco Ida, Amazon Annie, Kwango Kate, Sankuru Sadie,* and *Senegal Sal* be found?
14. What are the names of the four bird hosts for the Enchanted Tiki Birds?
15. What character is considered the host for the nighttime spectacular parade, SpectroMagic?

Walt Disney World
Magic Kingdom

Answers

1. Orange County, the same name in each state.
2. *Steamboat Willie, Plane Crazy, The Dognapper, Traffic Troubles, The Moose Hunt,* and *Mickey's Polo Team.*
3. The first airline was Eastern, which sponsored If You Had Wings. The second was Delta, which currently sponsors DreamFlight in Tomorrowland.
4. The original name was Flight to the Moon. Mission to Mars is expected to make way for a new Alien Encounters attraction.
5. January 15, 1975.
6. Ninety.
7. The Mad Tea Party.
8. The Liberty Tree, which stands in the courtyard of Liberty Square. It weighs thirty-eight tons and features thirteen hanging lanterns, each of which represents one of the original thirteen colonies.
9. "Grim Grinning Ghosts."
10. The Diamond Horseshoe Revue.
11. The two vultures can be found just before the big drop in the Frontierland attraction, Splash Mountain.
12. At the Frontierland Shootin' Arcade.
13. They are all boat names that make up part of the fleet on The Jungle Cruise.
14. Jose, Pierre, Michael, and Fritz.
15. Jiminy Cricket, whom you can actually see as the parade concludes.

EPCOT Center

1272-07c

EPCOT Center

1. Who provides the narration for Spaceship Earth?
2. What is Future World's largest pavilion?
3. An *Audio-Animatronics* figure of Leonardo Da Vinci can be found in what attraction?
4. What is the name of the film starring Goofy in Wonders of Life?
5. A replica of what cell compound can be found at the entrance to Wonders of Life?
6. When one enters The Living Seas, what model vessel from a Disney film can be seen on display?
7. The American Adventure is located between what two countries in World Showcase?
8. What means of conveyance are available on the walkway around World Showcase?
9. In what country's restaurant would one be likely to find pickled herring?
10. What two countries feature food facilities on the lagoon side of the walkway around World Showcase?

EPCOT Center

Answers

1. Walter Cronkite.
2. The Land Pavilion, presented by Nestlé.
3. World of Motion.
4. *Goofy About Health,* with segments taken from many of his classic cartoons.
5. A DNA molecule.
6. The *Nautilus* from *20,000 Leagues Under the Sea* (1954).
7. Italy and Japan.
8. Double-decker buses.
9. Norway.
10. Mexico and the United Kingdom.

Disney/MGM Studios
Theme Park

Disney/MGM Studios Theme Park

Questions

1. What is the name of the three-dimensional figure that Dr. Bunson Honeydew and his assistant, Beaker, invent at the "really super tippy-top secret Muppet Labs" in the film, *Muppet Vision 3-D*?

2. Comedian David Letterman and legendary voice actor Jim Macdonald combined to provide the preshow for what attraction?

3. What prop from the 1964 film *Mary Poppins* is on display inside the Chinese Theatre?

4. At the Disney/MGM Studios Theme Park, a film shows Mickey Mouse wearing what type of character watch?

5. In what attraction can a Mickey Mouse and a Donald Duck be found in hieroglyphic form?

6. What popular attraction combines live-action players, puppets, and a fantastic collection of special effects?

7. Whose private plane, bearing the marks N234MM, can one see while riding on the Backstage Studio Tour?

8. What actor provides the narration for the nighttime spectacular show, Sorcery in the Sky?

9. What is the name of the new section at Disney/MGM Studios Theme Park that attempts to recreate the Golden Age of Hollywood during the 1930s and 1940s?

10. What is the name of the thrill attraction that takes guests on a plunge of thirteen stories and uses an abandoned hotel to tell the story?

Disney/MGM Studios
Theme Park

....

Answers

1. Waldo C. Graphic.
2. The Monster Sound Show.
3. The carousel horse that Mary Poppins rode.
4. Mickey Mouse is shown wearing a Michael Eisner watch.
5. The Great Movie Ride.
6. The Voyage of The Little Mermaid.
7. Walt Disney's.
8. Vincent Price.
9. The new section is known as Sunset Boulevard.
10. The Twilight Zone, Tower of Terror.

Tokyo
Disneyland

Tokyo Disneyland

Questions

1. What is Tokyo Disneyland's equivalent to Main Street, U.S.A.?
2. What company sponsors the same facility on Main Street, U.S.A. in Disneyland, Walt Disney World Magic Kingdom, and in World Bazaar at Tokyo Disneyland?
3. What is the basic difference between the Cinderella Castles at Walt Disney World and at Tokyo Disneyland?
4. What is the name of the restaurant featuring an *Audio-Animatronics* character named Tony Solaroni and his intergalactic kitchen staff?
5. What Tokyo Disneyland attraction combines *Audio-Animatronics* and motion pictures to depict Japan's history and its encounters with other cultures?
6. What world-tour Circle-Vision film appeared in Tomorrowland at Walt Disney World in 1974 and was later shown at Tokyo Disneyland?
7. Which popular attraction opened in July 1989 at Tokyo Disneyland?
8. Name any one of the three railroad engines that make up the Western River Railroad at Tokyo Disneyland.
9. What is Tokyo Disneyland's equivalent to Frontierland?
10. What is the newest theme land to open at Tokyo Disneyland?

Tokyo Disneyland

Answers

1. World Bazaar.
2. Coca-Cola sponsors the Refreshment Corner at all three sites.
3. Cinderella Castle at Walt Disney World has King Stefan's Banquet Hall on the second floor; Cinderella Castle at Tokyo Disneyland features the Castle Mystery Tour in the basement.
4. Pan Galactic Pizza Port.
5. Meet the World.
6. *Magic Carpet 'Round the World.*
7. Star Tours.
8. Colorado, Missouri, and the Rio Grande.
9. Westernland.
10. Critter Country, home of Splash Mountain.

Euro Disney

Euro Disney

1. Name any one of the three railroad engines that make up the Euro Disneyland Railroad.
2. What is the name of the restaurant located on Main Street, U.S.A., that features fine dining based on American cuisine and includes original artwork used in the creation of Disney theme parks?
3. What popular Walt Disney World parade was transported to Euro Disneyland to be incorporated in their new nighttime entertainment?
4. What is the name of the attraction that houses the 360-degree Circle-Vision motion picture hosted by Time Keeper and Jules Verne?
5. The Carousel located in Fantasyland is named after whom?
6. What attraction appears in a different theme land in each of the four Magic Kingdoms?
7. What is Euro Disneyland's equivalent to Disneyland's Golden Horseshoe?
8. What is the name of the airship that marks the entrance to the state-of-the-art entertainment facility, Videopolis, at Euro Disneyland?
9. Which one of the Euro Disney resorts features a Manhattan skyline and a skating rink outside of the hotel that operates during the winter months?

Euro Disney

Answers

1. W. F. Cody, G. Washington, and C. K. Holliday.
2. Walt's, an American Restaurant.
3. The Main Street Electrical Parade.
4. Le Visionarium.
5. Sir Lancelot.
6. The Haunted Mansion. At Disneyland, the Haunted Mansion is located in New Orleans Square, while in the Walt Disney World Magic Kingdom, it is in Liberty Square. Tokyo Disneyland features this attraction in Fantasyland, and in Euro Disneyland its equivalent is known as Phantom Manor and appears in Frontierland.
7. The Lucky Nugget Saloon.
8. *Hyperion*.
9. Hotel New York.

The Art of the Lion King
The Disney Villain
The Disney Poster: The Animated Film Classics, from Mickey Mouse to Aladdin
A Dream Is a Wish Your Heart Makes: My Story by Annette Funicello
Walt Disney: An American Original
The Illustrated Treasury of Disney Songs
Tim Burton's Nightmare Before Christmas: The Film, The Art, The Vision
Disney's Art of Animation: From Mickey Mouse to Beauty and the Beast
Disney's Aladdin: The Making of an Animated Book
Mickey's Gourmet Cookbook
Birnbaum's Walt Disney World for Kids by Kids 1994
Birnbaum's Disneyland the Official Guide 1994
Birnbaum's Walt Disney World the Official Guide 1994
The Art of Mickey Mouse 1994 Calendar
Tim Burton's Nightmare Before Christmas: An Animated Flip Book
Disney's Mickey's Birthday Party: An Animated Flip Book
Walt Disney's Beauty and the Beast: An Animated Flip Book
Walt Disney's Aladdin: An Animated Flip Book
The Lion King: An Animated Flip Book
Walt Disney's Snow White: An Animated Flip Book
Walt Disney's Mickey Mouse in "The Little Whirlwind": An Animated Flip Book

We hope you've enjoyed our 999 Disney Trivia questions. Just like the Haunted Mansion that claims to house 999 happy haunts where there is always room for one more ghost, there is always room for one more trivia question. Now that you've heard ours, please write us with your own Disney trivia questions!

Kevin Neary
P.O. Box 15344
Philadelphia, PA 19111-0344

IDA

FINK

A

SCRAP

OF

TIME

AND OTHER STORIES

**TRANSLATED FROM THE POLISH
BY MADELINE LEVINE
AND FRANCINE PROSE**

SCHOCKEN BOOKS NEW YORK

The story "A Scrap of Time"
first appeared in *The New Yorker.*

Library of Congress Cataloging-in-Publication Data
Fink, Ida.
A scrap of time and other stories.
Translation of: Skrawek czasu-opowiadania.
1. Holocaust, Jewish (1939-1945)—Fiction.
I. Title.
PG7165.I44S513   1987   891.8'537   86-42982
ISBN 0-394-55806-5
ISBN 0-8052-0869-0 (pbk.)

Manufactured in the United States of America
First Schocken Paperback Edition

For Bronek

CONTENTS

A
SCRAP
OF
TIME

A
SCRAP
OF
TIME

I want to talk about a certain time not measured in months
and years. For so long I have wanted to talk about this
time, and not in the way I will talk about it now, not just
about this one scrap of time. I wanted to, but I couldn't, I
didn't know how. I was afraid, too, that this second time,
which is measured in months and years, had buried the
other time under a layer of years, that this second time had
crushed the first and destroyed it within me. But no. Today,
digging around in the ruins of memory, I found it fresh and
untouched by forgetfulness. This time was measured not in
months but in a word—we no longer said "in the beautiful
month of May," but "after the first 'action,' or the second,
or right before the third." We had different measures of
time, we different ones, always different, always with that
mark of difference that moved some of us to pride and
others to humility. We, who because of our difference were
condemned once again, as we had been before in our history, we were condemned once again during this time

measured not in months nor by the rising and setting of the sun, but by a word—"action," a word signifying movement, a word you would use about a novel or a play.

I don't know who used the word first, those who acted or those who were the victims of their action; I don't know who created this technical term, who substituted it for the first term, "round-up"—a word that became devalued (or dignified?) as time passed, as new methods were developed, and "round-up" was distinguished from "action" by the borderline of race. Round-ups were for forced labor.

We called the first action—that scrap of time that I want to talk about—a round-up, although no one was rounding anyone up; on that beautiful, clear morning, each of us made our way, not willingly, to be sure, but under orders, to the marketplace in our little town, a rectangle enclosed by high, crooked buildings—a pharmacy, clothing stores, an ironmonger's shop—and framed by a sidewalk made of big square slabs that time had fractured and broken. I have never again seen such huge slabs. In the middle of the marketplace stood the town hall, and it was right there, in front of the town hall, that we were ordered to form ranks.

I should not have written "we," for I was not standing in the ranks, although, obeying the order that had been posted the previous evening, I had left my house after eating a perfectly normal breakfast, at a table that was set in a normal way, in a room whose doors opened onto a garden veiled in morning mists, dry and golden in the rising sun.

Our transformation was not yet complete; we were still living out of habit in that old time that was measured in months and years, and on that lovely peaceful morning, filled with dry, golden mists, we took the words "conscription of labor" literally, and as mature people tend to read between the lines, our imaginations replaced the word "labor" with "labor camp," one of which, people said, was being built nearby. Apparently those who gave the order were perfectly aware of the poverty of our imaginations; that is why they saved themselves work by issuing a written order. This is how accurately they predicted our responses: after finishing a normal breakfast, at a normally set table, the older members of the family decided to disobey the order because they were afraid of the heavy physical labor, but they did not advise the young to do likewise—the young, who, if their disobedience were discovered, would not be able to plead old age. We were like infants.

This beautiful, clear morning that I am digging out of the ruins of my memory is still fresh; its colors and aromas have not faded: a grainy golden mist with red spheres of apples hanging in it, and the shadows above the river damp with the sharp odor of burdock, and the bright blue dress that I was wearing when I left the house and when I turned around at the gate. It was then, probably at that very moment, that I suddenly progressed, instinctively, from an infantile state to a still naive caution—instinctively, because I wasn't thinking about why I avoided the gate that led to the street and instead set off on a roundabout route, across the orchard, along the riverbank, down a road we called "the back way" because it wound through the outskirts of town. Instinctively, because at that moment I still did not know that I wouldn't stand in the marketplace in front of the town hall. Perhaps I wanted to delay that moment, or perhaps I simply liked the river.

Along the way, I stopped and carefully picked out flat stones, and skipped them across the water; I sat down for a while on the little bridge, beyond which one could see the town, and dangled my legs, looking at my reflection in the water and at the willows that grew on the bank. I was not yet afraid then, nor was my sister. (I forgot to say that my younger sister was with me, and she, too, skipped stones across the water and dangled her legs over the river, which is called the Gniezna—a pitiful little stream, some eight meters wide.) My sister, too, was not yet afraid; it was only when we went further along the street, beyond the bridge, and the view of the marketplace leapt out at us from behind the building on the corner, that we suddenly stopped in our tracks.

There was the square, thick with people as on a market day, only different, because a market-day crowd is colorful and loud, with chickens clucking, geese honking, and people talking and bargaining. This crowd was silent. In a way it resembled a rally—but it was different from that, too. I don't know what it was exactly. I only know that we suddenly stopped and my sister began to tremble, and then I caught the trembling, and she said, "Let's run away," and although no one was chasing us and the morning was still clear and peaceful, we ran back to the little bridge, but we no longer noticed the willows or the reflections of our running figures in the water; we ran for a long time until we were high up the steep slope known as Castle Hill—the ruins of an old castle stood on top of it—and on this hillside, the jewel of our town, we sat down in the bushes, out of breath and still shaking.

From this spot we could see our house and our garden—it was just as it always was, nothing had changed—and we could see our neighbor's house, from which our neighbor had emerged, ready to beat her carpets. We could hear the slap slap of her carpet beater.

We sat there for an hour, maybe two, I don't know, because it was then that time measured in the ordinary way stopped. Then we climbed down the steep slope to the river and returned to our house, where we heard what had happened in the marketplace, and that our cousin David had been taken, and how they took him, and what message he had left for his mother. After they were taken away, he wrote down again what he had asked people to tell her; he threw a note out of the truck and a peasant brought it to her that evening—but that happened later. First we learned that the women had been told to go home, that only the men were ordered to remain standing there, and that the path chosen by our cousin had been the opposite of ours. We had been horrified by the sight of the crowd in the marketplace, while he was drawn towards it by an enormous force, a force as strong as his nerves were weak, so that somehow or other he did violence to his own fate, he himself, himself, himself, and that was what he asked people to tell his mother, and then he wrote it down: "I myself am to blame, forgive me."

We would never have guessed that he belonged to the race of the Impatient Ones, doomed to destruction by their anxiety and their inability to remain still, never—because he was round-faced and chubby, not at all energetic, the sort of person who can't be pulled away from his book, who smiles timidly, girlishly. Only the end of the war brought us the truth about his last hours. The peasant who delivered the note did not dare to tell us what he saw, and although other people, too, muttered something about what they had seen, no one dared to believe it, especially since the Germans offered proofs of another truth that each of us grasped at greedily; they measured out doses of it sparingly, with restraint—a perfect cover-up. They went to such trouble, created so many phantoms, that only time, time measured not in months and years, opened our eyes and convinced us.

Our cousin David had left the house later than we did,

and when he reached the marketplace it was already known —not by everyone, to be sure, but by the so-called Council, which in time became the *Judenrat*—that the words "conscription for labor" had nothing to do with a labor camp. One friend, a far-sighted older man, ordered the boy to hide just in case, and since it was too late to return home because the streets were blocked off, he led him to his own apartment in one of the houses facing the marketplace. Like us, not comprehending that the boy belonged to the race of the Impatient Ones, who find it difficult to cope with isolation and who act on impulse, he left David in a room that locked from inside. What our cousin experienced, locked up in that room, will remain forever a mystery. Much can be explained by the fact that the room had a view of the marketplace, of that silent crowd, of the faces of friends and relatives, and it may be that finally the isolation of his hiding place seemed to him more unbearable than the great and threatening unknown outside the window—an unknown shared by all who were gathered in the marketplace.

It was probably a thought that came in a flash: not to be alone, to be together with everyone. All that was needed was one movement of his hand.

I think it incorrect to assume that he left the hiding place because he was afraid that they would search the houses. That impatience of the heart, that trembling of the nerves, the burden of isolation, condemned him to extermination together with the first victims of our town.

He stood between a lawyer's apprentice and a student of architecture and to the question, "Profession?" he replied, "Teacher," although he had been a teacher for only a short time and quite by chance. His neighbor on the right also told the truth, but the architecture student lied, declaring himself a carpenter, and this lie saved his life—or, to be more precise, postponed the sentence of death for two years.

Seventy people were loaded into trucks; at the last moment the rabbi was dragged out of his house—he was the seventy-first. On the way to the trucks they marched past the ranks of all those who had not yet managed to inform the interrogators about the work they did. It was then that our cousin said out loud, "Tell my mother that it's my own fault and that I beg her forgiveness." Presumably, he had already stopped believing what all of us still believed later: that they were going to a camp. He had that horrifying clarity of vision that comes just before death.

The peasant who that evening brought us the note that said, "I myself am to blame, forgive me," was somber and didn't look us in the eye. He said he had found the note on the road to Lubianki and that he didn't know anything else about it; we knew that he knew, but we did not want to admit it. He left, but he came back after the war to tell us what he had seen.

A postcard from the rabbi arrived two days later, convincing everyone that those who had been taken away were in a labor camp. A month later, when the lack of any further news began to make us doubt the camp, another postcard arrived, this one written by someone else who had been deported—an accountant, I think. After the postcard scheme came the payment of contributions: the authorities let it be understood that kilos of coffee or tea—or gold—would provide a family with news of their dear ones. As a gesture of compassion they also allowed people to send food parcels to the prisoners, who, it was said, were working in a camp in the Reich. Once again, after the second action, a postcard turned up. It was written in pencil and almost indecipherable. After this postcard, we said, "They're done for." But rumors told a different story altogether—of soggy earth in the woods by the village of Lubianki, and of a bloodstained handkerchief that had been found. These rumors came from nowhere; no eyewitnesses stepped forward.

The peasant who had not dared to speak at the time came back after the war and told us everything. It happened just as rumor had it, in a dense, overgrown forest, eight kilometers outside of town, one hour after the trucks left the marketplace. The execution itself did not take long; more time was spent on the preparatory digging of the grave.

At the first shots, our chubby, round-faced cousin David, who was always clumsy at gymnastics and sports, climbed a tree and wrapped his arms around the trunk like a child hugging his mother, and that was the way he died.

THE
GARDEN
THAT
FLOATED
AWAY

Once I saw a garden float away. It was our neighbors'
garden, just as beautiful and lush as ours, and there were
fruit trees growing in it, just as in ours. I saw it float away,
slowly and majestically, into the distance far beyond our
reach.

That afternoon was warm and peaceful. I was sitting with
my sister on the porch steps, and the two gardens—
Wojciech's and ours—were right there in front of our eyes.
They formed a single garden, for they were not divided by
a fence. A fence, we said, would be an intrusion. Only
a row of evenly spaced currant bushes stitched the two
gardens together.

It was a peaceful afternoon. The sun was lazy and golden.
Wojciech stepped onto his porch—the houses, too, were
twins—and called to us, "Let's go pick the russet apples."

We used to do the chores in both gardens at the same

time: we mowed the grass on the same day, painted the tree trunks white on the same day, and so, out of habit, he told us about the apple picking.

Right after he shouted we saw Wojciech's elder sister. She was carrying two large wicker baskets, just like the one we had in our attic. Wojciech's sister didn't say anything to us. She just went into the garden, placed her baskets under the largest golden russet, and returned to the yard for a ladder.

"Wojciech," she yelled, "get the newspapers ready!"

Every single apple first has to be gently and carefully plucked from the branch, then gently and carefully wrapped in paper to keep it from freezing over the winter, then gently and carefully placed in a wicker basket, and finally, up in the attic, they all have to be gently and carefully lifted out of the basket and set on the floor one by one, next to, but not touching, each other. This gentle carefulness, or careful gentleness, is essential in handling fruit.

Wojciech disappeared from the porch and returned a moment later with a stack of newspapers under his arm. And once more he shouted to us, "We're picking the russets!"

We were sitting on the porch steps, waiting for Father to finish talking with Mrs. Kasinska and call us in. Their conversation was taking place in his office, which was dusty and unused now, though sometimes a patient still appeared in the evening under cover of darkness with a loaf of black bread in his basket as payment. From time to time we could hear Mrs. Kasinska's animated voice, but we couldn't hear Father at all. They had been talking for a long time.

Wojciech climbed up the ladder; his sister stood under the tree and raised her arms, as if she were getting ready to dance the *kujawiak* or some other country dance. She would take the fruit that Wojciech picked and bend down over the basket, then straighten up and raise her arms again. I watched every movement of this fruit-gathering dance, so gentle and full of tenderness. We only wanted to watch, not to eavesdrop, but we couldn't help overhearing. True, they were speaking softly and not every word reached us, but sometimes you only have to hear a few words to know what someone is saying.

"Bare," they said. "Green."

"They are right," they said.

"What will happen in the winter?" they said.

They were saying that we had eaten up all our fruit while it was still green, and that we were right to do so, because who knows what would happen to us by winter. What they were saying was absolutely true.

I watched so attentively that my eyes began to hurt from watching. The sun ignited little fires on the masts of the trees. How could I have known that this was the signal to set sail?

Wojciech's garden, the garden of our childhood friend, suddenly shuddered, swayed, began to pitch and roll, and slowly, slowly, it started to float away, like a huge green ocean liner. It sailed away slowly but steadily; the distance between us grew quickly, the garden got smaller and disappeared. It had floated away to an inaccessible distance, far beyond our reach.

I felt confused and unhappy, because all through my childhood it had been close by. I don't know what would have happened next if my sister hadn't said, "Don't squint like that. When you squint anyone can see right away that you're Jewish."

As soon as she said that, everything suddenly returned to its place—the garden and the trees, the baskets and the ladder, Wojciech and his sister. But who could believe in such a return? Not me.

Father called us to his office, to the animated Mrs. Kasinska, who, once the price was agreed on, promised to make *Kennkarten* for us so we could be saved, so we would not be killed.

BEHIND
THE
HEDGE

Agafia stands in the doorway, leaning against the wall. She is short and sturdy with a shiny face; her eyes—small, shapeless, dark brown, filmed with a constant mist of tears—look like marinated mushrooms. Sometimes those mushrooms make me laugh, sometimes they infuriate me. It depends on Agafia's mood, not mine. Agafia announces her moods by slamming doors, by banging pots, and also by the flashes of light in her small shapeless eyes. Right now, I would like her to lower the windowshades—it's a stuffy day in July—but I don't say anything. I know that Agafia is preparing for one of her stories, which she has told me nearly every day for almost twenty years, and which, if they were written down, would make up a chronicle of our little town and its inhabitants. These stories are very complex, although they are about simple matters, and are full of tiny details that at first seem extraneous but which by the end turn out to be what make the stories vivid and complete.

Agafia's stories are my only link to the outside world. For years I have not left my chair, to which I am confined by the weakness in my legs. I see no one, and the muffled, distant echoes of daily life reach me across the high, thick hedge that my husband planted long ago.

Nonetheless, for a year now, that is to say, since we fell victim of the *Herrenvolk* and life began to abound with unheard-of cruelties, Agafia's reports have become my only way of participating—emotionally, passively—in the history of our days. I should also note that it was thanks to Agafia that my house—a spacious, one-family house, situated in an orchard of seventy-eight fruit trees—escaped being requisitioned as living quarters for German officers. To this day I do not know how she managed that. When I asked, she answered evasively, "Those bastards, I won't give them a goddamn thing, no lodging for them!" A few days later, when I discovered that my Rosenthal china was missing, it occurred to me that she had cunningly bribed them, especially since when I asked Agafia about it directly she flew into a rage. "People have nothing to eat and all you think about is your Rosenthals! Pfoo!" I fell silent, ashamed of myself. She was absolutely right.

The sun is broiling hot. A reddish haze of dust, shimmering in the rays of sun, rises from the heavy brocade drapes and from the carpets, which have not been beaten in a long time. Agafia's silence continues. She has a dingy cloth tied around her waist instead of an apron and is standing in the doorway—she always tells her stories standing up—with an empty tray in her hands. This time I foresee a symphony, an epic, and with great effort I get out of my chair and inch across the carpet towards the window to block out the sun. One pull on the cord obliterates the bright spot of green and the abundant sunflowers, gracefully bending towards the south; it silences the buzzing of the bees, shields me from the aroma of the hot grass. A sudden darkness the color of heavy red wine descends on the room. I struggle all the way

back to my chair and wait for her usual coarse comment—
"It won't hurt you. Exercise is good for you." But Agafia
isn't even looking at me; I can see that she is considering
the first words she will say as soon as I sit down again in
my worn chair. I sit facing the door, I raise my head slightly,
I am ready.

"Today they shot two truckloads of Jews in the pasture,"
Agafia begins, and looks me straight in the eye with her
teary mushroom gaze. Automatically I lift my hands to my
temples, but I let them drop instantly, rebuked by her
sharp gaze.

"We have to know." I remember her words when she first
told me about the horrors the Nazis were committing in our
town, and I protested weakly, "Agafia, dear, I can't listen
to that, I'm sick. Spare me."

"We have to know about it. And look at it. And remember," she replied, and after that I didn't dare interrupt her.

"They shot them in the morning; you were still asleep. I
woke up early; my brother and I were going to Lubianki for
some flour. There wasn't a bit of flour in the pantry! When
we got there it was seven o'clock. Mikolaj buried the sack
in the straw, and, though they offered us milk, we didn't
stop to drink any. We figured, it's time to go back, why
show ourselves to the Germans in daylight? Also, it's nice
to travel in the morning—it's cool out, birds are chattering
in the woods, the grass has dew on it, the white mist on the
fields looks just like flowering buckwheat. Mikolaj and I
got to talking about the old days when he was courting the
miller's daughter who married somebody else. Just remem-
bering it, Mikolaj almost died laughing. That mist on the
fields, it covered the world. When we came out of the
woods, we still couldn't see anything. The horse pricked up
his ears; something was making him nervous. You see, the

horse was the first to figure out that something awful was happening. But not us—not till we heard the first shot. Very close. The gray reared up. Mikolaj pulled on the reins and jumped down from the wagon. We were right on the road. What could we do? We heard voices—we couldn't tell if they were far or near—it was as if the fog had stuffed cotton into our ears. Every couple of minutes there was a shot, a little bit of screaming, and then silence. I got all soaked with sweat, especially here, between my breasts; my blouse was sticking to me like after a bath. 'Don't be scared,' Mikolaj said. 'They're shooting the Jews. Get down from the wagon and go into the woods. We can't drive past there now. We have to wait till they finish.' He turned the wagon around, slowly, quiet as can be, parked it in a hazel grove beside the road. Meanwhile the fog had lifted, so when I sat down on the grass at the edge of the woods, I could see everything, every single blessed thing . . ."

Agafia must have seen how pale I was, for she stopped and gave me an ironic look as I reached for a glass of tea. A bit of sugar sifted off the teaspoon; my hand was trembling.

"If I told people what a sensitive thing you are, they would laugh. Nowadays you have to have a tough tenderness. Tough. Any other kind isn't worth shit."

Agafia's marinated mushrooms glittered sternly. I put down the glass.

"There weren't very many of them—seventy people at most and a handful of Germans. They took them at night, in the outskirts, from that neighborhood near the pond. They're taking them pretty often now, to make sure that everyone left fits into the ghetto. The Germans walked up and down, with their guns loaded, and whenever one of them shouted, it was like barking dogs. The Jews were digging trenches, some of them were already lying on the ground. They dug quietly, seriously, not just any which way. Think about it—digging your own grave. What did they feel while they were digging? Do you know?"

I shook my head.

"But I know! Nothing, thank you. They didn't feel anything anymore. They were dead before they died. When they started shooting again, I jumped up and wanted to run into the woods, so I wouldn't have to see. But I didn't run. Something kept me there and said to me: 'Watch. Don't shut your eyes.' So I watched."

Agafia was silent. I sat motionless, feeling my helplessness more than ever before, the burden of being crippled. Agafia put down the tray, unpinned the cloth from her waist, and wiped her face. She came closer, pulled up a chair. Her sitting down was unusual and it terrified me.

"Do you know who was there with them?" she asked in a hushed voice, staring at me. "That young dark-haired girl, the one you chased away . . ."

I asked sharply, "And how do you know that, Agafia? You didn't see her!"

"I know."

And I knew that she was telling the truth.

"Didn't you say that she was pretty as a picture, with black hair and long braids? I know. I even know whose daughter she was."

She looked at me and I felt faint. I wanted to tell her to stop looking at me, that one thing has nothing to do with the other, but I couldn't speak. I moved my lips soundlessly and withdrew into myself. Suddenly I smelled flowers, I saw the pale, delicate face of the fifteen-year-old girl.

"Am I saying you're guilty of her death?" asked Agafia, who could read one's thoughts.

"I'm not guilty of anything!" I wanted to scream, but now, though I felt able to speak, I realized that I could not honestly say those words. And Agafia knew that I knew.

She stood up. Her short, sturdy figure seemed suddenly dignified and regal. She pinned the cloth around her waist again and picked up the tray and the plates from the table. In the doorway she turned around.

"She was standing there naked in the empty pasture, with the sun shining on her, waiting for them to kill her. But the one who was aiming at her couldn't shoot. He must have had an eye for beauty. He stood there and took aim, and she stood there and waited. Then another one of them ran up to him, a blond man, and shouted something in their language. He shoved the first one out of the way and fired the gun himself. She waved her little hands in the air, fell down, and lay still."

In the long silence that followed, we exchanged glances, Agafia and I. After a while I lowered my gaze and she left the room, slamming the door. The next sound that reached me was the noisy, metallic banging of pots being put away.

The hardest part is when I start to move. Then, when I feel the support of my cane, the effort of lifting my legs diminishes my sense of helplessness. After twenty years I have grown used to being crippled, just as I have grown used to Agafia's constant presence and to the isolation I sank into when my husband left me. Sometimes it even seems to me that the life I have spent inside the four walls of my house and the four green walls of my beautiful garden is a happy life. Step by step I hobble across the room in which the darkness, the color of wine—or of blood—is deeper; the sun has already moved from the south to the west. My rubber-tipped cane makes a dull sound. With my other hand I touch each piece of furniture, one by one: the oak table, the broad oak credenza, the bookcase. I walk slowly, deliberately, though common sense tells me not to move. I walk, obeying perhaps the gaze of Agafia, who can still make me feel a sickly child's fear.

Bright light, bursting through the open door, hurts my eyes. The orchard is silent; the bees, so noisy at midday, have grown quiet; there is only the sound of crickets and the chirping of the sparrows stripping the cherries from the trees. The sunflowers have turned their heads towards the sun, which is already going down. For me this is the most beautiful moment. I can't bear early mornings with their promise of full bloom, nor midday, priding itself on its gorgeous beauty. But sunset, slowly but inevitably descending into night, awakens in me neither anxiety nor sorrow.

A path bordered by currant bushes leads me to my destination. It was right here, among flowers that were once laid out in formal beds but now grow wild in a tangled mass, that I saw that girl, that child. She was lying on the ground half naked; her beauty went straight to my heart. Frail, delicate—only when she raised her eyes did I realize: a child.

"Shame on you!" I screamed at her. "For shame! At your age! In someone else's garden . . . Get out of here! Immediately!"

I didn't look at the boy, only at her. She got up from the ground and hastily, embarrassed, covered her nakedness.

"We're sorry," she whispered.

Her eyes were still warm with love, and her movements had a sensual heaviness that was strange and unnatural for her girlish body. They were beginning to walk away, but I kept on screaming about how rotten and debauched our young people were becoming.

"For shame," I repeated. "At your age . . . Shame on you!"

The more I shouted the colder and angrier the girl's eyes became. I thought she was going to strike me. But she spoke quietly, bitterly.

"We're not allowed to do anything. We're not even allowed to love each other, or make each other happy. All we're allowed to do is die. 'At your age,' you say. And will we get any older? Come on, Zygmunt," she turned to the boy, "let's get out of here."

They left by the same path that I had come on a moment earlier. The boy said, "Ssh. She's a jealous old woman, she's a cripple. Ssh . . ." And I realized that she was crying.

I watched them until they disappeared, expelled from paradise. Then I looked sadly at the broken flowers, the crushed grass. And I thought about how I hadn't even seen the boy. I know that there was a boy with her and he was named Zygmunt. But I didn't see him.

Now the flowers here grow straight, untouched. Theirs were the last feet that touched this grass. What am I looking for as I bend down towards the ground? That moment of love and happiness, which they tried greedily to save from their broken life? That I stole from them? What words are my lips whispering? She waved her little hands in the air, fell down, and lay still . . .

How fortunate it is that Agafia, who always knows when she's needed, is coming now. She walks briskly towards me, and her face is kindly, but still stern. Now she is beside me; I feel her hand grasping my arm.

"All right, all right," she says.

We walk back in silence. The only sound that can be heard is our breathing and the crunch of gravel on the path.

*   *   *   *   *

Hidden in the dark interiors of apartments, with our faces pressed against windowpanes damp from rain and from our rapid breaths, we, reprieved until the next time, looked out at the condemned, who stood in the marketplace, in the same spot where on fair days the cheerful town erects its stalls. Divided into groups of four, they were waiting for the command to set out. And the rain kept falling—it didn't stop for one minute that night, a night that those who survived will remember as the Night of the Old Men. Because those who stood in those groups of four were old, worn out with work, and many of them probably had trouble walking to their destination, which was the green ravine near the railroad station where our children—their grandchildren—used to go sledding. We also looked at the six SS-men. In the long capes that shielded them from the rain, in their high, shiny boots, they strutted around, spattering mud on the old men, and one of them, the youngest, kept running to the far end of the marketplace, where he would stand in the doorway of the pharmacy and watch for something. That watching made us anxious; and there was also a growing impatience in the faces of the SS. Only the old people waiting for the command to set out remained unconcerned. Finally, when the young SS-man had run to the pharmacy entrance for the fourth time and, cheerful now, shouted out something we didn't understand, but that was clearly good news, we saw the truck approaching the marketplace with shovels in the back. We also saw the young SS-man strike the driver in the face, while the others formed a black ring, encircling the groups of four. It was then—the old men of our town were already on their way and were passing their homes and the children and grandchildren hidden behind their windows—it was then that the door of one of those houses opened and we saw a woman running across the marketplace. She was thin, covered with a shawl, carrying her huge pregnant belly in front of her. She ran after those who were walking away, her hand raised in a gesture of farewell, and we heard her voice. She was shouting, *"Zei gezint, Tate! Tate, zei gezint!"**

And then all of us hidden in the darkness began to repeat, *"Zeit gezint,"* bidding farewell with those words to our loved ones who were walking to their deaths.

* Be well, Papa, be well.

A
DOG

Our dog was named Ching. We called him that because on the day he appeared in our home all the front pages of the newspapers carried the first reports of the Sino-Japanese incident.

After much discussion—Rex? Lux? Ami?—we settled on the Chinese name—and not only because of current events, but the dog had a squint that made him look Chinese, or so Agata said. This made no sense—Agata had never seen a Chinese person—but her suggestion stuck.

"Of course," we cried out, "he's a Chinaman, he's got slanted eyes and he squints!"

"Chinese people don't squint," our older, fourteen-year-old cousin snapped.

"But they can," my sister argued.

"He's the spitting image of a Chinaman," said Agata, ending the discussion.

Ching, whose mother was Santuzza, a purebred fox terrier owned by the music-loving veterinarian, took after his father, and in just a few weeks it was clear that he was turning out to be a charming mutt. The only sign of his fox terrier blood was the shape of his muzzle, as our neighbor the judge, a self-appointed canine expert, assured us. We often cited his opinion when we took Ching out on his leash for a walk and the children shouted after us, "Mutt on a string!"

"But he has a fox terrier's head," we would answer proudly.

"And what about his behind?" said the kids.

Ching knew how to beg, how to shake hands, and how to fetch. He obeyed all our commands, without enthusiasm or joy, but rather with a sad air of resignation, a kind of philosophical thoughtfulness, which Agata was the first to notice. One day, when she was carrying in a platter of steaming pirogi, she announced: "That Ching is a philosopher . . ."

"Of what school?" our well-read cousin joked.

"A sad one," Agata replied.

The dog was definitely sad. He didn't run around the garden. He disdained toy bones, the special little ball he'd gotten as a gift, and even the chickens that scratched all day in the yard. He could usually be found on the couch, on the soft, woolly hand-woven throw. He would be watching a fly strolling on the windowpane, and in answer to our solicitous "Ching-ching, why are you so sad?" we would hear his soft, tender, clarinet-like voice.

When he was two years old he moved into the servants' quarters permanently. He slept with our housekeeper, which earned him a new nickname, "Agata's lover." Agata really did love him. Elderly, a spinster past her prime, she lavished all her affection on the squint-eyed dog, and fussed over him as if he were a baby—so much so, that she would hold the dog in her arms while making jam, with no regard for hygiene.

"He won't climb into the pot," she'd say, ignoring all our complaints, angry at our coldheartedness, which seemed to her a hundred times worse than failing to observe the rules of cleanliness.

During the war our interest in Ching cooled off dramatically, so that we hardly paid him any attention. But in the evening, when we were getting ready for bed, frightened of the coming night, and with our underwear and clothing laid out so we could get into it as quickly as possible, then Agata would appear in our room holding Ching in her arms like a child and say, "Ching, kiss them good night." And Ching would bark ever so softly and just barely wag his tail, and then he would lick our faces. It was an extremely irritating ceremony. What night could be good? Who had any patience for a dog? But since our cousin, who would have known how to stop Agata, was no longer around, having been killed during the first action, we endured it until Agata and Ching left for the country and we moved into the ghetto.

Before that, however, Ching gave us proof of his heartfelt loyalty. It was a test that many more people than animals failed in those days. On the day before both our moves there was another action in our town, longer than all the previous ones, and one that showed us how incredibly far cruelty and bestiality could go.

We hid, the seven of us, in a former pigsty, which—in addition to its other dubious virtues as a shelter—also lacked a door. In the past it must have had a door, perhaps even a strong one, as the arched entrance studded with hooks and nails suggested. A shelter without a door is sheer madness. But this was one of the things that helped save us. Had they seen a closed door, the Germans searching the yard and outbuildings would certainly have kicked it in, thus assuring a sentence of death in Belzec for the seven people seated on the hay that was still there from the time of the pigs. But since what they saw was a yawning black hole left by a broken door, a hole that was barely concealed by a pile of dry leafless branches, they passed it by with a clear conscience, not suspecting that people were hiding inside. The moment when the silhouette of an SS-man appeared in the pointed arch of the pigsty and his hand carelessly brushed the apple tree, dried by the summer heat—that moment gave us a taste of suspension in that limbo between life and death.

That Agata should have stubbornly answered their shouted demands with "I don't know, I don't know" was absolutely predictable—so predictable that we hardly appreciated it, as often happens with those who love us faithfully. But what about poor, sad, forgotten Ching?

They took him out of Agata's arms, warning her not to say one word to him, fed him kielbasa, which, starved as he was, he gladly gobbled up, and then asked him in a gentle voice to find his "master."

"Where's your master? . . . mistress? . . . master? . . . mistress? . . ."

Ching looked at them calmly (afterwards Agata swore that he shook his head no) and didn't even tremble. He just looked at them and sat there. But they kept urging him in broken Polish: "Find your master . . . find your mistress . . ." Then, for the first time in his life, energy welled up in him, and not only did he begin barking at the top of his lungs, he even nipped at the German's calf.

Crouched in the pigsty, we could clearly hear the negotiations between the SS-men and the dog, from which the latter emerged triumphant. It is true that he got kicked for this, but he bore this blow in silence, although afterwards he trembled for the rest of the day, just like a person who, after some extraordinary effort, cannot calm down for the longest time.

Fate brought Ching a tragic end. He died an inhuman death. It happened a year later, several days after our escape from the ghetto, and it had all the earmarks of a cruel and ordinary SS death. It happened at lunchtime on a summer day in Agata's brother-in-law's front yard.

After leaving our house, Agata had moved in with her relatives in the country. And it was there that the Germans found her, sitting in front of their hut. They had been searching for us frantically for three days and were furious that they could find no one to reward for turning in the family that had fled the ghetto, and that their searches in the homes of that family's Polish friends and acquaintances had yielded nothing.

Their conversation with Agata was the last straw. Their rage, fueled by powerlessness—a feeling intolerable to the *Herrenvolk*—had to find an outlet. In an instant they expanded the scope of the Nuremberg Laws, to apply not only to Jewish great-grandmothers but also to Jewish-owned dogs.

"You're going to hang in their place!" they shouted, and when she told us the story, Agata shouted, too, and added that the faces of the murderers were as red as the peonies in her brother-in-law's garden.

She had to fetch a rope. There wasn't any strong rope around, but a thin string sufficed, because the dog was skinny. When they whistled for him, he came readily, his body trembling, as usual. They hanged him from a branch of a cherry tree, and rode off on a motorcycle, lighter by one more death.

JEAN-CHRISTOPHE

We were working on the Ostbahn. It was a good work assignment because our *Aufseherin* was a girl we knew; we had gone to school with her. She was pretty then, round-faced, with curly dark hair. She used to sleep with the clerks in the district office, and now she slept with the Germans, but she was a good girl—she only slept with them, that's all. It was a good assignment: planting embankments wasn't hard work, and we were in the woods, in a beautiful forest some five or maybe eight kilometers outside of town, amid the silence of the trees. Also, this *Aufseherin* didn't much care what we did or how we worked. She just sat under a tree, bored. She would have loved to talk to us, but she was probably afraid of losing her job. She wasn't pretty anymore; she had grown heavy and her complexion was blotchy.

Sometimes, during our dinner break, she would sit near us and say, "This is a lovely forest, isn't it?"

"It *is* lovely," we would reply.

It was obvious that she was sensitive.

On the day of the action in town she was tactful enough not to ask why we weren't working, why our shovels and hoes lay under the tree. She sat at the edge of the clearing with her back to us. We were lying on the grass, not saying a word, waiting for the thundering of the train, because then we would know it was all over—though not, of course, who was on the train, who had been taken and who had been spared.

We lay on the grass, not saying a word, as if our voices could have drowned out the thundering of the train, which would pass near the edge of the forest, not far from where we were working. Only one girl was crying. She wasn't the youngest, and, in fact, she was the only one of us who had no one left in the town, who was all alone. She cried quietly, moaning every once in a while. No one tried to comfort her. Another girl was braiding wreaths—large clumps of bluebells grew everywhere—but every time she finished one she would rip it apart and begin all over again. She pulled up every bluebell in the clearing. Another girl was gnawing on some bread; she chewed it slowly, thoughtfully, and when she had eaten her ration she grabbed someone else's bread and kept chewing. The oldest girl kept putting her ear to the ground.

It was silent in the forest. There were no birds, but the smell of the trees and flowers was magnificent. We couldn't hear anything. There was nothing to hear. The silence was horrifying because we knew that there was shooting going on and people screaming and crying, that it was a slaughterhouse out there. But here there were bluebells, hazelwood, daisies, and other flowers, very pretty, very colorful. That was what was so horrifying—just as horrifying as waiting for the thundering of the train, as horrifying as wondering whom they had taken.

One of us, a thin, dark-haired girl, had moved slightly away from the group and lay in the shade of the hazel trees. She alone wasn't straining to hear anything; she just lay on her stomach, reading a book. We could hear the soft, steady rustle of pages being turned. Not once did she lift her head and look at us. The book was thick; it was falling apart. When a strong wind blew up in the afternoon—the train still had not thundered past—several pages were suddenly whipped into the air. And as they fluttered over us like doves, she ran around, crying, "Catch them!" Then she gathered up the pages, put the book back together, lay down on her stomach, propped herself up on her elbows, and began to read again.

The girl who had been crying was now sobbing louder; all of us were aware that every passing minute brought the train's thunder nearer, that any moment now we would hear death riding down the tracks. One girl cried "Mama!" and then other voices cried "Mama!" because there was an echo in the woods.

Our *Aufseherin* finished hemming a kerchief, tossed her empty cigarette box into the bushes, stood up, and began pacing. Once she stopped beside the thin, dark-haired girl, obviously wanting to ask her something; instead, she walked away, humming softly and repeatedly checking her watch.

But the next time she passed near the girl, she couldn't help herself. "What are you reading?" she asked.

With great reluctance, the girl tore herself away from her book and looked up.

"*Jean-Christophe.*"

"*Jean-Christophe?*" The *Aufseherin* was surprised. "The title's just *Jean-Christophe?*"

"*Jean-Christophe,*" the girl replied.

"Is it good?"

She nodded.

"Is it about love?"

The girl thought for a moment. She was very thin, she wore a man's jacket instead of a blouse, and she looked very ugly. She answered seriously, "Love? That too."

"About love!" The *Aufseherin* burst out laughing. Maybe she laughed because she liked love. "Will you lend it to me when you're done?"

"Why not?" she answered. "I'll give it to you to keep."

"No, not to keep; lend it to me and I'll return it." She thought for a moment. "It must be good—you've been reading it all day; and especially on a day like this when they're taking your people away."

"I have to hurry," said the girl. "I want to make sure I finish it in time. There's one more section, and I'm afraid I won't be able to finish it." She looked carefully at the book to see how many pages she had left. "I'm afraid I won't have time to finish it," she repeated, to herself now, but the *Aufseherin* heard her.

"It must be *very* good. What's it called? I forget . . ."

"*Jean-Christophe.*"

"*Jean-Christophe,*" she repeated several times, and explained, "If you're not around to lend it to me, I'll look for it in the library."

Then she felt sorry and added, "But I'm sure you'll finish it. It's not *that* long."

The girl who had been crying began sobbing still louder. It wasn't weeping anymore, it was lamentation. The oldest one of us knelt down and placed her ear to the earth. But the earth was still silent.

THE
KEY
GAME

They had just finished supper and the woman had cleared the table, carried the plates to the kitchen, and placed them in the sink. The kitchen was mottled with patches of dampness and had a dull, yellowish light, even gloomier than in the main room. They had been living here for two weeks. It was their third apartment since the start of the war; they had abandoned the other two in a hurry. The woman came back into the room and sat down again at the table. The three of them sat there: the woman, her husband, and their chubby, blue-eyed, three-year-old child. Lately they had been talking a lot about the boy's blue eyes and chubby cheeks.

The boy sat erect, his back straight, his eyes fixed on his father, but it was obvious that he was so sleepy he could barely sit up.

The man was smoking a cigarette. His eyes were bloodshot and he kept blinking in a funny way. This blinking had begun soon after they fled the second apartment.

It was late, past ten o'clock. The day had long since ended, and they could have gone to sleep, but first they had to play the game that they had been playing every day for two weeks and still had not got right. Even though the man tried his best and his movements were agile and quick, the fault was his and not the child's. The boy was marvelous. Seeing his father put out his cigarette, he shuddered and opened his blue eyes even wider. The woman, who didn't actually take part in the game, stroked the boy's hair.

"We'll play the key game just one more time, only today. Isn't that right?" she asked her husband.

He didn't answer because he was not sure if this really would be the last rehearsal. They were still two or three minutes off. He stood up and walked towards the bathroom door. Then the woman called out softly, "Ding-dong." She was imitating the doorbell and she did it beautifully. Her "ding-dong" was quite a soft, lovely bell.

At the sound of chimes ringing so musically from his mother's lips, the boy jumped up from his chair and ran to the front door, which was separated from the main room by a narrow strip of corridor.

"Who's there?" he asked.

The woman, who alone had remained in her chair, clenched her eyes shut as if she were feeling a sudden, sharp pain.

"I'll open up in a minute, I'm just looking for the keys," the child called out. Then he ran back to the main room, making a lot of noise with his feet. He ran in circles around the table, pulled out one of the sideboard drawers, and slammed it shut.

"Just a minute, I can't find them, I don't know where Mama put them," he yelled, then dragged the chair across the room, climbed onto it, and reached up to the top shelf of the étagère.

"I found them!" he shouted triumphantly. Then he got

down from the chair, pushed it back to the table, and without looking at his mother, calmly walked to the door. A cold, musty draft blew in from the stairwell.

"Shut the door, darling," the woman said softly. "You were perfect. You really were."

The child didn't hear what she said. He stood in the middle of the room, staring at the closed bathroom door.

"Shut the door," the woman repeated in a tired, flat voice. Every evening she repeated the same words, and every evening he stared at the closed bathroom door.

At last it creaked. The man was pale and his clothes were streaked with lime and dust. He stood on the threshold and blinked in that funny way.

"Well? How did it go?" asked the woman.

"I still need more time. He has to look for them longer. I slip in sideways all right, but then . . . it's so tight in there that when I turn . . . And he's got to make more noise—he should stamp his feet louder."

The child didn't take his eyes off him.

"Say something to him," the woman whispered.

"You did a good job, little one, a good job," he said mechanically.

"That's right," the woman said, "you're really doing a wonderful job, darling—and you're not little at all. You act just like a grown-up, don't you? And you do know that if someone should really ring the doorbell someday when Mama is at work, everything will depend on you? Isn't that right? And what will you say when they ask you about your parents?"

"Mama's at work."

"And Papa?"

He was silent.

"And Papa?" the man screamed in terror.

The child turned pale.

"And Papa?" the man repeated more calmly.

"He's dead," the child answered and threw himself at his father, who was standing right beside him, blinking his eyes in that funny way, but who was already long dead to the people who would really ring the bell.

A
SPRING
MORNING

During the night there was a pouring rain, and in the morning when the first trucks drove across the bridge, the foaming Gniezna River was the dirty-yellow color of beer. At least that's how it was described by a man who was crossing this bridge—a first-class reinforced concrete bridge —with his wife and child for the last time in his life. The former secretary of the former town council heard these words with his own ears: he was standing right near the bridge and watching the Sunday procession attentively, full of concern and curiosity. As the possessor of an Aryan great-grandmother he could stand there calmly and watch them in peace. Thanks to him and to people like him, there have survived to this day shreds of sentences, echoes of final laments, shadows of the sighs of the participants in the *marches funèbres*, so common in those times.

"Listen to this," said the former secretary of the former town council, sitting with his friends in the restaurant at the railroad station—it was all over by then. "Listen to this: Here's a man facing death, and all he can think about is beer. I was speechless. And besides, how could he say that?

I made a point of looking at it, the water was like water, just a little dirtier."

"Maybe the guy was just thirsty, you know?" the owner of the bar suggested, while he filled four large mugs until the foam ran over. The clock above the bar rattled and struck twelve. It was already quiet and empty in town. The rain had stopped and the sun had broken through the white puffs of clouds. The sizzle of frying meat could be heard from the kitchen. On Sunday, dinner should be as early as possible. It was clear that the SS shared that opinion. At twelve o'clock the ground in the meadow near the forest was trampled and dug up like a fresh wound. But all around it was quiet. Not even a bird called out.

When the first trucks rode across the bridge over the surging Gniezna, it was five in the morning and it was still completely dark, yet Aron could easily make out a dozen or so canvas-covered trucks. That night he must have slept soundly, deaf to everything, since he hadn't heard the rumbling of the trucks as they descended from the hills into the little town in the valley. As a rule, the rumbling of a single truck was enough to alert him in his sleep; today, the warning signals had failed him. Later, when he was already on his way, he remembered that he had been dreaming about a persistent fly, a buzzing fly, and he realized that that buzzing was the sound of the trucks riding along the high road above his house—the last house when one left the town, the first when one entered it.

They were close now, and with horrifying detachment

he realized that his threshold would be the first they crossed. "In a few minutes," he thought, and slowly walked over to the bed to wake his wife and child.

The woman was no longer asleep—he met her gaze immediately, and was surprised at how large her eyes were. But the child was lying there peacefully, deep in sleep. He sat down on the edge of the bed, which sagged under his weight. He was still robust, though no longer so healthy looking as he used to be. Now he was pale and gray, and in that pallor and grayness was the mark of hunger and poverty. And terror, too, no doubt.

He sat on the dirty bedding, which hadn't been washed for a long time, and the child lay there quietly, round and large and rosy as an apple from sleep. Outside, in the street, the motors had fallen silent; it was as quiet as if poppy seeds had been sprinkled over everything.

"Mela," he whispered, "is this a dream?"

"You're not dreaming, Aron. Don't just sit there. Put something on, we'll go down to the storeroom. There's a stack of split wood there, we can hide behind it."

"The storeroom. What a joke. If I thought we could hide in the storeroom we'd have been there long ago. In the storeroom or in here, it'll make no difference."

He wanted to stand up and walk over to the window, but he was so heavy he couldn't. The darkness was already lifting. He wondered, are they waiting until it gets light? Why is it so quiet? Why doesn't it begin?

"Aron," the woman said.

Again her large eyes surprised him, and lying there on the bed in her clothing—she hadn't undressed for the night—she seemed younger, slimmer, different. Almost the way she was when he first met her, so many years ago. He stretched out his hand and timidly, gently, stroked hers. She wasn't surprised, although as a rule he was stingy with caresses, but neither did she smile. She took his hand and squeezed it firmly. He tried to look at her, but he turned away, for something strange was happening inside him. He was breathing more and more rapidly, and he knew that in a moment these rapid breaths would turn into sobs.

"If we had known," the woman said softly, "we wouldn't have had her. But how could we have known? Smarter people didn't know. She'll forgive us, Aron, won't she?"

He didn't answer. He was afraid of this rapid breathing; he wanted only to shut his eyes, put his fingers in his ears, and wait.

"Won't she, Aron?" she repeated.

Then it occurred to him that there wasn't much time left and that he had to answer quickly, that he had to answer everything and say everything that he wanted to say.

"We couldn't know," he said. "No, we wouldn't have had her, that's clear. I remember, you came to me and said, 'I'm going to have a child, maybe I should go to a doctor.' But I wanted a child, I wanted one. And I said, 'Don't be afraid, we'll manage it somehow. I won't be any worse than a young father.' I wanted her."

"If only we had a hiding place," she whispered, "if we had a hiding place everything would be different. Maybe we should hide in the wardrobe, or under the bed. No . . . it's better to just sit here."

"A shelter is often just a shelter, and not salvation. Do you remember how they took the Goldmans? All of them, the whole family. And they had a good bunker."

"They took the Goldmans, but other people managed to hide. If only we had a cellar here . . ."

"Mela," he said suddenly, "I have always loved you very much, and if you only knew—"

But he didn't finish, because the child woke up. The little girl sat there in bed, warm and sticky from her child's sleep, and rosy all over. Serious, unsmiling, she studied her parents' faces.

"Are those trucks coming for us, Papa?" she asked, and he could no longer hold back his tears. The child knew! Five years old! The age for teddy bears and blocks. Why did we have her? She'll never go to school, she'll never love. Another minute or two . . .

"Hush, darling," the woman answered, "lie still, as still as can be, like a mouse."

"So they won't hear?"

"So they won't hear."

"If they hear us, they'll kill us," said the child, and wrapped the quilt around herself so that only the tip of her nose stuck out.

How bright her eyes are, my God! Five years old! They should be shining at the thought of games, of fun. Five! She knows, and she's waiting just like us.

"Mela," he whispered, so the child wouldn't hear, "let's hide her. She's little, she'll fit in the coalbox. She's little, but she'll understand. We'll cover her with wood chips."

"No, don't torture yourself, Aron. It wouldn't help. And what would become of her then? Who would she go to? Who would take her? It will all end the same way, if not now, then the next time. It'll be easier for her with us. Do you hear them?"

He heard them clearly and he knew: time was up. He wasn't afraid. His fear left him, his hands stopped trembling. He stood there, large and solid—breathing as if he were carrying an enormous weight.

It was turning gray outside the window. Night was slipping away, though what was this new day but night, the blackest of black nights, cruel, and filled with torment.

They were walking in the direction of the railroad station, through the town, which had been washed clean by the night's pouring rain and was as quiet and peaceful as it always was on a Sunday morning.

They walked without speaking, already stripped of everything human. Even despair was mute; it lay like a death mask, frozen and silent, on the face of the crowd.

The man and his wife and child walked along the edge of the road by the sidewalk; he was carrying the little girl in his arms. The child was quiet; she looked around solemnly, with both arms wrapped around her father's neck. The man and his wife no longer spoke. They had said their last words in the house, when the door crashed open, kicked in by the boot of an SS-man. He had said then to the child, "Don't be afraid, I'll carry you in my arms." And to his wife he said, "Don't cry. Let's be calm. Let's be strong and endure this with dignity." Then they left the house for their last journey.

For three hours they stood in the square surrounded by a heavy escort. They didn't say one word. It was almost as if they had lost the power of speech. They were mute, they were deaf and blind. Once, a terrible feeling of regret tore through him when he remembered the dream, that buzzing fly, and he understood that he had overslept his life. But this, too, passed quickly; it was no longer important, it couldn't change anything. At ten o'clock they set out. His legs were tired, his hands were numb, but he didn't put the child down, not even for a minute. He knew it was only an hour or so till they reached the fields near the station—the flat green pastures, which had recently become the mass grave of the murdered. He also recalled that years ago he used to meet Mela there, before they were husband and wife. In the evenings there was usually a strong wind, and it smelled of thyme.

The child in his arms felt heavier and heavier, but not because of her weight. He turned his head slightly and brushed the little girl's cheek with his lips. A soft, warm cheek. In an hour, or two . . .

Suddenly his heart began to pound, and his temples were drenched with sweat.

He bent towards the child again, seeking the strength that flowed from her silky, warm, young body. He still didn't know what he would do, but he did know that he had to find some chink through which he could push his child back into the world of the living. Suddenly he was thinking very fast. He was surprised to see that the trees had turned green overnight and that the river had risen; it was flowing noisily, turbulently, eddying and churning; on that quiet spring morning, it was the only sign of nature's revolt. "The water is the color of beer," he said aloud, to no one in particular. He was gathering up the colors and smells of the world that he was losing forever. Hearing his voice, the child squirmed and looked him in the eye.

"Don't be afraid," he whispered, "do what Papa tells you. Over there, near the church, there are a lot of people, they are going to pray. They are standing on the sidewalk and in the yard in front of the church. When we get there, I'm going to put you down on the ground. You're little, no one will notice you. Then you'll ask somebody to take you to Marcysia, the milkmaid, outside of town. She'll take you in.

Or maybe one of those people will take you home. Do you understand what Papa said?"

The little girl looked stunned; still, he knew she had understood.

"You'll wait for us. We'll come back after the war. From the camp," he added. "That's how it has to be, darling. It has to be this way," he whispered quickly, distractedly. "That's what you'll do, you have to obey Papa."

Everything swam before his eyes; the image of the world grew blurry. He saw only the crowd in the churchyard. The sidewalk beside him was full of people, he was brushing against them with his sleeve. It was only a few steps to the churchyard gate; the crush of people was greatest there, and salvation most likely.

"Go straight to the church," he whispered and put the child down on the ground. He didn't look back, he didn't see where she ran, he walked on stiffly, at attention, his gaze fixed on the pale spring sky in which the white threads of a cloud floated like a spider web. He walked on, whispering a kind of prayer, beseeching God and men. He was still whispering when the air was rent by a furious shriek:

"Ein jüdisches Kind!"

He was still whispering when the sound of a shot cracked like a stone hitting water. He felt his wife's fingers, trembling and sticky from sweat; she was seeking his hand like a blind woman. He heard her faint, whimpering moan. Then he fell silent and slowly turned around.

At the edge of the sidewalk lay a small, bloody rag. The smoke from the shot hung in the air—wispy, already blowing away. He walked over slowly, and those few steps seemed endless. He bent down, picked up the child, stroked the tangle of blond hair.

"Deine?"

He answered loud and clear, "*Ja, meine.*" And then softly, to her, "Forgive me."

He stood there with the child in his arms and waited for a second shot. But all he heard was a shout and he understood that they would not kill him here, that he had to keep on walking, carrying his dead child.

"Don't be afraid, I'll carry you," he whispered. The procession moved on like a gloomy, gray river flowing out to sea.

A

CONVERSATION

When he entered her room and slowly, carefully closed the door, and then began pacing the two steps between the window and the table, she realized that something had happened, and she guessed that it had to do with Emilia.

She was sitting beside the stove because it was already winter, which meant that almost six months had gone by since Emilia had taken them in. She rested her feet on a bundle of firewood that Michal had split, and softly clicked her knitting needles. She was making a stocking out of black sheep's wool. Emilia had taught her how to do that; she hadn't known how to knit before. She was grateful to her because she could do something useful—fill this unproductive time to which she had been condemned, isolated from the world and from people, imprisoned in this tiny room. At first, she had been grateful to Emilia for everything, and she was grateful to her now, too, but in a different way, in an abstract, cool, cerebral way.

Everything made her nervous: her husband's footsteps; his high, mud-caked boots; his jacket, which belonged to Emilia's husband, who had been missing since the start of the war; his sunburned face, which was also not his own, because in the past he had always been so pale—that pale, Slavic face, so unusual in his swarthy, black-haired family.

Because he was making her nervous, and not to make it easier for him, she asked him first, without raising her head, which was bent over the needles:

"Is it about Emilia?"

"What makes you think that?"

The rough way he asked and the fact that he was standing perfectly still convinced her that she was right.

"Because I know. I have a lot of time, I think about things. I knew from the beginning that this would happen. Once I was standing near the window—don't be afraid, no one saw me—and I watched her. I saw how she looked at you, how she moved, her smile, it was completely obvious."

"Not to me. I had no idea until . . ."

"Why are you so upset? Calm down. You say you didn't know about it until . . ."

"Put down the needles," he said, furious. "I can't stand that clicking. And look at me, I can't talk like this."

"The clicking is what keeps me calm. It's a wonderful thing, this soft, monotonous clicking. I can talk while I'm doing it. You'd be surprised what I can do. So you had no idea . . ."

"Anna, why are you acting like this?"

"So you had no idea until . . ."

"Until she told me herself."

"How touching! And what did she tell you?"

"She just told me."

"That she can't take it anymore, that you are always together, and that since 1939, when her husband didn't return from the war, she has lived alone—poor thing. Is that right?"

"How did you know?"

"I told you, I just know. When did it happen?"

"A month ago."

"A month ago. And for a whole month you went on being together from dawn till night, together in the fields, together gathering wood in the forest, together going to town on errands . . . You know what? You really do look terrific, and she's very sharp, she spotted it right away that first evening. 'You can pretend to be my cousin, you're a born estate manager.' I never saw you as an estate manager, but that's probably because I never saw an estate manager in my whole life, I only read about them. She also sized me up right away. 'With your face, not one step outside this door . . .'"

"You're being unfair, Anna, ungrateful. . . ."

"I know. And have you and she . . . ? You can tell me."

"No."

He stood there in his mud-caked boots and Emilia's husband's jacket, leaning against the wall, sunburned and so tall that his head almost reached the ceiling. He smells of fresh air, she thought. And also, he has changed, he's not the same man.

"Stop it!" he shouted. "Put that stocking down! We're leaving, we have to leave. Now, today, at once!"

She didn't want the sound of the needles to stop, but they fell out of her hands. A soft, almost imperceptible shiver ran through her. She recognized it.

"Leave? Why?" she asked in a frightened voice, and immediately began to shake. Earlier, before Emilia took them in, she used to shake like that constantly.

"Why, Michal?"

He didn't answer.

"Michal, why? Is she driving us out?"

"We have to leave, Anna."

"But Michal, for God's sake, where to? We have nowhere to go, we have no one. With my face, without money . . . I won't survive, you know it. Talk to her, ask her . . ."

Suddenly she raised her head and looked into his eyes. For a moment she seemed about to scream. She looked panic-stricken, horrified; then just as suddenly she lowered her eyes and straightened up. She was no longer trembling. She sat stiffly, and in her black dress, with her smoothly combed black hair, she looked like a nun. She picked up the stocking from the floor and set the needles in motion: her white hands began to dance rapidly and rhythmically to the beat of the metal sticks. She pressed her lips into a horizontal, dark-blue line.

"All right," she said after a moment.

Because her head was bowed, she didn't, couldn't see the flush that passed across the man's face and left it a shade paler. But she heard his loud breathing.

"All right. You can tell her that everything's all right."

"Anna . . ."

"Please go now."

At the sound of the door closing she trembled slightly, but she did not put down her work or raise her eyes. She sat stiff and straight, the needles clicked softly. After a moment, her lips moved silently. She was counting her stitches.

THE

BLACK

BEAST

I was standing in the doorway, my hand still on the latch, when I saw him watching me. At first I saw nothing else; he drew all my attention. He looked at me intently, hostilely. I took this hostility as a bad sign. It's bad, I thought, not taking my eyes off him, the old man won't take me in. That's what I thought; but out loud I praised the name of God. I knew that the old man was there in the hut, sitting at the table, the smoke from his pipe was hurting my eyes. I knew this without seeing him.

A deep voice responded with "May He be praised forever." Only then did I tear my gaze from the huge form sitting next to the stove and focus on the owner of the place. He was a small, bony man, with bushy eyebrows. Matilda had described him perfectly, even the ugly hairy mole on his cheek, and the gray, twisted moustache that curled downwards. That was him, Matilda's uncle. So I announced that I had come from his niece in Dobrowka and that I was asking for a roof over my head for a week or two. There was a silence. The only sound was the panting of that black beast that I was afraid to look at. A branch was tapping at the window, and outside the night was dark and cold.

I took the pack off my shoulders; my legs felt so tired I sat down uninvited on the bench beside the door. The dog slurped loudly; it sounded as if he were giving permission and I sighed with relief.

"What a rogue that Tilda is! I didn't know she was hiding Jews." The old man laughed. The word he used to describe his niece was as inappropriate as his laughter. Anyone who had ever seen Matilda—a retired school-teacher, a tall, dignified woman—would have bridled at that, as I did. A rogue! Was he making fun of her?

"You been staying with her a long time, Mister?"

"Six months."

"So why is she sending you to me now?"

"She's afraid of a search, she's asking for a week or two."

"She didn't give you a letter?"

"She didn't want to, because if they had found it on me . . ."

"Well, that's absolutely right. Did you come on foot?"

"Yes."

"It's a long way. No one saw you?"

"I made it. But I was very frightened."

"Sure. I'd have been frightened, too, in your shoes. I'm pretty fearful, as a rule."

"Matilda said you wouldn't refuse."

"I wouldn't refuse? And why's that? Matilda always knows better than everyone else. Won't refuse? Of course I'll refuse."

He was arguing with her, not with me; it didn't sound too alarming. But a moment later he added seriously, "I can't."

He said it gently, almost regretfully. I understood that he was afraid and I got up from the bench. The dog, that black beast lying near the stove, jumped up on its sturdy legs. I don't know what breed it was, probably a mutt; heavy-boned, stocky, it resembled a wolf. It moved from the corner to the center of the hut, sniffed my legs, and growled softly. "He'd give me away," I thought, "that black beast would betray me." I took my pack from the floor and threw it over my shoulder. I didn't have the faintest idea where I'd go.

"Just a minute, just a minute," the old man said. "I won't let you go without some supper." He thought for a moment, then latched the door and hung a blanket over the window. "You can spend the night here with me. But only tonight."

Later he led me up to the attic. He stood in the passage, lighting the way with a lantern, and I climbed up the narrow, rotting ladder. I was on the top rung, just about to squeeze through the hatchway from which came the cloying smell of hay, when I looked behind me. Down below stood the dog, his head thrown back; he was keeping an eye on me.

A moment later I was lying in the hay, exhausted, half conscious, worn out from walking all day, and from terror. Even now the thought of my journey made me tremble. I marveled at the miraculous way I had managed to safely walk the fifteen kilometers from Dobrowka to Matilda's uncle's hut.

I didn't think about tomorrow. From below came the sounds of the old man's footsteps as he moved restlessly about the room; then they subsided and I sank into silence and sleep.

Suddenly I shuddered and woke up. My sharp, practiced ear had caught the sound of soft, almost inaudible steps. I froze in horror, even though I knew it was the dog. He climbed the ladder carefully, slowly, I could hear him breathing quietly. I recalled his hostile look, his enormous, heavy body, and what I had once read: they grab you by the throat. I crouched in the corner, cold sweat pouring down my face, I covered my face with my hands. When at last I lowered my hands, they were completely wet. The dog stood on the top rung of the ladder with his front paws resting on the sill of the loft. Two green flames were glowing at me. Drained by my needless panic, I said quietly, "Get out of here, go!" He turned obediently and ran down.

Early in the morning—I guessed it was morning by the strip of light streaming in through a crack in the roof—Matilda's uncle put a pan of milk and some bread down in front of me without saying a word.

"Do I have to go?" I asked. He didn't answer.

He never spoke to me, and if it weren't for the food that he left near the loft door twice a day one might think he didn't know I existed. But the black beast—that's how I thought of him—looked in on me every night when the hut grew still. He would silently climb the ladder and stand on the top rung with his eyes glowing. He would stand there till I said go away. I got used to those visits and after a week, I even waited for them. But it never entered my mind to call the dog although now, after everything that's happened, I think he expected me to and was waiting for it. Clearly, the terror that he aroused in me that first night was still with me, and my distrust had merely been lulled. One night I waited in vain. He didn't come. I waited a long time, and later had trouble falling asleep.

"What happened to the dog?" I asked the hand that slipped me the pot of milk the next morning.

"Matilda has sent word that you can go back."

It didn't even occur to me that he hadn't answered my question. I was overcome with emotion—joy at the thought of returning to kindly Matilda and my safe hiding place, and fear of the journey back.

The road wasn't safe. It led right through a large village, Siniawka, and there was no way around it. I left the loft filled with good and bad feelings.

When I thanked Matilda's uncle for his hospitality, he mumbled something into his whiskers. Only after I had already set off, he shouted after me, "Hurry, so you can walk through Siniawka before the fog lifts."

The fresh air startled me. I grabbed the fence and breathed deeply. It was very early, still dawn, and there was a thick fog. I closed the gate carefully and set out. I was trying to walk jauntily, which wasn't easy. For weeks I had been confined to two square meters, and now the open space terrified me. I suddenly regretted that I hadn't taken a stick with me, a walking stick. I could have used it to set a rhythm, I could have leaned on it. I was so busy thinking of the stick I didn't have that I went a good twenty meters or so before I heard those familiar, soft steps. I turned around; he had run after me.

"Goodbye, dog," I said, and for the first time, touched his coat. It felt warm and pleasant. He stretched his back beneath my hand, yawned loudly, and then, seized with a sudden rush of energy, shook as if after a bath and looked up at me.

"Get out of here! Go home, I have to go on," I said, but he didn't budge and followed me with his eyes. It was obvious that he was telling me something that people who understand the language of dogs would have understood.

But I had had very little to do with dogs and it never crossed my mind that you could talk to them.

Annoyed, I quickened my pace, but the dog, who used to be so obedient when I chased him from the loft, didn't listen. He trotted along beside me, rubbing against my legs from time to time. We walked in step, arm in arm, if you can use that expression—and you can, you really can, I know that now for a fact. I didn't know his name, so I called him simply "Dog."

I still hadn't figured out what he was up to. As we neared the place where the path through the meadow joined the highway, I assumed that here we would say goodbye. I was grateful to him for keeping me company on the first part of the trip, which was safer than what would follow—but more difficult, because the first minutes of solitude are always the loneliest. Luckily, one can get used to anything —it's one of the peculiar blessings fate bestowed on us in a moment of kindness.

The walk across the immense meadow was the beginning of my utter aloneness in the midst of that hostile world. Now, approaching the highway where I expected to say farewell, I realized that the grief that overcame me when I set out on my journey, the grief at not having a stick to lean on, was the desolate cry of a soul who has been abandoned by everyone.

This is what I was brooding about as I stood beside the ditch that divided the reddish autumn grass from the bumpy roadway. The fog was lifting, the sky was growing brighter, turning pink.

"Now go home, your master is waiting, go home, go home," I told the dog, who was running back and forth sniffing the ground along the deep ditch filled with rain-water.

"Enough, that's enough, go home," I called to him softly and pointed to the path that we had just left.

He paid no attention. He rooted in the ground, pawed at the grass, and suddenly bounded across the ditch. Now he was standing on the road, swinging his tail like a pendulum. He began to bark, and—a miracle!—I understood. "Jump," he was saying, "jump quickly!"

I stood as if fixed to the ground. But since he had jumped the ditch, since he was telling me to jump . . . I got a running start and flew across the filthy water and landed next to him on the road. I bent over and reached to stroke him. But he didn't want affection, he was in a hurry, he was already running straight ahead with his tail in the air. I had a hard time catching up with him.

The sun was shining, the first wagons appeared on the road. Their rumbling disturbed the early morning silence but not the peace I felt within me now because of the soft footsteps beside me. Only when the sun had risen higher and I looked down and saw the houses of Siniawka scattered about the valley did my serenity waver. But since we had already gone a good part of the distance, I left the road, and with him following me obediently, headed towards a grove to rest. I sat down, leaned against a tree, and the dog crouched down a few meters away from me. He was curious about his surroundings; he pricked up his ears, turned his head to the right, then to the left, and rhythmically thumped the ground with his strong tail. I was struck by his alert expression, which had so frightened me that first night and which I had foolishly thought hostile. Now, knowing him better, I read it differently—as heightened awareness, preparedness, a way of defending himself against surprises. I should have been turning *my* head from side to side, pricking up *my* ears on the alert. Instead, I sat there dully, worn out by the walk, wheezing slightly, my eyelids drooping sleepily.

"Listen," I said. He slowly turned his head towards me, baring his sharp, white fangs. "Listen, I'm going to take a little nap." I don't know if I said those words out loud or only thought them. Maybe I mumbled them, for I felt myself sinking into a warm whirlpool of sleep, falling into a blissful but not quite boundless abyss; I had slipped from a sitting position and was painfully aware of every place my body touched the ground.

The sleep that overwhelmed me so suddenly couldn't have been very deep since I could hear my own snoring—too loud for someone in my situation, and unwise. While I was sleeping I could see with perfect clarity the birch grove and the dog crouching beside me, keeping guard. And I was thinking very fast for a person deep in sleep, I was thinking that I could rest for just an hour, that I could postpone the difficult encounter with Siniawka for just an hour, since the dog was guarding me so diligently. But no sooner had I thought this than the dog jumped up and, with its tail down, raced towards the road. He was running away. I called to him, but since I didn't know his name I just said "dog" or "black beast." He was already disappearing from sight, getting smaller and smaller, first a patch of black, then a black stripe leaping along the road. I wasn't terribly sad at his sneaking off, I didn't have time, nor did I have room for sadness in me, I was too full of clammy terror at being alone once more.

I must have started in my sleep and shouted, because at the moment of waking my mouth was filled with sound and my face was wet. The black beast was standing over me, whimpering softly. He lifted his paw and gently touched my arms, once and then again.

We passed through Siniawka without incident. I didn't move stealthily between the fences as I did when I came through there the first time. We walked down the high road through the center of the village, in full view of everyone. The kids shouted, "What a big dog!" or, "Jesus! How black he is!" That "black" might have meant me, too, it might have led to another, more dangerous word. It might have. But I had a dog, I wasn't alone, and people like me didn't have dogs. I walked with the dignified pace of a farmer who has set out with his dog to visit a neighboring village.

We reached Dobrowka at four. Now I had to wait until sundown so I could sneak into Matilda's house under cover of darkness. We waited in the rushes by the pond. The frogs were croaking. The dog, sensing that our journey was ending, lay down at my feet and napped. From time to time he would lift his head and look at me, and then, reassured, would go back to sleep.

Late in the evening we walked up to Matilda's house. I ran up the stairs to the high porch and knocked at the window, as we had agreed. The door opened slightly and Matilda's tall, stern figure appeared in the doorway.

"Thank God. I was so worried about you."

"Matilda, please, give him something to eat, he's sitting there in the yard, he's hungry, you must have something."

"Who? What's wrong?"

"The dog."

She looked at me as if I were out of my mind.

"What dog? Please shut the door immediately, come in, quickly."

"He's sitting down there, next to the stairs. Your uncle's dog. He kept me company the whole way. Thanks to him I . . ."

I grasped her hand, she didn't believe me, she thought I was delirious. We ran down the stairs to the yard, but the yard was empty.

ARYAN
PAPERS

The girl arrived first and sat down in the back of the room near the bar. Loud conversation, the clinking of glasses, and shouts from the kitchen hurt her ears; but when she shut her eyes, it sounded almost like the ocean. Smoke hung in the air like a dense fog and curled towards the roaring exhaust fan. Most of the customers were men and most of them were drinking vodka. The girl ordered tea, but the waiter, who had no experience with drinks of that sort, brought beer. It was sweet and smelled like a musty barrel. She drank, and the white foam clung to her lips. She wiped them brusquely with the back of her hand; in her anxiety she had forgotten her handkerchief.

Perhaps he won't come, she thought, relieved, then instantly terrified, because if he didn't come that would be the end of everything. Then she began to worry that some-one would recognize her and she wished she could hide behind the curtain hanging over the door to the toilet.

When he entered, her legs began to tremble and she had to press her heels against the floor to steady herself.

"Good, you're here already," said the man and took off his coat.

"A double vodka!" he shouted towards the bar, "and hurry!"

He was tall, well built, with a suntanned face; his cheeks were a bit jowly, but he was good-looking. He was in his forties. He was nicely dressed, with a tasteful, conservative tie. When he picked up the glass she noticed that his fingernails were dirty.

"Well?" he asked, and glanced at the girl, who looked like a child in her plain, dark-blue raincoat. Her black eyes, framed by thick brows and lashes, were beautiful.

She swallowed hard and said, "Fine."

"Good," he said, smiling. "You see? The wolf is sated and the sheep is whole. As if there was a reason for all that fuss! Everything could have been taken care of by now."

He sat half turned away from her and looked at her out of the corner of his eye.

"Would you like something to eat? This place is disgusting but you must understand that I couldn't take you anywhere else. In a crummy bar like this even the informers are soused."

"I'm not hungry."

"You're nervous." He laughed again.

Her legs were still trembling as if she had just walked miles; she couldn't make them stay still.

"Come on, let's eat. This calls for a celebration."

"No."

She was afraid that she would pass out; she felt weak, first hot, then cold. She wanted to get everything over with as quickly as possible.

"Do you have it ready, sir? I brought the money . . ."

"What's this 'sir' business? We've already clinked glasses and you still call me sir! You're really something! Yes, I have everything ready. Signed and sealed. No cheating— the seals, the birth certificate—*alles in Ordnung!* Waiter, the check!"

He took her arm and she thought that it would be nice to have someone who would take her by the arm. Anyone but him.

The street was empty and dark; only after they reached the square did the streetlamps light the darkness and the passersby become visible. She expected that they would take a tram to save time, but they passed the stop and went on by foot.

"How old are you, sixteen?"

"Yes."

"For a sixteen-year-old you're definitely too thin and too short. But I like thin girls. I don't like fat on women. I knew you were my type the day you came to work. And I knew right away what you were. Who made those papers for you? What a lousy job. With mine you could walk through fire. Even with eyes like yours. How much did your mother give him?"

"Who?"

"The guy who's blackmailing you."

"She gave him her ring."

"A large one?"

"I don't know."

"One karat? Two?"

"I don't know. It was pretty. Grandma's."

"Aha, Grandma's. Probably a big stone. Too bad. So you see, I noticed at once that you had a problem, but I didn't know that you would admit it right away. At any rate, it's good that you happened to find me. I like to help people. Everybody wants to live. But why the hell did you spill it so fast?"

"I didn't care anymore."

"That's just talk! You knew I liked you, didn't you?"

"Maybe. I don't know."

"And why did your mother let the papers out of her hands?"

"They said that they wanted to check something and they took them away."

"And they said that they'd give them back once she came up with some cash. Right?" He laughed. "Was it always the same guys who came?"

"Yes."

"Naturally. Once you pay the first time, they'll keep coming back. They must have been making a pile. How much time did they give you?"

"Till the day after tomorrow. But we don't have any more money—really. The money I've brought for you is all we have."

He steered her through a gate and up to the third floor. The stairs were filthy and stank of urine.

"That means you want to leave tomorrow." And he added, "Send me your address and I'll come to see you; I've taken a liking to you."

The room was clean and neatly furnished. She looked at the white iron bed on which lay a pair of men's pajamas with cherry-red stripes.

If I throw up, she thought, he'll chase me out of here and it will all be for nothing.

"Please give me the documents, sir, I'll get the money out right away," she said.

"Sir? When you go to bed with someone, he's not a sir! Put your money away, we have time."

It probably doesn't take long, she thought. I'm not afraid of anything. Mama will be happy when I bring the papers. I should have done it a week ago. We would already be in Warsaw. I was stupid. He's even nice, he was always nice to me at work, and he could have informed.

"Don't just stand there, little one."

He sat down on the bed and took off his shoes. When he took off his trousers and carefully folded them along the crease, she turned her head away.

"I'll turn off the light," she said.

She heard his laughter and she felt flushed.

An hour later there was a knock at the door.

"Who's there?" he shouted from the bed.

"It's me, I've got business for you, open up!"

"The hell with you, what a time for business! What's up?"

"I'm not going to talk through the door. Do you have someone in there?"

"Yes."

"It's important and it ought to be taken care of fast. They could steal it from under our noses, and it would be too bad to lose all that good money."

"Get dressed," said the man. "You heard, someone's here on business. A man doesn't have a moment's rest! Don't put on such a mournful face, there's nothing to be sorry about! You'll be a terrific woman someday! Here you are, the birth certificates, the *Kennkarten*."

He counted skillfully, without licking his fingers. She could barely stand, and once again she felt queasy. She put the documents in her bag, the man opened the door and patted her on the shoulder. The other man, who was sitting on the stairs, turned around and looked at them with curiosity.

"Who's the girl?" he asked, entering the room.

"Oh, just a whore."

"I thought she was a virgin," he said, surprised. "Pale, teary-eyed, shaky . . ."

"Since when can't virgins be whores?"

"You're quite a philosopher," the other man said, and they both burst out laughing.

INSPECTOR
VON
GALOSHINSKY

He leaned against the door that had just shut and listened to the dull, ragged beating of his heart. The cell was dark, airless, thick with stale breath. At first he couldn't see anything, he could only hear the heavy breathing. But as he got used to the dark, he could make out the wooden planks that lined the walls and the small space that separated him from the door. He felt a sharp pain in his ribs and a weakness in his legs. He knew he couldn't keep standing much longer; and it was getting harder to breathe, but still he didn't move. From the darkness came a voice asking why he didn't lie down; then another, inquiring as to his name and how he had come to be there. He couldn't speak. His heart pounded dully, skipping beats; when it did that he felt he was going to faint. He finally roused himself and groped for an empty space on the bunk. He pulled himself up with effort, lay down on his right side so as to minimize the pain, and ordered himself: be calm. This was the final task of his life. He wanted to perform it conscientiously, to give his remaining time some human, moral significance. His lips were dry and cracked, it was all he could do to whisper: be calm, control yourself. When he ordered himself to be calm and self-controlled, did he really mean: be brave and dignified? He shut his eyes in order to concentrate, to lock himself into his thoughts, to shake off the numbness that reduces a man to a trapped animal. There wasn't much time, and he wanted to say an unhurried goodbye to his life. His heart slowed down, he was breathing more easily. This he noted, even though he was perfectly aware that the functioning of his body no longer mattered. He knew that Jews caught using Aryan papers were now shot within forty-eight hours. He had a last night and last day before him.

He wondered how much time had passed since they came for him. It seemed like a fraction of a second; everything had run together. That distant day a month ago, the last time he was with Teresa, surfaced in his memory, vivid, as if it were yesterday. The stairwell was so dark he could hardly see Teresa standing in the doorway. She said, "I want you to be with me, I don't want to be separated. Come back and stay with me."

"I'll come back. I can't go on like this anymore, either," he had answered.

He had stopped again half a flight down and looked up; she was gone. Why did you walk away so fast, he thought, I wanted to see you one more time. That's what had gone through his mind, and he'd felt a sudden pain in his heart, because those words sounded ominous.

A moment later he'd laughed at them, and at his stupid heart. He strode down the street, armed with his Aryan birth certificate, his employment papers from a German firm, and the pince-nez that had replaced his eyeglasses since his first day as an Aryan. That had been his one concession to his new life. Otherwise he lived normally, without any special precautions. His very Jewish appearance demanded either that he hide underground or cultivate an insane self-confidence. For two years he had been living like a madman with unfailing good luck.

"Where did they catch you?"

He opened his eyes and searched for the man who asked. Now he could see their faces, so similar in their pallor and exhaustion. They lay crowded together, with burnt-out eyes, seared by the fever of the life they had lost.

"They came to get me at work," he answered. "I tried to run away, but I tripped over something in the street and fell. If not for that, they wouldn't have caught me."

At the same time he was thinking, So it's with them that I'll be sharing the last bit of my life, their screams will be the last voices, the voices that will end the world for me.

"Who squealed on you?"

He was surprised by the question. He hadn't thought of that until this moment, and even now, when he reviewed in his mind the looks he had gotten recently, he found no answer.

"I don't know. I lived on the other side for two years and no one ever tried to trip me up." Then he added, "I was supposed to move to another city next week."

They laughed. Laughter was the last thing he would have expected. But in a moment he understood; their laughter was a sign of contempt.

"So you weren't in the ghetto? You didn't gasp for breath in a bunker? You didn't hear them shooting at your family? They didn't pull down your trousers? You are fresh, but the thirty of us here are well on our way to rotting by now."

He searched the darkness in vain; he couldn't see who was speaking. He figured that the guy must be young; he had a clear, mocking voice. How amazing that someone like that—someone whose strength you could sense—could wind up here, couldn't manage to save himself. But he remembered immediately that in these matters youth and strength made no difference. Everything was governed by accident and blind luck, which had granted him two years of relative peace.

"When was the last time they took people away?" he asked.

They were silent; he had touched their common wound. After a moment someone answered: "Four days ago. They used to take people every other day, but now they're liquidating the ghetto. The *Ordnungsdienst* said that the jail will go last."

They had been waiting four days! Suddenly the pain returned; it slammed him onto his back.

"You'll get used to it," that same young voice said. "You've just got to not give a damn, then you'll go to the killing grounds as light as a feather. True, it's harder for you—but we . . . we have experience."

He lay there with his face pressed into his shoulder and told himself, I'll think about Teresa, I'll think about everything that was beautiful and good in my life. It's the only way to protect myself. I'll think that way until the end. "Teresa," he whispered, "I want to say goodbye to you, I want you to be with me at the very end."

But he didn't see her, he saw only darkness, and whirling, reddish-yellow circles. He couldn't recall features that he knew by heart. He said to himself, "She has blond hair, she is tall and slender, she has a scar on her cheek . . ." But she did not appear, and that was horrible. He tried to jog his memory by summoning up the day she had entered his life; he remembered every detail: the raspberry ice cream in the little blue dishes, her green dress and white shoes; he saw the face of the waiter who said, "I can tell you're in love," although they weren't at all in love yet. But he did not see Teresa. It was torment, but he preferred to torture himself rather than die without a glimpse of her.

He heard himself say, "You're better off without me. You're blond, you look Polish, I look so Semitic." That was on the day when the regulation about the armbands was announced. They were both sitting in the room, with the light off, and Teresa was crying.

"It will be better that way," he said. "You'll go away, you'll be alone, it won't even occur to anyone. I'll come once a month."

"By train? You?" she asked—and he could still hear her pleading with him, "I can't, I won't be able to . . ."

But he forced her to do it, she went away, and he came once a month, just as he had promised. This time he was supposed to stay. They wanted to fix up the apartment; he had worked out a plan for a hiding place in the bathroom, just in case. Now what would happen if Teresa, worried by his silence and absence, came to the office and asked about him? Or showed up at his apartment? He bit his lip to keep from groaning.

He pictured her little alarm clock on the shelf. It says 8:00 P.M. The train he always takes arrives then. Teresa stands by the window and looks out at the street from behind the curtains. There is a bakery opposite the window, and chestnut trees line the sidewalk. A month ago they had buds on them—they must be green now. Teresa stands and looks, her eyes bright with joy. Then they grow dark, and she raises her hand to her mouth, as she always does when something frightens her. He can see her! At last he can see her. "Teresa!" he whispers, "take care of yourself, you have to survive . . ."

He felt the touch of someone's hand and shuddered as if he'd been awakened from sleep.

"Have they interrogated you?"

"No."

"They interrogate everyone, so don't be frightened."

"Where? Here?"

"Every day at ten Inspector von Galoshinsky makes his rounds."

"A German?"

"Of course he's German. Haven't you heard of him? He's well known in the ghetto. An oddball, a sadist. That's why I wanted to warn you."

"Did he interrogate you, too?"

"Yes."

He wanted to ask for details, but he felt enormously tired and longed to return to silence and solitude. He tried to find Teresa awaiting his arrival, but he had lost her. And not only her; everything had sunk into darkness, had vanished like smoke, irretrievable and unreal. Everything from over there. What remained was the darkness of the stinking cell, the people with whom he had to die, and this Galoshinsky.

"Calm down," he whispered, "so what if there's an interrogation? As long as it's fast, as long as I don't have to wait."

He didn't wait long. Footsteps echoed in the corridor, the cell door shook as someone kicked it with his boot. He jumped up and peered out; he didn't want to miss the moment when the door would open.

A powerful, booming voice searched out new arrivals: "*Ist jemand zugekommen?*"

"*Jawohl*," came the regulation response.

"Galoshinsky"—the whisper ran through the cell. He pulled himself together, enough to stop trembling.

"New people step forward!"

He slid down from the bunk and straightened his aching body. I am calm, Teresa, he said silently, and suddenly he saw her clearly beside him. She was smiling, squinting slightly, the wind was blowing her hair, and she held a large colored ball in her hands. A snapshot from our last vacation, he thought.

"To the middle of the cell, facing me," thundered Galoshinsky's voice.

He faced the closed door. A weak yellow light clicked on above, illuminating only the center of the cell. The bunks were in semidarkness.

"Name!"

He answered. He was still waiting for the moment when the door would open. He looked hard and saw an eye peering through the judas hole in the cell door.

"What are you?"

"I am a draftsman."

"You are a Jewish swine!" The voice grew louder; it was deafening. "Again! What are you?"

He took a deep breath.

"I am a Jew."

"I'll show you what you are. Lie down!"

Before he knew it he was lying down. The cement floor chilled him; it was damp and it stank.

"Stand up! Lie down! Stand up! Lie down!"

What for? he asked himself, but he couldn't control his body, and he bounced up and down like a ball. A hammer was beating in his temples; he no longer knew if it was his heart or that horrible booming voice.

"Dance! Do you hear? Dance, or I'll shoot! *Ein jüdisches Tanzele! Eins, zwei, drei!* Clap your hands! Faster, faster!"

I am a toy, a wound-up top, I want to stop and cannot. He was drenched with sweat, burning up.

"Stop! Take your clothes off! Strip naked! *Schneller, schneller!*"

Those weren't his hands flinging off his jacket, tearing at his trousers and underwear; that wasn't him standing naked.

"When was the last time you slept with your Sarah? Answer!"

Teresa! He called to her to help him and suddenly he grew sober.

"Answer, or I'll kill you like a dog!"

He stood motionless and looked straight ahead. He still couldn't make a sound, but he felt calm. My God, he said to himself, how could I, and for what?

"Answer me," boomed the voice, "or I'll shoot."

"Shoot!" he screamed. He stopped standing at attention and relaxed.

It grew quiet. He heard the rapid breathing of the prisoners and a faint whisper behind him.

"Shoot!" he screamed again. Now he was giving the orders, he was demanding. He didn't take his eyes off the judas hole; when the shot came, he wanted to be conscious, dignified, a human being.

The silence continued. Not even a rustle could be heard from outside the door. Then a thin ripple of laughter reached him. It was coming from deep inside the cell, growing bolder and more distinct. He turned around abruptly. The prisoners' amused faces were glowing; they could barely contain their laughter.

Suddenly he understood. He threw himself at the bunks like a madman.

A young prisoner was lying on the lowest bunk, in a dark corner with the cut-off top of a black galosh still in his mouth. He realized: Inspector von Galoshinsky! He raised his arm to swing at him, but his arm felt heavy and he lowered it.

"Animal!" he spat out.

He ran to his bunk, threw himself onto it, and hid his face in his hands.

"Hey you, new guy! Listen, don't make it into a tragedy. Put your clothes back on. Where's your sense of humor? After you've sat here a while you'll laugh like the rest of us. You can't imagine the kinds of things people say! About themselves, about their women. And nobody's caught on . . . You're the first to spoil the game. Do you know who banged on the door and turned on the light? Who was looking through the judas hole? The *Ordnungsdienst*; they get a kick out of it, too."

"How could you," he screamed. "You . . . you . . ."

"How could we? Another day or two and we'll all be feeding the worms."

They took them out that same night, just before dawn. The stars were already growing pale, the smell of spring was in the air. But they could not see the sky, they could not feel the wind. A canvas cover hid the world. When the truck started rolling more smoothly, they realized that they had left the city and were riding on the highway. Someone said,

"The first turn to the left is Krzemionki, the killing grounds."

Through an opening in the torn tarpaulin he looked out. An early morning fog covered the fields. They'll kill us before the sun rises, he thought.

In a moment yellow road signs loomed out of the fog, and he just had time to hiss, "Now, a crossroads . . ."

They froze; they held their breath. The truck slowed down, listed to one side, and made a sharp right turn. The road sign said: Auschwitz. Someone grabbed his hand; he heard muffled sobbing. In the pale film of light he caught sight of a young, boyish face. Von Galoshinsky was crying.

THE
PIG

The man was hiding in a barn. He was no longer young, and he had been through a lot. He had been hiding behind a straw partition for two weeks. It wasn't much of a shelter. Nor was this his first hiding place. For weeks he had wandered in and out of attics, barns, cellars, even family graveyards, all bought dearly, with cash. Each day and night of those weeks could fill a book, if only the pen could take on this burden of despair and helpless loneliness.

But he was alive. By now, the nearby town in which he had been born and which he knew as well as his own face, was half dead, gutted by *Sonderkommandos*. The area had been reduced to a few inhabited buildings; the doors of the other houses had been sealed, and through the windows you could see bedding, pots, and clothing strewn about the floor.

It was a glorious summer, sweltering, auguring a good harvest. But it was stuffy in the hayloft; dust from the dry straw floated in the air of these few square meters. The man made a small chink for himself in the outside wall of the barn; through this chink he could keep an eye on a scrap of the world: the meadow in front of the peasant's fenced-in yard and a strip of road. The house was right next to the main road that linked the small town with the county seat of T——. He spent entire days at the chink in the wall. He took turns and looked first with one eye, then with the other. He witnessed fragments of daily events: the peasant's wife walked past, a cart drove by, a child fell down.

He couldn't smoke because of the danger of fire. So that chink kept him going. At least he could see.

He had already pondered his entire life; for hours at a time he held imaginary conversations; he recited Latin texts that he had to struggle to recall; he was close to developing a split personality, which he diagnosed with a doctor's objectivity. He listened attentively to shots from the town; he listened attentively to the silence. Then he counted. He counted the steps of people walking around the farmyard, the blows of the ax when they chopped wood. What kept him alive in this attic was the chink. He saw.

That day he was awakened by the sound of motors. It was gray outside and he couldn't see very much. But he knew it was the sound of trucks driving from T—— to the town. He recognized the big trucks by their heavy rumbling. He dropped onto the floorboards and after a while he could no longer hear the rumbling diesel engines, his heart was beating so loudly. He knew what they signified; he thought about how the last time, when he was still in the town, twenty trucks packed solid had driven out of there. "They're coming back for the rest of the living," he whispered to himself, "for the rest of the living."

Silence soon fell over the outskirts of town and dawn broke slowly. The yellow flowers on the meadow, whose names he could not recall, shone in the sunshine. He kept his eyes glued to that little bit of highway visible through the chink, although nothing was happening there. For the moment nothing was happening there.

Then he placed his ear against the crack and listened. After an hour that seemed to him like a century he heard a distant scream. He swayed and shut his eyes, but closing his eyes didn't save him. He saw everything with the precise, experienced eyes of a witness to four actions, all of which, by some miracle, he had survived intact.

The screams were growing in intensity, or perhaps it only seemed that way to him. Still, the shots could not be a hallucination. Dulled by a distance of two kilometers, they came one after the other, chaotically, from several directions. He cowered in a corner with his hands over his eyes. Whom had they taken? Whom were they torturing? He knew them all, he had treated them.

Suddenly he shook off his weakness and pressed himself against the chink. They were returning. Impulsively he jabbed his finger into the opening to make it larger; now he could see clearly.

The meadow beside the highways was crowded with gaping onlookers. He even recognized the children of the peasant couple who were hiding him. They stood there, full of curiosity, looking towards the town, from which the rumbling trucks straining uphill could be heard.

"I can't," he said, and slumped into a corner, but he stood up again and watched without blinking.

He saw the first two trucks clearly. It seemed to him that he recognized a woman, the one standing at the back with her arms hanging limply at her sides. But the third truck he saw as if through a mist. No one screamed, no one shouted, no one wailed.

He had counted six trucks when suddenly he heard an inhuman shriek. He froze. A commotion rippled through the crowd; everyone swarmed to the roadway.

What had happened? Had someone tried to escape? But

the trucks didn't stop nor were there any shots. The rumbling of the motors was drowned out by the wailing of the spectators. The crowd broke up and angrily dispersed, loudly discussing what had happened.

He could barely contain himself until his peasant arrived that evening; he was trembling with excitement.

"What happened?"

"What happened was . . . ," the peasant responded in his singsong Volhynian accent, "the devil take them! They ran over a pig!"

That evening he did not touch his food, that night he didn't close his eyes.

There was one more attic, then a forest; he endured the last months of the war buried in a hole beneath a pigsty. The woman was poor but she gave him food, protected him, and when he was very ill, she swore from the goodness of her heart that she would bury him under the most beautiful apple tree in her orchard. It was at her place that he survived the war. When she pulled him—filthy, covered with lice, unable to walk—from his underground hiding place, he said, "You know, when they ran over that pig, I didn't believe there were any human beings left . . ."

"Yes, yes," she answered him, as if talking to a child. And being a sober, sensible woman, she thought to herself, "The poor thing has gone crazy from happiness. He's babbling about pigs!"

TITINA

Perhaps because Ludek was the youngest, the commandant ordered him, "Bring Titina." That's all, he didn't give him a list like he gave the others who had just left the *Judenrat* building and scattered through the town. Ludek asked, "By myself?" but the short, bald commandant didn't answer and slammed the door in his face. A storm of voices was raging behind the door.

It was a warm, windy night. The ice was breaking up on the river, and the sound of the water could be heard everywhere in town. There wasn't a single light in the houses, just thick darkness, sleep.

He walked quickly. The river's voice grew stronger. Titina lived next to the bridge. "Good evening," he imagined himself saying, and heard Titina answer, *"Bonsoir, jeune homme."*

"Bonsoir, Madame," he corrected himself—she insisted he speak to her only in French. The little desk under the window, the worn volume from Larousse, the gilded binding of *Letters from My Windmill*. And the smell of mold from the dark room. Even back then she showed signs of becoming a madwoman. That mustiness. She never opened the windows. Dark, slender spruce trees outside. She referred to her little house as "Spruce Manor," and rolled her r's as befits a teacher of French.

"Comment va ta maman?"

"Merci, elle va bien."

His mother in her nightgown, her wrinkled neck, her slack, goose-bump skin. She hadn't even had the time to dress.

"Ludek, they've sent for you." And she began to weep, "My child . . ."

He dressed efficiently—trousers, tunic, the cap with the shiny visor. "Mama, where's my truncheon?"

"I'll ask the Marciniaks, you can hide in their barn."

A month before, she was crying because the *Judenrat* didn't want him. She walked kilometers, tried all her connections, spent hours cooling her heels in the corridor outside the *Judenrat* president's door. "I want to save you," she used to say.

"Don't be hysterical, Mama."

She raised her hands to her neck as if to choke herself. That was her strongest gesture of despair; it was what she kept doing the night they took his father away.

"I didn't know. I didn't expect . . . ," she could hardly talk. She grabbed his arm. He freed himself gently but firmly.

"Stop it, Mama, I have to go," he said.

She wanted to embrace him, but he stopped her with a look, although he knew what that embrace was supposed to mean. She was asking for his forgiveness.

"Elle ne va pas bien."

Dear Zofia, *la belle Sophie*, and her little boy! Titina's voice is low and hoarse, like that of a sorceress. Her long dress shimmers and rustles; on her nails is a gleaming, blood-red shell.

"I don't want a candy, no!"

"He'll get used to it," says the hoarse voice of the sorceress, and his mother laughs lightheartedly.

"Why don't you air out your house, Titina?"

A scream came from the direction of Castle Hill. He stopped and listened. Silence now, nothing, only the sound of the river. The river and his own heart. "She's half mad, or maybe by now she's gone completely mad," he said out loud. Again he stopped. No, he wasn't mistaken. The center of town was already awake. Someone was running, someone screamed once, then again; someone kept shouting and shouting. He took off his cap, bared his head to the wind. Spring was in the air. If I don't do it they'll throw me out. From the other end of town, near the railway station, came the sound of motors. They'll drive by the bathhouse and wait there. How many trucks? Six? Five? How many names were on the list? Old people, cripples, madmen. How many people did they want? He leaned over the bridge railing. One thrust of his body and he would be floating away, carried along by the current into the heart of that roar. "Ludek, take care of Mama, be brave and obedient." What does brave and obedient mean? To shift his center of gravity a centimeter beyond the bridge railing and let his hands hang over? To get crazy Titina? To float away with the river?

Suddenly he saw them coming. So that's what it looks like. Completely normal. They're walking, leading the others by the arm. So silently. Jozek's broad shoulders, Heniek's boyish silhouette, and between them two bags of bones. A man gets smaller in old age. They stopped. Jozek was so angry he could barely speak:

"So, you're admiring the landscape, mama's boy? Let us do all the work, right? You scum! You heard them—if something goes wrong, then two of *us* will have to go. And it won't be me, that's for sure."

One bag of bones is a man, the other a woman. He drew back to let them pass. The woman took tiny steps, bent over as if she might fall any minute. Her eyes were closed.

Titina's house was behind the garden; the spruce trees came right up to the porch. He had a hard time opening the gate; it was frozen solid. He sank up to his knees in snow. It probably hadn't been shoveled since the start of winter. He turned on his flashlight: there weren't any footsteps. Had she not left the house all winter? Maybe she was dead. God, let her be dead. A white snowy porridge had drifted over the rotted steps; three steps, he still remembered that. The spruce trees had grown as high as the roof.

He pushed the door with his shoulder. It gave way; there was no key in the lock. The entranceway, the familiar damp odor of mold.

"Don't be afraid," Mama had said, "she's a little strange, an eccentric old maid, but she knows the language so well, she lived in Paris for many years. Now she's old and very poor."

"And loony." He smiled.

"Shush, Ludeczek, please. Don't act so badly brought up. 'Strange' is what I said. Bow to her politely."

He wanted to shout, but could only manage a sharp whisper. "Miss Titina!" I'm hoarse, he thought.

He shouldn't have called out "Titina." That wasn't her real name, only a nickname; probably no one even knew what her real name was. But the commandant had also said it: "Bring Titina." He remembered that when he began to study French he asked his mother where she had gotten such a funny name, and his mother sang him the song "Titina, oh Titina, Let's play the concertina." The gay melody flew out of his mother's lips like a swift little bird, and his mother, with her head cocked to one side, looked like a comic little bird with a round neck. Then she told him a long story about a ball, a complicated story which she must have found amusing because she kept stopping to laugh, and his father became angry at her for telling such nonsense to a child. He was seven then; his mother thought it the proper age for studying foreign languages. It was then, at the ball that Mother had described, that the name Titina stuck forever to the queer, old woman whom he now had to lead to the square in front of the bathhouse.

His whisper got no response. He felt for the light switch; it sparked once, but the house stayed dark. He forgot about his flashlight, and with his arms outstretched, walked to the end of the hall where, just as he remembered, double doors led into the big dark room.

He stopped in front of the doors and pressed his ear against them. There was a ringing silence, which turned into the ringing of a church clock striking eleven. There was one hour left.

He waited until the final, eleventh chime faded away. He thought, she's probably dead, I'll go back, I'll say she's no longer alive. There are no footprints in the snow and the door is locked.

But he remained there with his ear to the door and now it was neither the silence nor the clock that rang, but his own heart ringing inside him, sounding an alarm.

"Miss Titina," he said once more, cajolingly. He was begging her: don't be alive.

"Who's there?"

He was horrified and jumped back.

"*Entrez*," said the low, hoarse voice that he recognized immediately.

He entered.

She was sitting up in bed, barricaded behind a pile of pillows. All he could see was her head with its straggly gray hair sticking straight up like wires. She was holding a candlestick in her raised hand.

As he approached, his shadow suddenly leapt onto the wall beside the shadow of her medusa head and then slowly, steadily covered it.

The face that peered out from the bedding was huge, mottled with liver spots. "A wreck," he thought aloud, and repeated with a strange satisfaction, "a wreck, a wreck."

She was watching him closely. He sensed that she was struggling to remember him. He felt a cramp in his stomach, a quiver of nausea, and undid the collar of his tunic.

"Please get up," he said. "All Jews have to be at the *Judenrat* now."

She didn't move. A slight tremor passed across her face and she smiled.

"You're probably here for a lesson."

"No. You have to get up. I'll take you to the *Judenrat*. Everyone . . ."

"Unfortunately, I'm not giving lessons at the moment."

He bent over her and, fighting nausea, said sharply, "Please get up."

I can't do it, they'll throw me out, he thought. She won't

go, I won't be able to make her go. If only I had someone to help me.

"Get up!" he shouted.

She dropped the candlestick on the floor. He picked up the candle and kicked a pot away with his foot. Bread crusts, hard as bone, scattered all over the floor. He gathered them up carefully.

"What a way to speak to me!" said Titina. "And whom do I have the pleasure? . . ."

He didn't answer. Once more he repeated, calmly, and now politely, "Please get up and get dressed. I shall be escorting you to the *Judenrat*. All Jews have to assemble at the *Judenrat*."

"*Tiens, tiens.*" She twisted her head. "To the *Judenrat*? I've never had anything to do with the *Judenrat*. And I don't want to have anything to do with them. *Voilà*, young man. And now you may leave."

"Miss Titina!" he screamed. "The Germans ordered . . ."

"*Les sales boches!*"

"I'll help you."

Her shapeless bag of a face was up against his; her eyes were swimming with tears. She grabbed his hand. "Whose son are you, child?" she asked. And without waiting for an answer she whispered, "Son . . . you are the son of . . ."

"Of Zofia," he answered obediently, despite himself.

"*Mon Dieu*, Zofia's son—*la belle Sophie*! How could I . . . I knew you would come. Why haven't you come for so long? Do you have your notebook and grammar?"

"Miss Titina, you have to come with me. The Germans have ordered . . ."

"I remember, I was at a ball with your mother, ah . . .

she was the only one who remembered that a lonely woman needs some diversion. The garrison commander danced the mazurka with me. *Mon Dieu*, so she hasn't forgotten about me. Sit down at the desk, open your notebook. *Elle était si belle, ta maman . . .*"

He sat down. He was very tired. Titina's hoarse voice reached him from far away. He was thinking: What am I doing here? Why? And also: It would be so nice to fall asleep and wake up when all this is over. All what? All this.

His mother used to run from the president to the secretary, from the secretary to the vice president, and return home weak, broken, ill. He noticed her stockings had holes in them. People are ungrateful, she said. They owe your father so much and now, when they've killed him, no one will help me. They say that you're too young. She cried in front of him. Until one day she returned home a different, a much younger, woman.

"Ludeczek, you won't go to the camp!" she called out. "They agreed, they swore to me!"

He was neither happy nor sad. "And what will I do, Mama?" he asked.

"What do you mean, what? You will be an orderly. That's a good post." Everyone said "post" now. He didn't like that word—orderly! And tonight she was choking herself again.

The heavy fall of the church bell. He jumped up as if he'd been scalded.

"It's been years since anyone has come, I've been alone for years. They all forgot . . . not a single lesson . . ."

This madwoman keeps going around in circles, he thought in a rage.

"No one, no one . . ."

"But now they've remembered you," he suddenly heard his own voice, his own unrecognizable voice, and he noticed that these words got through to her.

"They've remembered," he repeated louder and more emphatically. And with a growing fury such as he had never felt before, he added, "The commandant wants to study French with you."

Having said this, he backed away. His heart was pounding, in his throat. But it was too late now.

Titina straightened up, with more strength than he had expected.

"*Monsieur le commandant veut prendre des leçons chez moi?*"

"Yes! Now, at once," he screamed.

You scum, he said to himself. You filthy scum.

The loading was finished now, the square was empty, the snow trampled flat. The SS were standing near the trucks; a group of policemen, with their bald-headed commanding officer, were off to one side.

At the sight of Ludek leading the bizarre figure dressed in a long coat and a hat festooned with flowers, the SS roared with laughter. One of them pointed his riding crop at the steps which led up into a truck and graciously extended his hand to Titina.

"*Merci, Monsieur,*" she said before she disappeared into the dark interior of the truck filled with stale human breath.

The bald man handed Ludek a flask and told him, "Take a drink, it'll make you feel good." Ludek obediently pressed it to his lips and gulped it like water. He felt as if he were on fire.

He flung the flask onto the ground and took off running. He ran blindly through the empty town, and then across the fields, he ran sinking into the drifts of snow, he kept falling and getting up and running towards the ever closer, ever more threatening roar of the river.

NIGHT
OF
SURRENDER

I met Mike in a park, in a pretty little town on the Alsatian border. I had been imprisoned there briefly in 1943, which was complicated, considering that I was a Jew using Aryan papers. Now the war was ending, the front was falling apart around Stuttgart, and the surrender was expected any day.

Mike was a very nice fellow, and in those first days of freedom I was feeling very lonely and sad. I used to go to the park every day. It was immaculately kept and the rhododendrons were in full bloom, covered with pale violet flowers. I would walk to the park, sit on a bench, and tell myself that I should be happy to have survived, but I wasn't happy, and I was upset to be so sad. I went there every day and the girls from the camp figured that I had met a boy; they were envious and curious. Their suspicions were confirmed on the day Mike walked me back to the camp; and from then on he would come to get me every day at four and we would go for a stroll.

Michael was very tall, he had funny long legs, his uniform trousers fit tightly, his waist was as slender as a girl's. He wore large eyeglasses with rectangular frames. He smiled like a child, and if he wasn't so big, you could have mistaken him for a teenager; but he was a serious grown man, a professor of mathematics, already twenty-seven, ten years older than I.

He would take my hand—my head came up to his elbow —and we would go strolling in the park or along the Rhine, and he would always whistle the same tune. Much later, I found out that it was Smetana's *Moldau*, but at that time I didn't know its name or who had composed it. My knowledge of the world and of life was one-sided: I knew death, terror, cunning, how to lie and trick, but nothing about music or poetry or love.

This is how I met him: One day I was sitting on the bench beside the pale violet rhododendrons. It was evening and I should have gotten up and returned to the camp for supper, but I kept on sitting there, I didn't feel like getting up even though I was hungry, and I didn't notice the lanky boy with the glasses and the American uniform who had sat down on the edge of the bench. When he asked, "What are you thinking about?" I was terrified, and he burst out laughing.

I answered in my broken English, "I was in a German prison here,"—though I hadn't been thinking of that at all, only about supper, because I was hungry.

"Did they beat you?"

"No."

He looked closely at me, then said, "That's funny."

I didn't know what was funny—the fact that I had been in prison or that they hadn't beaten me. Some kind of moron, I thought, but he kept on asking me questions.

"And why did the Germans lock you up in prison?"

I looked at him as if he were a creature from another world.

"Don't worry. I just wanted to know what it was like for you."

He looked at me seriously, and his eyes shone with a warm, golden light. Maybe he's not such a fool, I thought. But watch out, I told myself, wait a bit. You held out for so many years, you can hold out for another week or two. The war is still going on.

But already I anticipated the enormous relief it would be to say those three words—their weight was growing more unbearable each day. I smiled faintly, and in that teary voice befitting the revelation of one's life story, said: "Ah, my history is very sad, why return to those matters? I don't want to."

"Poor child!" He stroked my hair and took some chocolate out of his pocket. "But you will tell me some day, won't you?"

It was milk chocolate. I love milk chocolate; it's light and melts in your mouth. The last time I ate chocolate was before the war, but I didn't say anything, I just got up to go to supper—the potatoes and canned meat in gravy we got every day.

The next afternoon Mike brought me some enormous, dark violets, and I rewarded him with the life story I had patched together over the last three years; it moved him as it was meant to. I was sorry that I was still lying, but consoled myself with the fact that the true story would have been a hundred times more horrifying.

The girls from the camp were jealous, and in the evening they would ask in detail about everything. After a week, they asked, "Has he kissed you?" and when I answered, "No," they were very disappointed. And that was the truth. Mike brought me more chocolate (because I had told him, after all, that not since before the war . . .). He bought me ice cream, he held my hand, and sometimes, when we lay near the Rhine, he stroked my hair and said it was silken and shiny. He also told me about his home and the school where he taught, and about the garden he worked himself. It all sounded like a fairy tale from a storybook for well-brought-up children, and sometimes I smiled to myself, especially when he talked about flowers and mowed grass. I never asked him if he had a girlfriend in America. It was obvious that he did, but he never mentioned her.

Sometimes we didn't say anything. The water in the Rhine glittered like fish scales, the weeds flowered in the ruins, airplanes circled overhead and they too were silvery and long, like fish. But there was no reason to fear them, and now, without getting that tightness in your throat, you could watch them dive, grow huge, and mark the earth with the shadow of a cold black cross.

"Ann," Mike would say, giving my name, Anna, its English form, "isn't this nice?"

"Very nice," I would answer, and he would say, "Very, very nice, my dear," but it wasn't very nice at all and it couldn't be very nice as long as I was lying to him.

That day, when we were returned from the park, the rhododendrons were already yellow and withered. Mike asked, "Why won't you tell me everything about yourself? It would make you feel better."

I was well trained. I replied instantly, "But I told you."

"Not everything, Ann. I'm sure that was only a part, maybe not even the most important part. Why don't you trust me?"

Again he had that warm, golden glow in his eyes, and I thought: I am mean and nasty.

"The war taught all of you not to trust anyone. I'm not

surprised. But listen, the war is over. You have to learn to believe in people, in happiness and goodness."

"You're talking like a professor, and a stupid one. You think everything can change just like that? Believe in people? It makes me laugh"—I wanted to say throw up—"when I hear such idiotic stuff."

"Ann, I want to ask you something."

My heart began to pound, because that was what everyone said before they asked, "Are you a Jew?"

"Well, ask," I said, but he didn't say anything; he just looked at me and I couldn't help seeing the tenderness and concern in his glance. I felt like touching his face, pressing close to him, asking him not to go away, telling him that I didn't want to be alone anymore, that I was tired of standing outside myself and watching every move.

"Well, ask. I'm waiting," I said.

We were standing at the gate to the camp. It was suppertime. A crowd of DPs with aluminum mess kits for their potatoes and canned meat with gravy were crossing the large square where, every morning, roll call and edifying prayers were held.

I looked at Mike and noticed that a muscle in his right cheek was quivering.

"Would you go away with me?"

"With you? Well . . . where?" I asked only to gain time and calm down. I knew very well what he meant.

"Where? Where? To the moon!" All at once, he grew serious. "You know what I'm asking and you know that I mean it. I've thought about it for a long time and I've come to the conclusion that it's very nice for us both when we're together. Right?"

"You're saying this out of pity, aren't you?" I laughed.

"A poor victim of the war, she lost her parents in the uprising, she's all alone in the world."

"Stop it, that's horrible. You know that isn't true. It's not pity, I just want things to be nice for us. I know that together . . . Don't answer now. Think about it. I'll come tomorrow. You can tell me then. We've known each other for almost a month, and I want you to stay with me. But Ann," he didn't let go of my hand, "get rid of all those defenses. Trust me. I want to bring you up all over again, teach you to live again."

For the first time he looked like a serious, grown-up man.

"All right, Professor," I said, and then ran away. The next day the surrender came and everyone was going wild. I waited for Mike for a whole hour on the low wall in front of the camp. By the time he arrived that evening, I had lost hope. Lying on my bunk in the empty room—all the girls had gone to a party—I thought, with the army you never can tell, they might have transferred him suddenly, and goodbye! I lay there dazed, trying to recall the melody he always whistled, and which I still didn't know the name of. But I couldn't, so I tried to summon up his smile and his long funny legs. When he walked into the room, I was very happy—but only for the second it took me to remember that today I had to tell him everything. Though I very much wanted to be rid of the burden of those three words, I was frightened. Mike seemed like a total stranger. But that feeling, too, lasted only a moment, because he said, "My God, you look like a schoolgirl, like a child, and I'm an old man." He began singing to that *Moldau* melody, "Such an old man, but so very much in love," and we laughed till tears came to our eyes. Only on the way to the Rhine did I remember the gnawing fear inside me and though the night was quite warm, I felt cold.

The river no longer looked like a silver scale; it was dark and the water babbled against the shore. From the direction of town came songs, shouts, the noise of fireworks.

I thought, what a shame to ruin this night. We should be drinking and celebrating like normal people.

"Ann," Mike said softly, "today is doubly important. Right? The war has ended and we are beginning a new life. The two of us. I know your answer; I can read it in your eyes. I know—you'll stay with me."

He kissed me tenderly on the mouth; his lips were soft and gentle.

"Michael," I said, "before I tell you I'll stay with you, you have to know the truth about me. You have to know who I am."

"Do you think I don't know? You're a small, lost child of the war. You're seventeen years old, but you're just a little girl who needs protection and tenderness."

I looked at the sky. A rain of man-made stars showered down, falling like fiery fountains. The water in the river was sparkling with color, the ruins of the town were colored, the whole night was colored.

"Michael." I looked into his eyes. Now I couldn't afford to miss even the tremor of an eyelid. "I am Jewish."

Perhaps it was because I was hearing those words for the first time in three years, those words I had carried inside myself constantly, or because none of the things I had feared registered on Mike's face, but I felt tears well up, and I opened my eyes wide so as not to burst out crying.

"And that's what you were hiding from me so carefully? Whatever for?"

I spoke quickly, feeling lighter with every word.

"You don't know, and you can't know. You don't know what it means to say, 'I am Jewish.' For three years I heard those words day and night but never, not even when I was alone, did I dare to say them aloud. Three years ago I swore that until the war ended no one would hear them from me. Do you know what it means to live in fear, lying, never speaking your own language, or thinking with your own brain, or looking with your own eyes? Michael, it's not true that my parents died in the uprising. They were killed right in front of me. I was hiding in the wardrobe that the Germans forgot—just think, they forgot!—to open. You don't know what an action means. You don't know anything, and I won't tell you. When I came out of the wardrobe, I found my parents' bodies on the floor. I ran out of the house. I left them there just as they were, it was night, deathly still. I ran to the village where friends of my father lived and they gave me their daughter Anna's birth certificate. I got on the train and got off in a big city, but there was a round-up in the station—you don't even know what a round-up is!—and they shipped me directly to Germany to do forced labor. I was lucky, very few people had such good luck, because others saw their parents' bodies and then were tortured and killed. But I milked cows, mowed grass, knew how to lie, to invent stories at the drop of a hat. I was lucky, no one found me out, and except for the few days spent in prison, I lived in peace until the end of the war. But at night I dreamed all the time that I was hiding in a wardrobe and was afraid to come out. But I don't want to tell you about it, why did I tell you? Tonight is such a joyous night, and I've ruined it completely."

His kind eyes were so sad. He didn't stop stroking my hand and I didn't want him to stop. I longed to go to sleep, I felt as if I had been in labor, with its healthy pain and healthy exhaustion.

"What's your real name?" he asked.

"Klara."

"Klara," he repeated. "Clear one . . . but you'll always be Ann to me."

The sky above us was golden and red. We could hear the noise of the rockets, and red stars were falling into the river. I bowed my head and heard that wondrous music: the beating of a human heart.

"I will do everything to make you forget that nightmare. And you will forget," Mike said after a moment. "You're very young. You'll see, time will cover over all this the way grass grows over the earth. But promise me one thing: that you will remain Ann—and not just in name. It will be better that way, believe me."

I felt a chill down to my fingertips.

"For whom?" I asked clearly, because suddenly it seemed to me that the river was making a lot of noise and that my words were drowning in that noise.

"For you, for us. The world is so strange, Ann, it will be better if no one other than me knows about Klara."

"Michael, *you too?*"

"Oh, you child, it's not a question of anti-Semitism. I have no prejudices, it'll simply be easier that way. You'll avoid a lot of problems, it'll be simpler for you to cast off the burden of your experiences. You've suffered so much already! I'm not saying this out of prejudice, but for your own good. And since you've already left it behind . . ."

The river was still roaring, the river that was flowing inside me.

"If you don't want to I won't insist. You can decide for yourself, but believe me, I have experience, it'll be easier for you this way."

He touched his lips to my hair; in the glare of the rocket exploding into light above us I saw the anxiety in his eyes. I felt cold and once again I didn't know how to cry.

"Let's not talk about this now, it's not important," he pleaded. "Not tonight, the night of the surrender . . ."

He didn't finish. He wasn't stupid.

I silently shook my head. Maybe he didn't notice, maybe he didn't understand.

The water in the river was burning with the fire of victory and in the pure air of the May night we could clearly hear the singing that welcomed the end of the war.

THE
TENTH
MAN

The first to come back was Chaim the carpenter. He turned
up one evening from the direction of the river and the
woods; no one knew where he had been or with whom.
Those who saw him walking along the riverbank didn't
recognize him at first. How could they? He used to be tall
and broad-shouldered; now he was shrunken and withered,
his clothes were ragged, and, most important, he had no
face. It was completely overgrown with a matted black
thicket of hair. It's hard to say how they recognized him.
They watched him from above, from the cliff above the
river, watched him plod along until, nearing the first houses
of the lower town, he stopped and began to sing. First they
thought he had gone mad, but then one of the smarter ones
guessed that it was not a song, but a Jewish prayer with a
plaintive melody, like the songs that could be heard on
Friday evenings in the old days, coming from the hundred-
year-old synagogue, which the Germans had burned down.
The synagogue was in the lower town; the whole lower
town had always been Jewish—before the Germans came
and during the occupation—and no one knew what it

would be like, now that the Jews were gone. Chaim the carpenter was the first to come back.

A dark cloud from the burnt-out fire still lingered over the town, the stench still hung in the air, and gray clouds floated over the marketplace the Germans had burned.

In the evening, when the news had spread, a crowd gathered in front of Chaim's house. Some came to welcome him, others to watch, still others to see if it was true that someone had survived. The carpenter was sitting on the front steps in front of his house; the door of the house was nailed shut. He didn't respond to questions or greetings. Later, people said that his eyes had glittered emptily in the forest of his face, as if he were blind. He sat and stared straight ahead. A woman placed a bowl of potatoes in front of him, and in the morning she took it away untouched.

Four days later the next one came back. He was a tenant on a neighboring farm and had survived in the forest with the help of the farm manager. The manager brought the tenant back by wagon, in broad daylight. The old man was propped up, half reclining, on bundles of straw. His face, unlike the carpenter's, was as white as a communion wafer, which struck everyone as strange for a man who had lived so long in the open.

When the tenant got down from the wagon he swayed and fell face down on the ground, which people ascribed more to emotion than to weakness. In fact, it was possible to think he was kissing the threshold of his house, thanking God for saving him. The manager helped him up, and supporting him on his arm, led him into the entrance hall.

A week passed and no one came back. The town waited anxiously; people came up with all sorts of conjectures and calculations. The stench of burnt objects faded into the wind and the days became clear. Spring blossomed suddenly as befitted the first spring of freedom. The trees put forth buds. The storks returned.

Ten days later three more men came back: a dry goods merchant and two grain dealers. The arrival of the merchant upset the conjectures and calculations, since everyone knew that he had been taken away to the place from which there was no return. He looked just as he had before the war; he might even have put on some weight. When questioned, he smiled and explained patiently that he had jumped out of a transport to Belzec and hidden in a village. Who had hidden him, and in what village, he didn't want to say. He had the same smile on his face that he used to have before the war when he stood behind his counter and sold cretonnes and percales. That smile never left his face, and it astonished everyone, because no one from this man's family had survived.

For three days the grain dealers slept like logs. They lay on the floor near their door, which was left slightly ajar, as if sleep had felled them the moment they walked in. Their high-topped boots were caked with dried mud, their faces were swollen. The neighbors heard them screaming in their sleep at night.

The grain dealers were still sleeping when the first woman returned. No one recognized her. Only when she reached the teacher's house and burst out sobbing did they understand that she was his wife. Even then, they didn't recognize her, so convincing was her beggar woman's disguise. She had begged in front of Catholic and Orthodox churches, had wandered from church fair to church fair and market to market, reading people's palms. Those were her hiding places. From beneath her plaid kerchief peered the drawn face of a peasant woman.

They asked in amazement: "Is it you?"

"It's me," she answered in her low voice. Only her voice was unchanged.

So there were six of them. The days passed, the gardens grew thick and green. They're being careful, people said, they're waiting for the front to move—it had been still for so long that an offensive seemed likely. But even when the offensive began and the front made a sudden jump to the west, only a few more came back.

A wagon brought the doctor back. He had lain for nine months in a hole underneath the cowshed of one of his patients, a peasant woman. He was still unable to walk. The accountant and his son and the barber and his wife returned from a bunker in the forest. The barber, who had once been known for his mane of red hair, was bald as a bowling ball.

Every day at dusk, the dry goods merchant left his house and walked towards the railway station. When asked where he was going, he explained, "My wife is coming back today." The trains were still not running.

The farmer, a pious man, spent more and more time by his window; he would stand there for hours on end. He was looking for a tenth man, so that the prayers for the murdered might be said as soon as possible in the ruins of the synagogue.

The days kept passing, fragrant and bright. The trains began to run. The people in the town no longer conjectured and calculated. The farmer's face, white as a communion wafer, shone less often in his window.

Only the dry goods merchant—he never stopped haunting the railway station. He would stand there patiently, smiling. After a while, no one noticed him anymore.

CRAZY

. . . everybody thinks I'm crazy, but I'm not. I know—every crazy person says that, but really, there's nothing wrong with my head. If only God *would* make me crazy! It's my heart that's sick, not my head, and there's no cure for that.

You can see, I have crooked legs and a hump. I'm four feet eleven inches. I have a face that frightens children. But my children were such good children, and every morning and every evening they would kiss me on both cheeks and say, "Good morning, Papa. Good night, Papa."

Doctor, have you heard people say that beautiful children are born to ugly people? Have you? My children were *beautiful*! They had blond hair like silk, and straight legs, plump as sausages. My wife, who was a good woman, my wife and I used to say, "God is just; He has given the children what we don't have any of." There were three of them, all girls. The oldest was seven and the youngest three.

I'm a garbageman. I swept the streets. There was plenty to sweep and it was a hard way to earn my bread, Doctor, breathing in that stench. After work, in the bathhouse, I could never wash myself clean enough. In that bathhouse! My oldest girl was already going to school and she brought home a report card—all A's from top to bottom. Sometimes in school they would shout at her, "Your father's a garbageman," but she . . . a heart of gold . . . such a child! Can you understand, Doctor? No, it's impossible.

Later I swept the ghetto; at least it was called sweeping.

But who worried about garbage? I had a broom and I walked around with that broom. The children were hungry, and as I walked around, sometimes something would turn up. Sometimes someone gave me something . . .

The younger ones didn't understand, but the oldest . . . a golden child. It was still "Good morning" every day, "Good night" every evening. I used to tell her, "Sleep peacefully." Peacefully!

When the first action was organized everyone said they would take me, because they took cripples, and I'm a dwarf with a hump. I hid on the roof. During the second action we ran away to the woods. When the third action happened, I was walking down the street with my broom, because I used to start work at five in the morning, and the action began at five-thirty. Do you know what those brooms are like? They're made out of twigs, long and thick. Do you see how tall I am? Four feet eleven inches.

When the trucks drove into the square in front of the bathhouse, I squatted in a corner between two houses, and the broom hid me. No one, not the SS nor the *Ordnungsdienst*, suspected there was anyone there, they only saw a broom. I was shaking so hard that the broom was swaying. I heard everything, because they locked them up in the bathhouse till they loaded them on the trucks. I was saying: O God, O God, O God. I didn't know myself what I wanted of God. Did I even know if there was a God? How could I?

Someone was running, trying to escape, and he touched the broom with his hand. It fell down and now if someone had looked at that corner it would have been the end of me. I was afraid to pick it up, because they were already leading them to the trucks.

Doctor! My children were on the first truck, my three

girls. I saw that the oldest understood, but the others were crying from plain fright. Suddenly they stopped crying and the youngest, the three-year-old, cried out, "Papa! Papa, come to us!"

They saw me. They were the only ones who saw me in that corner.

Doctor! So what did I do? Their father, I came out, ran over to them, and together we . . . right?

No. I put my finger to my lips and shook my head at them, they shouldn't cry out, they should be quiet. Sha!

The two youngest called to me again, but that one, my firstborn, she covered their mouths with her hand. Then they were quiet . . .

Now please give me a certificate that says I am not crazy, or they'll throw me out of work and lock me up in a hospital. Better yet, give me some medicine so I won't have to hide and shout, "I'm coming! I'm coming!" because in any case they can't hear me anymore.

JUMP!

Anka used to come with her parents, in a pink dress and gleaming patent leather shoes. The adults would drink tea in the parlor, while we children went out to the garden, and there the persecution of the small, well-dressed guest would begin.

It would start quite innocently with an ordinary game of "school," which we played by throwing a ball against the wall of the house and performing a series of pirouettes, turns, and hand clappings before we caught the ball again. The wall was covered with dark stains, the plaster was scaly and peeling; those were the results of our strenuous practice sessions, through which we had achieved perfection.

But she—perhaps she wasn't allowed to damage the walls of her house, perhaps she didn't like this game—she always "flunked out" in the first round, and then, impeccably pink, would stand politely under a tree and watch us clap our hands, whirl, and bounce a white tennis ball under our bent knees. Easily, without "flunking," we moved from one round to the next, until we reached the height of success—"graduation."

"We" were Elzbieta and I, and our friend Tadeusz, who had taught us this new expression "flunked out" when his brother failed his high-school graduation exam.

After we'd finished we would ask her, "Would you like to start over?" Well-mannered, she nodded silently, though intimidated by our circus performances, and obligingly took the ball, which would bounce into the tangle of raspberry bushes during the first difficult trick. When the winner ended the game of "school" by acquiring the title of "triple-professor," it would be time for mumblety-peg.

"You have to be careful," we warned her every time, "it's a dangerous game." Tadeusz would lift the bottom of his shorts to reveal the thick, ugly caterpillar on his thigh, a scar from a recklessly thrown pocketknife.

"When they sewed up his leg he squealed like a pig," we'd tell her proudly.

Turning pale, she would reluctantly take hold of the rusty knife. I don't know what frightened her more—the ugly caterpillar on Tadeusz's thigh or having to eat grass, which was the penalty for losing. She would welcome the end of the visit and leave with her parents, clean and fragrant as always. We would hang on the fence, watching them. When they disappeared around the bend in the street, Tadeusz would spit out the word that both Elzbieta and I feared like fire: "Sissy!"

That is how I remember her from those days. And the two Ankas—one pink, with a bow in her hair, the other unconscious, dying in the hut of a Ukrainian deacon—refuse to be reconciled in my mind, even though time brought all of us something quite different than what our childhoods promised.

Back then, as a child, she was pretty, and later she became even prettier, with a flawless, classical beauty. By that time the ball and the pocketknife were things of the past, and a high swing had been hung in the garden.

Only Anka's face was beautiful, but its loveliness made up for her somewhat heavy figure and her legs, which

Tadeusz once said were Jewish legs because they were red. Tadeusz had whispered that to Elzbieta and then to me, and we had immediately checked our own legs to see if he was right. Our legs were burnt brown by the sun and were covered with scratches and scabs, without a trace of red.

"That's because you're not real Jews," he explained. "Real Jews are scared, and you're not afraid to jump off the swing. You're not real and that's why your legs aren't red."

We were sitting on the grass and Anka was standing near the swing; it was her turn. She stood there and looked towards the house, listening for the voice that would herald the end of her visit—her reprieve.

"Climb up," we told her, "and bend your knees. It's easy."

We were playing "douse the candles." Chandeliers of blooming lilac grew around the swing, and you had to make the swing go as high as you could and then spit down onto them. After this came the dramatic finish, a big jump into the soft, fluffy grass.

It was a good swing, all you had to do was pump your legs gently and it would pick up speed and sail way up over the barn roof, over the lilac chandeliers, which you were supposed to extinguish.

The swing posts creaked. "Bend your knees," we shouted. "Don't be afraid, bend your knees!"

Flying high in the air, she looked like a beautiful doll. The wind billowed the pink sail of her dress, revealing the red pillars of her legs in all their splendor. She was already high above the lilacs. We waited for her to spit.

"She's dried up out of fear," Tadeusz said contemptuously.

"Jump!" we shouted. "Jump now!"

Her lovely face turned to stone. Many years later, she jumped.

After the war, I heard what had happened to her and her parents. I could visualize their destiny as if it were sketched out before me. At first it looked so serene, even lazy, like the surface of our river, unbroken by waves. Then suddenly it began churning, and caught in a whirlpool, it plunged into the abyss. There was nothing exceptional in this sudden convulsion of fate that trapped one in a fatal whirlpool. Nevertheless, this pattern, almost like a geometric drawing, had never seemed so clear to me until I learned about Anka.

At first, her fate promised to be as serene as her beauty. School went by without any triumphs but also without any failures, and was followed by an early, prosperous marriage. She had already begun to resemble her mother, and would surely have relived her mother's life—a fine home in a small town, pretty children, pretty dresses, the annual trip to a health resort—if the sentence of time hadn't made tragic heroes even of those least suited to play the part.

I last saw her when things were still relatively peaceful. She was strolling through town with her husband; they were walking arm in arm, stately and dignified. Her face was still beautiful, though no longer quite so perfect; perhaps this new, almost imperceptible flaw was the mark of time, which disfigured the less perfect of us so much more brutally. She was wearing pink. Maybe it was this gay, childish color, or the fact that, at the time, even eighteen-year-olds were nostalgic for the past. In any case, I said to her, "Do you remember 'douse the candles'?"

She looked at me in amazement. She did not remember.

And shortly after that, she descended into hell. In whispers, frightened by the import of their words, people talked about how she became a widow. The story was told in detail; it had happened out in the open, in public. There were people who saw and heard how the SS-man directing the action from in front of the *Judenrat* building took out an index card and read off the name. They saw how her father, a member of the *Judenrat*, looked thunderstruck. It was his son-in-law's name.

They saw him walk off, stop for a moment, move his arms in a nervous gesture, walk and stop, walk and stop. But he kept on walking.

There were no witnesses, however, to the scene in their home, to his knocking at the entrance to the hiding-place, to his calling out his son-in-law's name, telling him to come out. There are no witnesses because all of them were killed.

Everyone saw the two men returning. They walked side by side, without speaking.

How did she live under the same roof with her father after that? Did they look each other in the eye? What did they say? I don't know. Some questions should not even be thought. The facts alone suffice.

They weren't together for long. She fled to a different city, and a month later people heard that she had been deported to Belzec. Soon after that her parents were killed.

But not her. Anka did not die in Belzec.

Did someone in that train racing through the forest shout, "Jump! Jump now!"?

Surely someone must have shouted; one person after another jumped. She jumped into the darkness. All this is known because a young Ukrainian deacon found her at the edge of the forest, helpless, half-conscious. She lay in his hut. He said that she was beautiful, that he wanted to save her. He called a doctor, bought medicine for her, prayed to his God. But fate wouldn't listen. She died several weeks later without regaining consciousness.

THE
OTHER
SHORE

I looked up and saw that someone was approaching. It annoyed me. I wanted to get up and leave, but I was too lazy. I searched through my purse for my glasses. It was a woman—small, frail, elderly. She walked slowly, stepping carefully, as if she were walking on glass. But the path that led down to the pond was a good one—soft and loamy even during hot dry spells. I know that, because every summer I spend a few days in Z—— with friends, who own a cottage there and a magnificent wild orchard. We pick fruit and tend the overgrown flower beds. It's a long way from their house to the pond. You have to go through the village, then down the road to the very last farm and only then turn right, down a wide path lined with poplars. The path leads to the edge of the pond, where there are two flat tree stumps. Farther along, there are rushes and reeds, and no way to cut through.

She was coming towards me, no doubt heading for the other stump. And I had had such high hopes for this evening! There are thoughts that wither under the gaze of others, that are wounded by the breath of others, that the slightest disruption destroys. I saw the woman as my enemy. As she got closer, I could see her more clearly; she wasn't so small or so old. She was no more than forty, with a gentle, kind face. But she was still walking strangely, haltingly. When she emerged from the trees she stopped briefly, hesitated. Only then did she wade into the grass, lifting her legs high, as if she were being stung by nettles. But there weren't any nettles.

She's certainly timid, I thought. A moment ago I was ready to drive off the enemy, but now I could hardly repress a friendly hello. But she wasn't looking my way; I don't think she even saw me.

She walked up to the edge of the pond. The water there was muddy, but a dozen or so meters out, it suddenly grew clear, pure blue. The pond was oval, egg-shaped, overgrown with reeds, and not at all picturesque. But it was fragrant with sweet flag. She stood there for a long time, scanning the water; it puzzled me. What was she looking for?

I sat down and watched her. She was just a few steps away from me, delicate, meticulously dressed. And yet . . .

It was some time before she slowly and gracefully turned her head. She met my gaze without the least bit of surprise. So she had known that I was there. She said, "It's a beautiful warm evening."

And I had been thinking God knows what! I felt bad and answered her with a smile, "It's pleasant by the pond."

"Except for the mosquitoes. There's an awful lot of them."

We both reached for our cigarettes at the same moment. I gave her a light, she sat down next to me, on the other stump. We smoked in silence. The sun went down, and mist rose from the water.

"This is the first time I've been here since that day," she

said suddenly. She seemed amazed at her own words and at herself for saying them. "That's why I was so . . . so . . . ," she groped for the right word. "That's why I didn't acknowledge you. There was no one here then."

So I was right! I kept silent. It didn't matter what I said or if I said anything at all. Unasked, uninvited, she was going to tell me everything—to me, an absolute stranger, on the first meeting. One pebble had fallen; I awaited the avalanche.

"I wasn't brave enough. I was afraid to come, and whenever the day approached, I looked for obstacles, arguments to prove I didn't have to. Only this year was different. At the beginning of the month I said to myself, you have to paint the apartment and a trip costs money. Except that I didn't want to paint the apartment, I wanted to come. I wanted to see . . ."

She looked at me.

"Am I boring you?"

I shook my head no. She seemed pleased and went on.

"It was today, exactly. The same day, the same time. I didn't have a watch then, but the sun had already gone down and it was chilly, like it is now. See that little house? The last one on the road? That's where I was hiding with a friend of the family. It was near the end. They had already shot my sons and my husband. I remember that people were saying, 'How can she do it? Why should she save herself? For whom?' But you know, the life force has such strong roots, you can't tear it out. Even after those we love most have died. But you are young, what do you know about that?

"I was living with them in a room, not in the cellar, in a regular room. It was small and dark, but it had a bed. A bed and a chair. At night I would sit on the bed, because

I couldn't sleep, and during the day, on the chair. I patched sacks, I sewed, I had to do something. One idle moment and I would have gone mad. Even I wondered, why are you sitting here? For whom? But I kept on sitting. There were only women in the house: the grandmother, the mother, two daughters. Men would sometimes drop by at night, stay for a day or two, and disappear. I knew something was up but I didn't want to ask.

"One day I was sitting in the chair darning stockings when the grandmother came in. She was shaking, and my first thought was that someone had betrayed us. I knew what the penalty was. But all she said was, 'Paula, you have to run away. There's going to be a search here. My daughter's husband has been caught. And he wasn't the only one. They're looking for my son, too. They could be here any minute. When it quiets down you'll come back.'

"She spoke as if I were a child; once upon a time she had been my teacher. I suddenly felt like a schoolgirl, and I said, 'What a misfortune. Of course, I'm on my way.' Perhaps I even curtsied, I don't know. Anything was possible then.

"Where should I go? I thought. The ghetto no longer existed, the city was *judenrein*. It wasn't even my city. I had no friends here, no one, not a soul. I was penniless. As soon as I left—out the window, straight out into the garden —I realized that, with all that sitting, I had forgotten how to walk. My joints had grown rusty. Did you see how I was walking? Like a stork.

"Their garden was full of beautiful flowers I had never seen in the city. My eyes ached from so much color. And the orchard! I would gladly have stayed in the orchard. It had been a long time since I had seen trees, grass, but I couldn't, because of the owner.

"So I set out on the road, that one over there." She pointed with her hand. "It was straight and white and flat as an ironed ribbon. The road was wide but I felt as if I were walking a tightrope. I turned right, away from town. I was looking for a forest to hide in. It must have been far off, maybe in the other direction. I couldn't see it. With every step—and I'd only taken a few—I felt wearier. It wasn't the physical effort, it was everything. Again I asked myself: For whom? Why? My strength had left me. Those roots, you know, those roots, they suddenly tore loose.

"When I saw the poplars, and then the thicket and the reeds, I thought to myself: that way. I'd heard them mention this pond—the children were forbidden to come here unsupervised. So I knew that that was where I must go. And all at once I grew calm. It was the right road.

"I walked slowly, still looking. It was pretty here, green, though not quite the same green as today. Paler, dusty, it hadn't rained for weeks.

"I passed these stumps and entered the water right here. Just as I was; I didn't even take off my shoes. It was warm, murky, dirty. I thought: What good luck that I didn't meet anyone, that I can do this peacefully, alone. I walked out farther and farther, deeper and deeper. I began to think about my children and my husband and about how much crueler their end had been than mine. Dusk was falling, it was warm and quiet, and I was peaceful and calm.

"The water was already up to my waist, then higher. The bottom dropped off very gently. It was difficult to walk. My legs kept sinking into the muck and I had to keep pulling them out. I said to myself, one more step, one more, there, in the center it's deep. Sweat was pouring down my face, this slow dying was so hard. Then the water grew cold and transparent. I saw that I was almost there. I moved faster,

I was rushing now. I couldn't catch my breath, there was a roaring in my ears. I was afraid I wouldn't have the strength to get to the place where the ground would slip out from under my feet. I raised my head to catch my breath and then . . . Do you know what happened then? Right in front of me—distinct, nearby—I saw the other shore. The pond was shallow. It was normally shallow, and now with the drought and no rainfall . . . I collapsed on the ground, exhausted, wet . . . alive."

I thought she would keep talking, but she was silent, staring at the other shore, and her face, shadowed by twilight, was still gentle and kind.

"Thank you," she said after a moment.

I wanted to ask her what happened next, but I knew she wouldn't say more. The deepening twilight revealed the stars. A late bird took flight from a branch and flew low over the water, rippling the surface with its wings.

SPLINTER

The girl touched his arm with her hand, her delicate, manicured hand, blossoming with polished pink nails.

She said, "Let's not talk about that any more. You promised."

They were walking along a steep road in the hills of a defeated country, in a region unscathed by war, clean and radiant. The meadows with their lush, long, unmown grass looked especially lovely—bright with flowers and alive with the chirping of crickets. Summer had come unusually early this year. It was only the beginning of June and already the air was heavy with the smell of the lindens.

They were both very young and they were going on a picnic. When she asked him to stop talking, the boy fell silent in embarrassment. He smiled sheepishly and said, "Look, I've got to tell everything to the end. And since I don't have anyone but you . . . It's like a deep splinter that has to be removed so it won't fester. Do you understand?"

"I understand, I understand, only you can't talk about it all the time, without stopping. You haven't stopped for"— she hesitated, they had known each other scarcely a week— "*days*. It's for your sake that I want you to stop. But if you think it helps to . . ."

She raised her beautiful hands in a gesture of helplessness. She was giving in.

"It's beautiful here," said the boy. "This picnic was a good idea. Your idea. You always have the good ideas, I'm still not much good for anything."

"Don't worry. At first I used to think pretty clothes would never make me happy again." She laughed. She was wearing a bright print dress flowered like the meadow.

"You! You were lucky. You spent the whole time in the country, you fed chickens. Come on, don't get angry, that's really terrific luck, and that's why you're so lovely and calm and why I need you. You have such beautiful legs! I'd like to paint them someday. I always wanted to paint. Always, before the war, that is. But I was thirteen then."

The sun was setting when they entered the dense forest; the pine trees stood in rows like soldiers. The soft needles gave way beneath their feet.

"Speaking of good ideas," said the girl, "let's go to the movies tonight. Or to a dance. Okay?"

The boy bent down, picked up a pine cone, sniffed it. "Let's take a little rest," he said.

They lay down on their backs and looked up at the pure, pale blue sky suspended over the woods.

"My mother would be very happy," he began. His eyes were closed, his long lashes emphasized his pallor. He waited a moment, but the girl did not ask why. So he went on:

"She would have been very happy to know that I am lying here in the woods with a girl I love, that I'm lying around on such a splendidly happy day, with nothing threatening me. Because she was probably thinking of that when . . ."

Again he fell silent. The girl lay motionless with her hands under her head and gnawed on a blade of grass.

"What happened with my mother was the worst thing possible," he said after a moment. "Worse than the bunker in the forest where I ate leaves and roots for a week—remember I told you?—worse than a beating in the camp. You have hands just like my mother's. She was very beautiful. We were living in a small, dirty room. Father was already in the camp, and we had nothing to eat. But my mother was still beautiful and cheerful and never showed any fear in my presence. I was terribly afraid. She was, too, I knew it, her quiet crying would often wake me up at night, but I would lie still as a mouse so she could cry in private. Before what I am about to tell you happened, my mother was crying less often at night, because we were supposed to get papers and cross to the other side. Now I couldn't fall asleep, I was so worried about whether our papers would arrive in time. She was calm; she taught me different prayers and how to cross myself, and carols, because it was almost Christmas.

"I didn't sleep *that* night either. I heard them come through the gate, but I was speechless with terror. I lay there stupefied, I couldn't even call out 'Mama.' I heard wailing from the ground floor; they were beating people. I didn't scream until they were walking up the stairs. Those stairs used to creak, I can still hear them creaking, it's funny, isn't it?"

He paused, listening intently. The wind was blowing and several pine cones fell from the trees. It was hot, as before a storm.

"How did she do it? It was unbelievable—it took her just a few seconds. Later I often thought that she must have rehearsed that moment beforehand, she acted so quickly and efficiently. She jumped out of bed, scooped up the bedding in one motion and stuffed it into the bureau drawer; in a second she had folded up her cot and slipped it behind the wardrobe. Then she grabbed my hand and shoved me into the corner by the door, and before they could pound on it, she opened it wide and hospitably. The heavy oak door pressed me against the wall and hid me. There was only one bed and one person in the room. I heard her ask in German, "What's the matter?" Her voice was so calm she could have been speaking to the mailman. They struck her in the face and ordered her, just as she was, in her nightgown, to go downstairs."

He took a deep breath. "That's almost all there is to say. Almost . . . Because you know, when my mother pressed me against the wall with the door, I grabbed the handle and held on to it, even though it wouldn't have shut on its own, since it was a heavy door and the floor was uneven."

The boy fell silent; he brushed away a bee. Then he added, "I would give a great deal to let go of that handle . . . . ," and then, with a smile that begged forgiveness, he added, "You'll have to have a lot of patience with me. All right?"

He turned over lazily and looked at her face. The girl was gorgeous, slightly pink. Her warm lips were parted, she was breathing calmly, evenly. She was asleep.

THE
SHELTER

That summer I happened to be traveling on a line I rarely take. It was a local route punctuated with frequent stops, and the passenger train lumbered slowly and noisily through the monotonous countryside. Occasionally it ran alongside a forest, but mostly it kept stopping at villages and small towns with unfamiliar names. After an hour of this, I was cursing my wretched plan for this trip. I felt filthy, black with soot, unkempt. I tried to sleep, I tried to read, I basked in the sunshine like a cat and tried to kill my boredom with cigarettes—a method as unhealthy as it was useless.

The train was empty. Practically no one was traveling in my direction except for peasant women in white kerchiefs with bulging baskets that smelled of the milk and sour cream they were carrying to market. They got on at one station only to get off at the next. In the corridor several men were arguing loudly about the Sunday soccer game; it seems it was all the goalie's fault. The conductor was dozing.

We were stopped at one of those tiny stations—two posts and a board with some writing on it, evidently the name of a village some distance from the track—when I saw a man and a woman boarding the train. In the city, I wouldn't have noticed them, but there, in that open field . . . The woman was beautiful, carefully groomed, dressed in a simple but elegant suit and narrow, flat-heeled shoes that fit her feet like second skins. The man was somewhat older, graying at the temples, tall, thin, with strong features. His raincoat was slung carelessly over his arm. They had an overnight bag and a huge, soft-sided suitcase.

I looked out the window: nothing, only oats, rye, clover, a narrow road through the fields, along which a wagon, on its way back from the station, trailed behind it a cloud of gray dust. They must have come in that wagon. From where? From whom? They had the air of people who had lived in the city for generations, and I would have bet anything that they were not returning from a visit to relatives.

They entered my compartment. The man lifted their baggage onto the luggage rack and helped the woman off with her jacket. In her blouse she looked younger, more girlish, though its whiteness emphasized her eyes, which were red from crying. She sat down in the corner, away from the window, although the window seat was free. She took the man's hand with a fearful gesture as if seeking his support. But what kind of support could he give her? The cigarette in his hand was trembling.

The train made a gentle arc; small houses scattered beside the river suddenly appeared and just as suddenly disappeared behind dark clouds of trees.

"Shh, shh," I heard him whisper. Turning, I saw that the woman was crying. She cried softly, silently, the tears flowing down her cheeks in thin rivulets. It was a pitiful kind of weeping, and the man kept repeating "hush, hush" as if he were comforting a child. But suddenly he glanced in my direction, bent over the weeping woman, and whispered distinctly, "Stop that now."

She couldn't stop. She was crying loudly, hiding her face in her hands.

"A temporary indisposition," her husband explained. "It will pass in a moment."

"Lie down, dear." By now his voice had taken on a slightly impatient tone; the word "dear" had an edge. "Why don't you just laugh it off?"

"Laugh?" she cried out.

There was a deep, raw bitterness in her cry, and I thought: It's not a laughing matter. She's right. I stood up; they should be left alone. I took my suitcase down from the rack and was about to leave, when he spoke to me.

"No, please stay. It will be easier if we're not alone."

I felt stupid. I didn't know what to do. I reached for my book but he, clearly dreading silence, immediately said, "May I ask what you are reading?"

I told him the title. Of course he knew it. "It's about the occupation, isn't it?" he asked. Now they both burst out laughing, and even though it was an uneasy laughter, I still could not hide my amazement.

"They warped people. Why waste words on it?" he said at last. "Where were you?"

"In a camp."

"We were in hiding. Not far from here, in the village where we got on the train."

"Yes," I said, "I understand. It's hard enough just returning to those years in memory, not to mention going back . . . I understand your being so upset."

Suddenly the woman's voice rang out. "That's not it! You're mistaken."

She began her story. A week ago they received a letter from their aunt and uncle, inviting them to come to a name day party and see their new home. The aunt and uncle—she didn't use any other name for them—were the people who had hidden them in 1943. They had come upon them quite by chance. After weeks of wandering in the forest, when they no longer had any rusks or onions in their knapsacks, when their legs were swollen, and autumn had blown away all the berries, they knocked at the door of the first hut on the edge of the woods.

It was evening, and a good-looking, youngish woman was bustling around inside. "What do you want?" she asked.

They didn't know how to answer. Was it only bread they were asking for?

"Aha, so that's it." She took a better look at them. They looked like wild animals. "Where are you from?"

They didn't answer. A pot of milk was on the stove. They looked at the milk. Heavy and big-boned, she walked up to them, and still eyeing them suspiciously, she gave them some milk. They lapped up the milk like dogs. Then she told them to go.

They just stood there, so she repeated, "And now get out of here fast, before someone sees you."

She was chasing them out, but they stood there rooted to the spot.

The train screeched, braking, and the woman fell silent. Her husband wiped his sweaty forehead, stood up, closed the window, and then opened it again. The voices of the people boarding the train drifted in from the corridor. A man with a child in his arms opened the compartment door and backed out, saying, "Ugh, it stinks of smoke in here, this is not for us."

"All aboard!" yelled the conductor. A bridge rattled under the wheels, the little town outside was silent and dead. A moment later we entered the forest.

"We couldn't leave," the woman continued. "The warmth made us tired, we longed to sleep. I thought, she's good, she gave us milk. So when she came closer, angry and impatient, ready to shove us out the door, I grasped her hands and begged her shamelessly. I felt her dry, strong fingers in my hands, roughened from the brambles in the forest, and I pleaded with her the way a believer pleads with God. Her fingers grew limp; it was her heart softening. She opened the door to a small room and said, 'Wait here till my husband comes home.'

"We collapsed onto our knapsacks. That same night Olek had a long talk with the husband. The money we had was only enough to feed two people for two or three months—really almost nothing. But we promised to pay the cost of a new house—if we survived. Their hut was dilapidated, and you could smell poverty in every corner. They took us in. We cried like children; it was the first night we'd spent under a roof in many weeks.

The next night the husband began building a shelter. As a young man he had been a mason, so the work went quickly. It was a bricked-in storage area in the cellar, so narrow it could scarley hold two people. But we went down there only as a last resort, when a visitor came, or when there were Germans in the village. Otherwise, we sat in the small room during the day, and at night when the doors were locked, in the main room of the hut. Olek played cards with the husband, and we read books aloud.

"But towards the end of the war, when troops were quartered in the area, we didn't leave our shelter for two months. Those two months were very hard. I had pains in my joints; but being sick was the least of it. It was impossible to lie down. We had to sit all the time. We played 'geography'—all the rivers that begin with *A*, the cities with *B*; we asked each other Latin words. Eventually, we didn't even feel like eating. We just sat there. Sometimes Germans spent the night in the hut. We could hear their footsteps; they would go down to the cellar, they were right there on the other side of the thin wall with potatoes piled against it. The day the couple came downstairs and said it was over, I couldn't even rejoice. We were ill for a long time afterwards, seriously ill, it seems, because the husband, who came to visit us in the hospital, looked at Olek and said, 'That's the end of my house.'

"Afterwards we started all over from the beginning. We had only the clothes on our backs, and if it were not for my husband . . ."

"What of it?" the husband interrupted. "I began to work, and slowly, slowly things fell into place. I sent the first money we saved up to Aunt and Uncle; we sent money every month, for three years. They came to visit us. Why not? We were all alone, no one in our families survived; so they became like . . .

"They finished building the new house in the spring— three rooms and a kitchen. They asked us to come and see it, but somehow it turned out that either I had to work, or my wife was sick, always those joints. A week ago we got a letter; they were inviting us to Uncle's name day party in their new home."

He took a deep breath, lit another cigarette. It was quiet for a moment. Had they not had the courage to go?

She was the first to break the silence.

"So we finally went. We were five years older. What am I saying? *Fifty* years older! I said to Olek, 'Look, that bridge, we slept here. Do you remember the town of W——? And the station at N——? We bought our tickets there and were afraid to get on the train. Just think,' I said to him, 'we are alive, we are together, nothing threatens us.' I was happy.

"I waved out the window to Uncle, who was waiting for us at the station. We climbed into his wagon, which was filled with straw. My heart was pounding. I waited for the hut and the garden to appear around the turn. I forgot that a new house would be standing there. It was pretty—but seeing that hut would have touched my soul. The house? It looked just like any other house. With a red roof. His wife stood in the doorway, dressed in her holiday clothes, and though I smiled and kissed her, I felt bad because I missed the old hut. They asked us in. It was clean, the red floors were newly waxed, there were cretonne curtains on the windows. The table was set with cold meats and vodka. Olek knew right away what was bothering me and said quietly, 'Don't get hysterical,' but out loud he exclaimed over how nicely they had furnished it. Uncle poured out the vodka, he wanted to make a toast, but his wife said, 'No, first take a look around.'

"We began in the kitchen, then we went into the living room, the bedroom, and another room for the son who had returned from the army. We thought they had shown us everything, but then they said, 'And we kept you in mind, too. Here, take a look!'

"The husband pushed aside a wardrobe and I looked— a white, blank wall. But when he went down and touched the floor, I grabbed Olek's hand. I didn't see anything yet, but that gesture was familiar.

"He lifted a red, waxed board and told us to look closely. 'There, now, just in case something happens, you won't have to roost like chickens, a shelter as pretty as a picture, with all the comforts!'

"I leaned over and saw stairs leading down into a small, dark room, without any windows or doors. It had two beds, two chairs, and a table."

The train shook as it switched tracks and picked up speed. We were approaching the city. The sky had turned pale, and the little houses on the outskirts appeared outside the windows, behind low, evenly trimmed hedges.

"What are we supposed to make of that?" asked the man. "Sentenced to a hiding-place, sentenced to death once again? And by whom? By good people who wish us well. It's appalling. To build a hiding-place out of the goodness of one's heart! That's what's so horrible. There, in that house, it was as if I were kneeling above my own grave."

"Horrible," I repeated. I said something else about how the war twisted people, and I felt ashamed; it was so banal, so polite. But they didn't hear me. They were hurrying towards the exit, and their quick, nervous steps gave the impression of flight.

TRACES

Yes, of course she recognizes it. Why shouldn't she? That was their last ghetto.

The photograph, a copy of a clumsy amateur snapshot, is blurred. There's a lot of white in it; that's snow. The picture was taken in February. The snow is high, piled up in deep drifts. In the foreground are traces of footprints; along the edges, two rows of wooden stalls. That is all. Yes. This is where they lived. She recognizes those stalls; they used to be market stalls and were converted to living quarters. Well, perhaps she has put it badly, they were simply enclosures made with boards.

There were about a dozen of those stalls, on both sides of the narrow market street. Three or four families lived in each stall. The loose-fitting boards gave no protection from rain or snow.

"That's the ghetto," she says again, bending over the photograph. Her voice sounds amazed.

Of course she is amazed. How did they survive there? Such . . . such, well, it's hard to express. But in those days no one was surprised at anything.

"They did such terrible things to us that no one was surprised at anything," she says out loud, as if she has just now understood.

The person who took the photograph must have been standing next to the building in which the *Judenrat* was housed. That was an actual house, not a stall. Three windows in front, and an attic under the roof.

She pushes the photograph away. "I prefer not to be reminded . . ."

"So, in the last stage, the ghetto was reduced to this one little street?"

Yes, of course. It was a tiny street, Miesna, or Meat, Street. There used to be butcher shops in those stalls and that's why, at the end, the ghetto was called "the butcher shop ghetto."

How many people were there? Not many. Maybe eighty. Maybe less.

Again she reaches for the photograph, raises it to her nearsighted eyes, looks at it for a long time, and says, "You can still see the traces of footprints." And a moment later, "That's very strange."

That's the direction they walked in. From the *Judenrat* down Miesna Street. She looks at the footprints, the snow, and the stalls once again.

"I wonder who photographed it? And when? Probably right afterwards: the footprints are clear here, but when they shot them in the afternoon it was snowing again."

The people are gone—their footprints remain. Very strange.

"They didn't take them straight to the fields, but first to the Gestapo. No one knows why, apparently those were the orders. They stood in the courtyard until the children were brought."

She breaks off: "I prefer not to remember . . ." But suddenly she changes her mind and asks that what she is going to say be written down and preserved forever, because she wants a trace to remain.

"What children? What trace?"

A trace of those children. And only she can leave that trace, because she alone survived. So she will tell about the children who were hidden in the attic of the *Judenrat*, which was strictly forbidden under pain of death, because children no longer had the right to live. There were eight of them, the oldest might have been seven or so, although no one knew for sure, because when they brought them over they didn't look at all like children, only like . . . ach . . .

The first tears, instantly restrained.

They heard the rumbling, a horse cart drove up to the yard, and on it were the children. They were sitting on straw, one beside the other. They looked like little gray mice. The SS-man who brought them jumped down from the cart, and said kindly, "Well, dear children, now each of you go and run to your parents."

But none of the children moved. They sat there motionless and looked straight ahead. Then the SS-man took the first child and said, "Show me your mother and father."

But the child was silent. So he took the other children one by one and shouted at them to point out their parents, but they were all silent.

"So I wanted some trace of them to be left behind."

In a calm voice she asks for a short break. With an indulgent smile she rejects the glass of water they hand her. After the break she will tell how they were all shot.

THE
TABLE

A PLAY FOR
FOUR VOICES
AND BASSO
OSTINATO

CHARACTERS:

FIRST MAN, 50 years old
FIRST WOMAN, 45 years old
SECOND MAN, 60 years old
SECOND WOMAN, 38 years old
PROSECUTOR, 35–40 years old

The stage is empty and dark. Spotlights only on the witness, seated in a chair, and the prosecutor, seated at a desk.

PROSECUTOR: Have you recovered, Mr. Grumbach? Can we go on? Where did we stop? . . . Oh, yes. So you remember precisely that there was a table there.

FIRST MAN: Yes. A small table.

PROSECUTOR: A *small* table? How small? How many people could sit at a table that size?

FIRST MAN: Do I know? It's hard for me to say now.

PROSECUTOR: How long was it? A meter? Eighty centimeters? Fifty centimeters?

FIRST MAN: A table. A regular table—not too small, not too big. It's been so many years . . . And at a time like that, who was thinking about a table?

PROSECUTOR: Yes, of course, I understand. But you have to understand me, too, Mr. Grumbach: every detail is crucial. You must understand that it's for a good purpose that I'm tormenting you with such details.

FIRST MAN: (*resigned*) All right, let it be eighty centimeters. Maybe ninety.

PROSECUTOR: Where did that table—that small table—stand? On the right side or the left side of the marketplace as you face the town hall?

FIRST MAN: On the left. Yes.

PROSECUTOR: Are you certain?

FIRST MAN: Yes . . . I saw them carry it out.

PROSECUTOR: That means that at the moment you arrived at the marketplace the table was not there yet.

FIRST MAN: No . . . Or maybe it was. You know, I don't remember. Maybe I saw them carrying it from one place to another. But is it so important if they were bringing it out or just moving it?

PROSECUTOR: Please concentrate.

FIRST MAN: How many years has it been? Twenty-five? And you want me to remember such details? I haven't thought about that table once in twenty-five years.

PROSECUTOR: And yet today, while you were telling your story, on your own, without prompting, you said, "He was sitting at a table." Please concentrate and tell me what you saw as you entered the square.

FIRST MAN: What did I see? I was coming from Rozana Street, from the opposite direction, because Rozana is on the other side of the market. I was struck by the silence. That was my first thought: so many people, and so quiet. I noticed a group of people I knew; among them was the druggist, Mr. Weidel, and I asked Weidel, "What do you think, Doctor, what will they do with us?" And he answered me, "My dear Mr. Grumbach . . ."

PROSECUTOR: You already mentioned that, please stick to the point. What did you see in the square?

FIRST MAN: The square was black with people.

PROSECUTOR: Earlier you said that the people assembled in the marketplace where standing at the rear of the square, facing the town hall, and that there was an empty space between the people and the town hall.

FIRST MAN: That's right.

PROSECUTOR: In other words, to say, "The square was black with people," is not completely accurate. That empty space was, shall we say, white—especially since, as you've mentioned, fresh snow had fallen during the night.

FIRST MAN: Yes, that's right.

PROSECUTOR: Now please think, Mr. Grumbach. Did you notice anything or anyone in that empty white space?

FIRST MAN: Kiper was sitting in a chair and striking his boots with a riding crop.

PROSECUTOR: I would like to call your attention to the fact that none of the witnesses until now has mentioned that Kiper was walking around with a riding crop. Are you certain that Kiper was striking his boots with a riding crop.

FIRST MAN: Maybe it was a stick or a branch. In any case, he was striking his boots—*that* I remember. Sometimes you remember such tiny details. Hamke and Bondke were standing next to him, smoking cigarettes. There were policemen and Ukrainians standing all around the square —a lot of them, one next to the other.

PROSECUTOR: Yes, we know that already. So, you remember that Kiper was sitting in a chair.

FIRST MAN: Absolutely.

PROSECUTOR: So if there was a chair in the marketplace, wouldn't there have been a table as well?

FIRST MAN: A table . . . just a minute . . . a table . . . no. Because that chair seemed so . . . wait a minute . . . No, there wasn't any table there. But they carried out a small table later. Now I remember exactly. Two policemen brought a small table out from the town hall.

PROSECUTOR: (*relieved*) Well, something concrete at last. What time would that have been?

FIRST MAN: (*reproachfully*) Really, I . . .

PROSECUTOR: Please, think about it.

FIRST MAN: The time? . . . God knows. I have no idea. I left the house at 6:15, that I know. I stopped in at my aunt's on Poprzeczna Street, that took ten minutes, then I walked down Miodna, Krotka, Okolna, and Mickiewicza streets. On Mickiewicza I hid for a few minutes inside the gate of one of the houses because I heard shots. It must have taken me about half an hour to walk there.

PROSECUTOR: How much time elapsed from the moment you arrived in the square to the moment when you noticed the policemen carrying the table out from the town hall?

FIRST MAN: Not a long time. Let's say half an hour.

PROSECUTOR: In other words, the policemen carried a table into the marketplace around 7:15. A small table.

FIRST MAN: That's right. Now I recall that Kiper pointed with his riding crop to the place where they were supposed to set the table down.

PROSECUTOR: Please indicate on the map you drew for us the exact place where the policemen set the table down. With a cross or a circle. Thank you. (*satisfied*) Excellent. Kiper is sitting in a chair, the policemen carry in the table, the length of the table is about eighty centimeters. How was the table placed? I mean, in front of Kiper? Next to him?

FIRST MAN: I don't know. That I couldn't see.

PROSECUTOR: If you could see them carrying in the table you could see that, too—perhaps you just don't remember. But maybe you can remember where Kiper sat? At the table? Beside it? In front of it?

FIRST MAN: Obviously, at the table. When someone waits for a table, it's so he can sit at it. He was sitting at the table. Of course. That's what people do.

PROSECUTOR: Alone?

FIRST MAN: In the beginning? I don't know. I wasn't looking that way the whole time. But later—this I know—

they were all there: Kiper, Hamke, Bondke, Rossel, Kuntz, and Wittelmann.

PROSECUTOR: (*slowly*) Kiper, Hamke, Bondke, Rossel, Kuntz, and Wittelmann. When you testified a year ago you didn't mention either Rossel or Wittelmann.

FIRST MAN: I must have forgotten about them then. Now I remember that they were there, too.

PROSECUTOR: Were they all sitting at the table?

FIRST MAN: No. Not all of them. Some of them were standing next to it.

PROSECUTOR: Who was sitting?

FIRST MAN: What I saw was that Kiper, Hamke, Bondke, and Kuntz were sitting. The rest were standing. There were more than a dozen of them, I don't remember all the names.

PROSECUTOR: How were they seated, one beside the other?

FIRST MAN: Yes.

PROSECUTOR: Is it possible that four grown men could sit one beside the other at a table that is eighty centimeters long?

FIRST MAN: I don't know. Maybe the table was longer than that; or maybe it wasn't big enough for all of them. In any event, they were sitting in a row.

PROSECUTOR: Who read the names from the list?

FIRST MAN: Hamke or Bondke.

PROSECUTOR: How did they do it?

FIRST MAN: People walked up to the table, showed their *Arbeitskarten*, and Kiper looked them over and pointed either to the right or to the left. The people who had good

Arbeitskarten went to the right, and those whose work wasn't considered important, or who didn't have any *Arbeitskarten*, they went to the left.

PROSECUTOR: Was Kiper the one who conducted the selection?

FIRST MAN: Yes. I'm positive about that.

PROSECUTOR: Did Kiper stay in that spot during the whole time the names were read? Or did he get up from the table?

FIRST MAN: I don't know. Maybe he got up. I wasn't looking at him every minute. It took a very long time. And anyway, is it that important?

PROSECUTOR: I'm sorry to be tormenting you with these seemingly unimportant details . . . In other words, is it possible that Kiper got up and walked away from the table, or even left the square?

FIRST MAN: I can't give a definite answer. I wasn't watching Kiper every minute. It's possible that he did get up from the table. That's not out of the question. Still, he was the one in charge at the marketplace. Kiper—and no one else. And he was the one who shot the mother and child.

PROSECUTOR: Did you see this with your own eyes?

FIRST MAN: Yes.

PROSECUTOR: Please describe the incident.

FIRST MAN: The woman wasn't from our town, so I don't know her name. She was young, she worked in the brickworks. She had a ten-year-old daughter, Mala. I remember the child's name; she was a pretty little girl. When this woman's name was called she walked up to the table with her daughter. She was holding the child by the hand. Kiper gave her back her *Arbeitskarte* and ordered her to go to the right. But he ordered the child to go to the left. The mother started begging him to leave the child with her, but he wouldn't agree. Then she placed her *Arbeitskarte* on the table and walked to the left side with the child. Kiper called her back and asked her if she knew the penalty for disobeying an order, and then he shot them—first the girl, and then the mother.

PROSECUTOR: Did you actually see Kiper shoot?

FIRST MAN: I saw the woman approach the table with the child. I saw them standing in front of Kiper. A moment later I heard two shots.

PROSECUTOR: Where were you standing at that moment? Please mark it on the map. With a cross or a circle. Thank you. So, you were standing near the pharmacy. How far was it from the table to the pharmacy?

FIRST MAN: Thirty meters, maybe fifty.

PROSECUTOR: Then you couldn't have heard the conversation between Kiper and the mother.

FIRST MAN: No, obviously. I didn't hear what they said, but I saw that the mother exchanged several sentences with Kiper. It was perfectly clear what they were talking about. Everyone understood what the mother was asking. Then I saw the mother place her *Arbeitskarte* on the table and go to the left with the child. I heard Kiper call her back. They went back.

PROSECUTOR: They went back and stood in front of the table, correct?

FIRST MAN: That's correct.

PROSECUTOR: In other words, they were blocking your view of the men who were sitting at the table, or at least of some of the men sitting at the table.

FIRST MAN: It's possible. I don't remember exactly. In any case, I saw them come back to the table, and a moment later there were two shots, and then I saw them lying on the ground. People who stood closer to them clearly heard Kiper ask her if she knew the penalty for disobeying an order.

PROSECUTOR: Was Kiper standing or sitting at that moment?

FIRST MAN: I don't remember.

PROSECUTOR: So, you didn't see him at the exact moment you heard the shots. Did you see a gun in his hand? What kind of gun? A pistol? A machine gun?

FIRST MAN: He must have shot them with a pistol. Those were pistol shots.

PROSECUTOR: Did you see a pistol in Kiper's hand?

FIRST MAN: No . . . perhaps the mother and child were blocking my view; or maybe I was looking at the victims and not at the murderer. I don't know. But in any case, I did see something that told me it was Kiper who shot them, and no one else.

PROSECUTOR: Namely?

FIRST MAN: Namely . . . immediately after the shots, when the mother and child were lying on the ground, I saw with my own eyes how Kiper rubbed his hands together with a disgusted gesture, as if to cleanse them of filth. I won't forget that gesture.

PROSECUTOR: (*summarizing*) And so, Mr. Grumbach, you saw Kiper sitting at a table in the company of Hamke, Bondke, Rossel, and Kuntz. Then you saw Kiper carrying out the selection and Kiper brushing off his hands immediately after you heard the shots that killed the mother and child. But you didn't see a gun in Kiper's hand nor the shooting itself. Is that correct?

FIRST MAN: Still, I assert with absolute confidence that the murderer of the mother and child was Kiper.

PROSECUTOR: Was Kiper sitting behind the table when your name was called?

FIRST MAN: (*hesitating*) I was one of the last to be called. My *Arbeitskarte* was taken and returned by Bondke. I don't remember if Kiper was present or not. By then I was already half dead.

PROSECUTOR: Of course. What time would it have been when your name was called?

FIRST MAN: What time? My God, I don't know, it was already past noon.

PROSECUTOR: Did you witness any other murders committed that day?

FIRST MAN: That day more than four hundred people were shot in the town. Another eight hundred at the cemetery.

PROSECUTOR: Did you see any member of the Gestapo shoot someone?

FIRST MAN: No.

PROSECUTOR: Were you one of the group that buried the victims in the cemetery?

FIRST MAN: No.

PROSECUTOR: Is there anything else that you would like to say in connection with that day?

FIRST MAN: Yes.

PROSECUTOR: Please, go ahead.

FIRST MAN: It was a sunny, cold day. There was snow in the streets. The snow was red.

FIRST WOMAN: It was a Sunday. I remember it perfectly. As I was walking to the square, the church bells were ringing. It was a Sunday. Black Sunday.

PROSECUTOR: Is that what the day was called afterwards?

FIRST WOMAN: Yes.

PROSECUTOR: Some of the witnesses have testified that the day was called Bloody Sunday.

FIRST WOMAN: (*dryly*) I should think the name would be unimportant. It was certainly bloody. Four hundred corpses on the streets of the town.

PROSECUTOR: How do you know the exact figure?

FIRST WOMAN: From those who buried the victims. The *Ordnungsdienst* did that. Later they told us, four hundred murdered in the town alone. A hard, packed snow lay on the streets; it was red with blood. The worst one was Kiper.

PROSECUTOR: Slow down. Please describe the events in the square as they occurred.

FIRST WOMAN: At six they ordered us to leave our houses and go to the marketplace. First I decided not to go, and I ran up to the attic. There was a window there, so I looked out. I saw people pouring down Rozana, Kwiatowa, Piekna, and Mickiewicza streets towards the square. Suddenly I noticed two SS entering the house next door. They stayed inside for a moment, then came out leading an elderly couple, the Weintals. Mrs. Weintal was crying. I saw that. They were elderly people. They owned a paper goods store. The SS-men ordered them to stand facing the wall of the house, and then they shot them.

PROSECUTOR: Do you know the names of the two SS-men?

FIRST WOMAN: No. One was tall and thin. He had a terrifying face. I might be able to recognize him in a photograph. You don't forget such a face. But they were local SS, because there were no outside SS in town that day. *They* did it, the locals. Four hundred murdered on the spot, twice that number in the cemetery.

PROSECUTOR: Let's take it slowly now. So, you saw two SS leading the Weintal couple out of the building and putting them against the wall. You lived on Kwiatowa Street. Was their house also located on Kwiatowa?

FIRST WOMAN: I lived on Kwiatowa at number 1; it was the corner building. The Weintals lived in a building on Rozana.

PROSECUTOR: What number?

FIRST WOMAN: I don't know, I don't remember . . .

PROSECUTOR: Did you see which of the two SS shot them? The tall one or the other one?

FIRST WOMAN: That I didn't see, because when they ordered them to stand facing the wall, I knew what would happen next and I couldn't watch. I was afraid. I moved away from the window. I was terribly afraid.

PROSECUTOR: Afterwards, did you see the Weintal couple lying on the ground dead?

FIRST WOMAN: They shot them from a distance of two meters; I assume they knew how to aim.

PROSECUTOR: Did you see the bodies afterwards?

FIRST WOMAN: No. I ran downstairs from the attic, I was afraid—with good reason—I was afraid that they would search the houses for people who were trying to hide, but I didn't go out into the street, I took the back exit to the garden and made my way to the marketplace by a round-about route.

PROSECUTOR: Would you recognize those two SS in photos?

FIRST WOMAN: Perhaps. I'm fairly certain I could recognize the tall thin one. You don't forget such a face.

PROSECUTOR: Please look through this album. It contains photographs of members of the Gestapo who were in your town; but there are also photographs here of people who were never there.

FIRST WOMAN: (she turns the pages; a pause) Oh, that's him.

PROSECUTOR: Is that one of the men you saw from the window?

FIRST WOMAN: No, it's that awful murderer. It's Kiper. Yes, I remember, it's definitely him.

PROSECUTOR: Please look through all the photographs.

FIRST WOMAN: (a pause) No, I can't find that face. Unfortunately.

PROSECUTOR: You said "awful murderer". Did you ever witness a murder committed by Kiper?

FIRST WOMAN: (*laughs*) Witness? You're joking. The witnesses to his murders aren't alive.

PROSECUTOR: But there are people who saw him shoot.

FIRST WOMAN: I did, too. Sure—in the square, he fired into the crowd. Just like that.

PROSECUTOR: Do you know who he killed then?

FIRST WOMAN: I don't know. There were fifteen hundred of us in the square. But I saw him rushing around like a wild man and shooting. Not just him, others, too. Bendke, for example.

PROSECUTOR: When was that?

FIRST WOMAN: In the morning. Before the selection. But it's possible it also went on during the selection. I don't remember. I know that they fired into the crowd. Just like that.

PROSECUTOR: Who read the names from the list?

FIRST WOMAN: An SS-man. I don't know his name.

PROSECUTOR: How did they do it?

FIRST WOMAN: Very simply. Names were called out, some people went to the right and others to the left. The left meant death.

PROSECUTOR: Who conducted the selection?

FIRST WOMAN: They were all there: Kiper, Bendke, Hamm, Rosse.

PROSECUTOR: Which one of them reviewed the *Arbeitskarten*?

FIRST WOMAN: I don't remember.

PROSECUTOR: Who ordered you to go to the right? Kiper? Bendke? Hamm? Rosse?

FIRST WOMAN: I don't remember. At such a time, you know . . . at such a time, when you don't know . . . life or death . . . I didn't look at their faces. To me, they all had the same face. All of them! What difference does it make whether it was Kiper or Bendke or Hamm or Rosse? They were all there. There were ten or maybe fifteen of those murderers. They stood in a semicircle, with their machine guns across their chests. What difference does it make which one? They all gave orders, they all shot! All of them!

PROSECUTOR: Please calm yourself. I am terribly sorry that I have to provoke you with such questions. But you see, we can only convict people if we can *prove* that they committed murder. You say that all the members of the local Gestapo were there. But it could be that one of them was on leave, or possibly on duty in the *Dienststelle*. And didn't shoot.

FIRST WOMAN: Every one of them shot. If not that day, then another. During the second or third action, during the liquidation.

PROSECUTOR: The law requires proof. And I, as the prosecuting attorney, am asking you for proof. I am asking for the names of the murderers, the names of the victims, the circumstances in which they were murdered. Otherwise, I can do nothing.

FIRST WOMAN: (*quietly*) My God . . .

PROSECUTOR: Excuse me?

FIRST WOMAN: Nothing, nothing.

PROSECUTOR: Please think: which one of them was in charge of the selection in the square?

FIRST WOMAN: They all participated in the selection. Kiper, Bendke, Hamm, Rosse. They were standing in a semicircle.

PROSECUTOR: Standing? Were all of them standing? Or perhaps some of them were seated?

FIRST WOMAN: No, they were standing. Is it that important?

PROSECUTOR: It's very important. Do you remember seeing a table in the marketplace at which several Gestapo men were seated? The others were standing near the table.

FIRST WOMAN: A table? I don't remember. There was no table there.

SECOND MAN: Here's the map. The marketplace was shaped like a trapezoid. At the top was the town hall, a beautiful old building that had been built by a Polish nobleman in the seventeenth century. The jewel of the town. The square sloped down towards the actual market where the stores were, as if the town hall reigned over the place. On the left, by the ruins of the old ramparts, stood those whose *Arbeitskarten* were taken away and also those who did not have *Arbeitskarten*. Note that the streets radiate out like a star. Here's Rozana, then Sienkiewicza, then Piekna, then Male Targi, then Nadrzeczna. There was no river in the town, but maybe once upon a time there was one, and that's why it was called Nadrzeczna—Riverside. Then came Zamkowa Street. All the streets I've named were later included in the ghetto, with the exception of Piekna. Beyond Male Targi there was a cemetery. Yes. That's where they were shot. Nadrzeczna was adjacent to the cemetery. Most of the people who lived on Nadrzeczna were Poles, but it was incorporated into the ghetto nonetheless, because of the cemetery. Because the cemetery played a major role in our life then. Between Rozana and Sienkiewicza there were shops. First, Weidel's pharmacy—he was killed in the camp; then Rosenzweig's iron shop—he was shot during the second action. Then Kreitz's dry goods store, the Haubers' restaurant and hotel—they were the wealthiest people among us, their daughter lives in Canada—and then two groceries, one beside the other, Blumenthal's and Hochwald's. They were rivals all their lives, and now they're lying in the same grave. Oh yes, I can draw every single stone for you, describe every single person. Do you know how many of us survived?

PROSECUTOR: Forty.

SECOND MAN: How do you know?

PROSECUTOR: They are my witnesses.

SECOND MAN: And have you found all of them? And taken their testimony?

PROSECUTOR: I have found almost all of them, but I still haven't taken testimony from everyone. Several witnesses live in America; they will be questioned by our consular officials, and if necessary, subpoenaed for the trial. Two live in Australia, one in Venezuela. Now I would like to ask you about the details of the selection that took place during the first action. When was it, do you remember?

SECOND MAN: Of course. It was a Sunday, in December, towards the end of the month. It was a sunny, cold day. Nature, you see, was also against us. She was mocking us. Yes, indeed. If it had rained, or if there had been a storm, who knows, perhaps they wouldn't have kept shooting from morning till night. Darkness was already falling when they led those people to the cemetery. Oh, you want proof, don't you? The snow on the town's streets was red. Red! Does that satisfy you?

PROSECUTOR: Unfortunately, Mr. Zachwacki, snow doesn't constitute proof for judges, especially snow that melted twenty-five years ago.

SECOND MAN: The snow was red. Bloody Sunday. Four hundred fifty corpses on the streets. That's not proof? Then go there and dig up the mass graves.

PROSECUTOR: I'm interested in the selection. Who was in charge of it?

SECOND MAN: Kiper. A thug, a murderer. The worst sort. I can't talk about this calmly. No. Do you mind if I smoke? These are things . . . I'm sixty, my blood pressure shoots right up. A cutthroat like that . . .

PROSECUTOR: How do you know that Kiper was in charge of the selection?

SECOND MAN: What do you mean, how? I gave him my *Arbeitskarte* myself. He peered at me from under his brows and snarled, *"Rechts!"* I went to the right. Saved. Saved until the next time.

PROSECUTOR: Please describe the scene in more detail.

SECOND MAN: I was standing some distance away. We all tried to stand as far away from them as possible, as if that could have helped. I was standing near the Haubers' hotel. It was one in the afternoon. The church bell struck one, and since it was quiet in the square, you could hear the bell clearly even though the church was in a different part of town, near Waly Ksiazece. By then they had been calling out names for about an hour. Suddenly I hear, "Zachwacki!"

PROSECUTOR: Who called your name?

SECOND MAN: One of the Gestapo, but I don't know which one.

PROSECUTOR: Didn't you notice which of them was holding the list?

SECOND MAN: No, you're asking too much. There was a list, because they read the names from a list, but I didn't see it. If a person saw a scene like that in the theater, maybe he could describe it in detail. This here, that there, and so on. But when a tragedy like this is being played in real life? You expect me to look at a list when my life is hanging by a thread? I was standing there with my wife. She had an *Arbeitskarte* from the sawmill—that was a good place to work—and I had one from the cement works. Also a good place. When they called my name, my wife grabbed my arm. "Let's stay together!" she cried. Dr. Gluck was standing nearby, a kind old doctor. He told my wife, "Mrs. Zachwacki, calm down, your husband has a good *Arbeitskarte*, you have a good *Arbeitskarte*, get a grip on yourself." But she kept saying, "I want to stay together, if we don't we won't see each other ever again. Albert," she said, "I'm afraid." I literally had to tear myself away, she was holding on to me so tight. There, you see, so much for instinct, intuition . . . I never saw her again. All the women who worked in the sawmill were sent to the left. (*he clears his throat*)

PROSECUTOR: (*a short pause*) Then what happened?

SECOND MAN: I dashed through the crowd. There was an empty space between us and them, you had to walk about thirty meters to cross the empty square. First—I remember this—someone kicked me, who I don't know. I took a deep breath and ran as hard as I could to get to the town hall as fast as possible. When I handed them my *Arbeitskarte* my hand was trembling like an aspen leaf, although I'm not a coward. Not at all!

PROSECUTOR: To whom did you hand your *Arbeitskarte*?

SECOND MAN: I already told you, to Kiper. He opened it, read it, handed it back to me and snarled, *"Rechts!"* I was young, tall, strong. He gave me a reprieve.

PROSECUTOR: At the moment that you handed him your *Arbeitskarte*, was Kiper standing or sitting?

SECOND MAN: He was standing with his legs apart, his machine gun across his chest. His face was swollen, red.

PROSECUTOR: And the rest of the Gestapo?

SECOND MAN: I didn't see. I don't remember if any of them were standing next to Kiper.

PROSECUTOR: Did you see a table?

SECOND MAN: Yes, there was a table, but it was further to the right, as if it had nothing to do with what was happening there.

PROSECUTOR: A small table?

SECOND MAN: No, not at all. It was a big, long oak table, like one of those trestle tables you see in monasteries. It was probably one of those antique tables from the old town hall.

PROSECUTOR: Long, you say. What were its dimensions, more or less?

SECOND MAN: How should I know? Two, three meters. The Gestapo sat in a row on one side of the table; and there was quite a large group of them sitting there. Bondke was sitting, Rossel was sitting—them I remember. And there were at least six others.

PROSECUTOR: Did you by any chance notice whether Kiper was sitting at the table earlier and whether the reviewing of the *Arbeitskarten* took place at the table?

SECOND MAN: I didn't notice. When I was called, Kiper was standing several meters from the table.

PROSECUTOR: Who do you think was in charge of the action?

SECOND MAN: Kuntze. He had the highest rank.

PROSECUTOR: Did you see him in the square?

SECOND MAN: I don't remember if I saw Kuntze. Presumably he was sitting at the table. But I only remember Bondke and Rossel.

PROSECUTOR: Was the table already there when you got to the square?

SECOND MAN: Yes.

PROSECUTOR: Who was seated at it?

SECOND MAN: No one.

PROSECUTOR: Some people claim that Kiper was sitting in a chair even before the table was brought out and that afterwards he sat at the head of the table. That he took the *Arbeitskarten* while he was sitting.

SECOND MAN: It's possible. Everything is possible. When I was called, Kiper was standing.

PROSECUTOR: Mr. Zachwacki, do you recall an incident with a mother and child who were shot in the square?

SECOND MAN: Yes, I do. It was Rosa Rubinstein and her daughter Ala. They were from another town and had lived in our town only since the beginning of the war. I knew them.

PROSECUTOR: Who shot them, and under what circumstances?

SECOND MAN: I was standing in the group of workers on the right side of the square, beside the well.

PROSECUTOR: Please indicate the place on the map. With a circle or a cross. Thank you. There was a well there, you say. No one has yet mentioned that well.

SECOND MAN: It was an old well, wooden, with a wooden fence around it. All around it, in a semicircle, there were trees, poplars. At one moment I heard a shot, and people who were standing somewhat closer said that Rosa Rubinstein and her daughter had been shot. It seems that both of them had been sent to the left, but they went to the right. People said that Kiper ran after them and shot them.

PROSECUTOR: You said, "I heard a shot." Do you mean you heard a single shot?

SECOND MAN: Those were my words, but it's hard for me to say if I heard one shot, or two, or three. No doubt he fired at least twice.

PROSECUTOR: Did you see the shooting with your own eyes?

SECOND MAN: No. I saw the bodies lying on the ground. They were lying next to each other. Then the *Ordnungsdienst* picked them up. A red stain was left on the snow.

PROSECUTOR: You were part of the group that helped to bury the victims afterwards?

SECOND MAN: That's correct. There were so many victims that the *Ordnungsdienst* had to take twenty men to help. Four hundred and fifty people were killed in the town—in the square and in the house searches—and eight hundred and forty were shot in the cemetery. My wife was one of them.

PROSECUTOR: (*pause*) But you didn't see any murders with your own eyes? Can you say, "I saw with my own eyes that this one or that one shot so-and-so or so-and-so?"

SECOND MAN: I saw thirteen hundred victims. The mass grave was thirty meters long, three meters wide, five meters deep.

SECOND WOMAN: No, I wasn't in the square. Because I worked as a cleaning woman for the Gestapo, and in the morning, when everyone was going to the marketplace, Mama said to me, "See if they'll let you stay at work." I took my pail and a rag and a brush and said goodbye to my parents on the corner of Mickiewicza and Rozana. We lived on Mickiewicza Street. My parents kept going straight, and I turned onto Rozana. I had gone a few steps when suddenly I caught sight of Rossel and Hamke; they were walking towards me and I got terribly frightened, so I ran into the first gate, and they passed by, they didn't notice me. Later I saw them entering the building at number 13. I kept going.

PROSECUTOR: Who lived in the house?

SECOND WOMAN: I don't know, I was young, I was thirteen years old, but I said I was sixteen because children, you know, were killed. I was well developed, so I said I was sixteen and they let me work for them. That was good luck. That day the Gestapo were going around to all the houses looking for people who hadn't gone to the square, and if they found someone, they shot him either in his apartment or on the street.

PROSECUTOR: Was there a family named Weintal in the house at number 13?

SECOND WOMAN: Weintal? No, I never heard of anyone with that name. I stayed at the Gestapo all day long, hiding. I knew the building, I knew where I could hide. Well, I must say, I certainly was lucky.

PROSECUTOR: Which Gestapo members were in the building that day?

SECOND WOMAN: I don't know. I was hiding in an alcove next to the stairway to the cellar, at the very end of the corridor. Once I thought I heard Wittelmann's voice; he seemed to be on the telephone and was yelling something awful.

PROSECUTOR: Did you ever witness an execution while you worked there?

SECOND WOMAN: I know that they took place, and I know where. But I never saw them shoot anyone. I was afraid, and as soon as they brought someone in, I would hide, get out of their way. I was afraid that they might shoot me, too. They killed them against the fence.

PROSECUTOR: Which fence?

SECOND WOMAN: There was a courtyard at the back surrounded by a fence, and behind the fence there was a trench. That's where they were shot. I know, because afterwards the *Ordnungsdienst* would come and collect the bodies. Once I saw them carrying a doctor whom they had killed. His name was Gluck. But that was after the first action, in the spring. Another time I saw a group of Gestapo men walk out into the courtyard and immediately afterwards I heard a burst of machine-gun fire.

PROSECUTOR: Who did you see then?

SECOND WOMAN: Bondke, Rossel, Hamke, and Wittelmann.

PROSECUTOR: All together?

SECOND WOMAN: Yes. All together. I was washing the stairs to the cellar then.

PROSECUTOR: Were they all armed? Did each of them have a weapon?

SECOND WOMAN: Yes.

PROSECUTOR: Those shots you heard then, were they from a single machine gun or from several?

SECOND WOMAN: I don't know. I didn't pay attention. I wasn't thinking that someday someone would ask me about that. Maybe one of them shot, maybe two. Maybe they took turns. How should I know?

PROSECUTOR: When was that?

SECOND WOMAN: That was even before the first action, probably in the fall.

PROSECUTOR: Do you know how many people were shot then? Do you know their names?

SECOND WOMAN: I don't. I didn't see their bodies being taken away. I saw them collect the dead only once or twice. I don't know who was killed then.

PROSECUTOR: And you never saw a Gestapo man fire a gun?

SECOND WOMAN: No. I only worked there until the second action. I couldn't stand it any longer, I preferred to go to a camp. In general they were nice to me and never did anything bad. Once Bondke gave me cigarettes. The best-mannered was Kiper. He was an educated man, like Kuntze. But the others, no. Kiper had a lot of books in his room. He wanted fresh flowers in a vase every day. Once, when I didn't bring flowers, he yelled at me. Once he broke the vase because the flowers were wilted. On the desk in his room was a photograph of an elegant woman with a dog. But it was Hamke who had a dog. I used to prepare food for the dog. His name was Roosevelt. A wolfhound, very well trained. He tore the druggist Weidel's child to pieces. I heard Hamke boasting about him: *"Roosevelt hat heute ein Jüdlein zum Frühstück bekommen"*—Roosevelt had a little Jew for breakfast today. He said that to Kiper, and Kiper screwed up his face in disgust. Kiper couldn't stand Hamke and used to quarrel with Bondke. In general, he kept to himself. He didn't drink. That Sunday he was the first to come back from the marketplace.

PROSECUTOR: How do you know it was Kiper? Did you see him?

SECOND WOMAN: I heard his voice.

PROSECUTOR: Who was he talking to?

SECOND WOMAN: He was talking to himself. I thought he was reciting a poem. Anyway, that's what it sounded like. Then he went to his room and played his violin—I forgot to say that he was a trained musician. Bondke used to make fun of him and call him *Gestapogeiger*—Gestapo-fiddler. I don't know much about music, but I think he played very well. I heard him play several times. Always the same thing. I don't know what melody it was, I don't know much about music.

PROSECUTOR: Did you see him that day?

SECOND WOMAN: No, I only heard him playing.

PROSECUTOR: What time would that have been?

SECOND WOMAN: I don't know. It was growing dark.

PROSECUTOR: Could you hear the shots from the cemetery inside the Gestapo building?

SECOND WOMAN: I don't know. Maybe not. The cemetery is on Male Targi, and the Gestapo headquarters was on St. Jerzy Square. That's quite a distance. But maybe in the silence, in the clear air . . .

PROSECUTOR: Did you hear any shots when Kiper returned?

SECOND WOMAN: I can't say. Because the way I felt that Sunday and for several days afterwards, I was hearing shots all the time, and my parents thought I had lost my mind. I kept saying, "Listen, they're shooting . . . ," and I'd run and hide. Mama took me to Gluck, who gave me a powder, but it didn't help. I kept on hearing shots for a week. It was my nerves.

PROSECUTOR: When did the other Gestapo men come back?

SECOND WOMAN: I don't know. When it got dark, I sneaked out through the courtyard and returned home. The city was empty, as if no one was left alive. I was astonished: the snow was black. That was the blood. The most blood was on Sienkiewicza Street, and on Rozana. I didn't meet anyone in the marketplace either. It was empty. In the center of the square, lying on its back with its legs in the air, was a small, broken table.

ABOUT THE AUTHOR

Ida Fink was born in Poland in 1921. Her music studies were interrupted by the Nazi occupation. She lived in a ghetto through 1942, and then in hiding until the end of the war. In 1957 she emigrated to Israel with her husband and daughter. Ida Fink is the author of numerous short stories and radio plays; the radio play "The Table" has been broadcast in Israel and Europe, and dramatized on German and Israeli television. A *Scrap of Time* has already appeared in Hebrew, German, and Dutch translations, and in 1985 was honored with the first Anne Frank Prize for Literature. A Polish edition was published in London in 1987.

SCHOCKEN CLASSICS

THE TRIAL

by Franz Kafka, translated from the German by Willa and Edwin Muir

The terrifying story of Joseph K., his arrest and trial, is one of the great novels of the twentieth century.

"Here we are taken to the limits of human thought. Indeed everything in this work is, in the true sense, essential. It states the problem of the absurd in its entirety."

—Albert Camus

0-8052-0848-8 paper, $6.95

THE CASTLE

by Franz Kafka, translated from the German by Willa and Edwin Muir and with an Homage by Thomas Mann

Franz Kafka's final great novel, the haunting tale of a man known only as K. and his endless struggle against an inscrutable authority to gain admittance to a castle, is often cited as Kafka's most autobiographical work.

"One of the classics of twentieth-century literature."　　　—*New York Times*

0-8052-0872-0 paper, $8.95

THE METAMORPHOSIS, THE PENAL COLONY, AND OTHER STORIES

by Franz Kafka, translated from the German by Willa and Edwin Muir

This powerful collection brings together all the stories Franz Kafka published during his lifetime, including "The Judgment," "The Metamorphosis," "In the Penal Colony," "A Country Doctor," and "A Hunger Artist."

0-8052-0849-6 paper, $7.95

THE DIARIES OF FRANZ KAFKA

Edited by Max Brod

For the first time in this country, the complete diaries of Franz Kafka are available in one volume. Covering the period from 1910 to 1923, the year before Kafka's death, they reveal the essential Kafka behind the enigmatic artist.

"It is likely that these journals will be regarded as one of [Kafka's] major literary works; in these pages, he reveals what he customarily hid from the world."

—*New Yorker*

0-8052-0906-6 paper, $12.95

LETTERS TO FELICE

by Franz Kafka, edited by Erich Heller and Jürgen Born, translated by James Stern and Elizabeth Duckworth

Kafka's correspondence with Felice Bauer, to whom he was twice engaged, reveals the writer's complexities as a lover and as a friend.

"The letters are indispensable for anyone seeking a more intimate knowledge of Kafka and his fragmented world." —*Library Journal*

0-8052-0851-8 paper, $13.95

THE FAMILY CARNOVSKY

by I. J. Singer, translated from the Yiddish by Joseph Singer

This family saga traces the lives of three generations of German Jews, up to the Nazis' rise to power.

"A titanic, overwhelming novel . . . filled with life, with people of every conceivable type, with suffering, and yet with an unbreakable optimism." —Joyce Carol Oates

0-8052-0859-3 paper, $11.95

YOSHE KALB

by I. J. Singer, translated from the Yiddish by Maurice Samuel, with an introduction by Irving Howe

A brilliant, haunting novel set in the world of competing hasidic dynasties in late nineteenth-century Galicia.

"This is a powerful novel, dashing and turbulent in style, and deeply interesting in its glimpses of Jewish customs." —*Saturday Review*

0-8052-0860-7 paper, $8.95

PAST CONTINUOUS

by Yaakov Shabtai, translated from the Hebrew by Dalya Bilu

A grand, hypnotically rendered panorama of life in the quintessential modern city— Tel Aviv.

"Urgent, innovative, extraordinary." —*New Republic*

0-8052-0868-2 paper, $11.95